CRISIS AT BIHAC

CRISIS AT BIHAC
Bosnia's Bloody Battlefield

INCLUDING
The Carter Peace Initiative
Croatia Reclaims Western Slavonia
The Fall of the Krajina Serbs

Brendan O'Shea

Foreword By Robert Fisk: the *Independent*
Journalist of the Year 1995/6

SUTTON PUBLISHING

First published in the United Kingdom in 1998 by
Sutton Publishing Limited · Phoenix Mill
Thrupp · Stroud · Gloucestershire · GL5 2BU

British Library Cataloguing in Publication Data
A catalogue record for this book is available from the British Library

ISBN 0 7509 1927 2

 ™ ALAN SUTTON™ and SUTTON™ are the
trade marks of Sutton Publishing Limited

Typeset in 10/13pt New Baskerville.
Typesetting and origination by
Sutton Publishing Limited.
Printed in Great Britain by
WBC Limited, Bridgend.

My friends, this is a difficult period for me. Someday someone will write a book about it. It is a very special responsibility to command an encircled unit.

General Atif Dudakovic
Commander, 5th Corps Armija
Bihac Pocket, Bosnia-Hercegovina

12 March 1995

Contents

List of Plates

Between pages 108 and 109.

Foreword

One dark winter's evening in early 1995, I watched the Serbs vainly trying to defend the town of Velika Kladusa from the Bosnian army. It was a miserable day, the trees and hedgerows rimed with frost, the Serb soldiers hollow-cheeked with hunger and tiredness. A dead dog sat at the roadside, staring at my car as I skidded slowly down the broken laneways. It must have sat down to rest one afternoon and simply frozen to death. I was to see it many times on that road, always watching, dead eyes open, as the rabble of Serb soldiery pulled their field guns down to Fikret Abdic's great fortress.

Its battlements that day were shrouded in a grey mist as the thump of explosions shook the ground. Beside the roadway, Abdic's Muslim troops and their Serb allies – explaining these crazed alliances to newspaper readers in 800 words was always a nightmare – were harnessing nags to the guns. The Abdic Muslims wore armbands to distinguish them from the pitiful Muslim prisoners from the Bosnian army's 5th Corps who were being marched up the icy road under the guard of men in Partisan hats. Some of the horses tried to bolt. It was a scene from the First World War. So were the local atrocities.

At a prison camp half a mile away, the Serbs showed us their latest captives; they were being forced to dig for mines with their bare hands. 'We are treating them according to the rules of war,' a blue-uniformed Serb policeman announced to me, pointing to a warm barn which he claimed was their prisoners' hut. I suspected it belonged to the camp guards. And while I walked past these cowed, fearful men, all pawing the ice-hard ground with their hands, the Serb gun batteries in the surrounding forests banged away into the fog. When I watched carefully, I could see a big, golden fire flicker behind the winter trees, their branches showing up for a millisecond like the veins in a corpse. Then the fog would cover them as the gun crew reloaded.

For a journalist, these battles and their attendant horrors were always accompanied by the awkward feeling that, even if the physical shape of war was explicable, the politics of the Bosnian conflict was impenetrable to readers. We often saw the men from the European Community Monitoring Mission in their white shirts and trousers – spacemen, we called them – hovering around the battlefields, observers of a grisly game whose participants were often happy to meet them or try to use them or lie to them and, on rare and terrible occasions, to kill them. From time to time, I would be given the opportunity of reading their carefully prepared, often grim, occasionally very eloquent reports. One day, I thought, they should write down their own experiences and use this wealth of documents to ensure that the base nature of this particular war was placed on the historical record. Brendan O'Shea's book is one of the first to do that.

The Bihac Pocket was one of those odd crises thrown up by larger wars, conflicts in microcosm which deserve their own account long after television pictures have briefly helped the world to realise – and then to forget – their brutality. Fikret Abdic was (and still is) a Bosnian Muslim businessman who ran much of Bihac, in the north-west of Bosnia, bordering Croatia, as a personal fiefdom, appropriately administered from his forbidding castle in Velika Kladusa. Employing thousands of local Muslims in his multimillion-dollar agro-commercial enterprises, he was a little king with attendant lords who decided – for reasons made clear in Brendan O'Shea's book – to ally himself with the Serbs rather than the Bosnian government in Sarajevo.

When the Bosnian Muslim army in Bihac, encircled with its starving civilian population, took the offensive against Abdic's men and the Serbs, another of Bosnia's great population shifts got underway, a tide of Muslim refugees – Abdic's refugees – seeking sanctuary among the Serbs and Croats. I came across 30,000 of these Muslims, camped out in one of Abdic's abandoned chicken farms, a place of thick mud and leaking corrugated iron roofs and perpetual cold. Walk into their stinking huts or tents, and the visitor would be met by the stench of excreta and suppurating wounds. It was in this world – cynical, cruel, preposterous, incredible as it was – that O'Shea and the European monitors moved.

It is curious, reading through this book's usually dispassionate but sometimes angry pages, to see how many times the ECMM men and the journalists reached the same conclusions – without necessarily discussing the events we separately witnessed. Take the case of the Croatian Serbs living in the region of Krajina, a part of Croatia, but a district populated by Serb families since the sixteenth century. The Serbs there had staged a putsch against the Croatian authorities on the break up of Yugoslavia and the Croat argument in recapturing the land was that the Serbs did not really belong to the Krajina – that they were strangers, aliens, that they had never really lived there. It was a lie. But flying into Zagreb one afternoon on Croatian Airlines, I noticed in the in-flight magazine an interview with Peter Galbraith, the US ambassador to Croatia, in which he referred to the occupants of Krajina as 'the so-called local Serbs'.

Could there be a more obvious way of signalling America's support for the Croatian lie?

So it is with some satisfaction that I note how often the sinister figure of Galbraith was observed by Brendan O'Shea, creeping to the edge of battlefields to smile or offer strange, dangerous advice to refugees or local political leaders. European monitors knew all too well what was happening in the later stages of the Bosnian war when they noticed more and more American officials – defence attachés, former US generals, 'training' officers, CIA operatives and FBI men – leaving Croatian and Bosnian military headquarters.

US Special Forces 'on active' duty were turning up by January of 1995 to support first the Croats and then the Bosnian Muslims. The United States was flying pilotless 'drone' photo-reconnaissance aircraft over the Serb lines from Brac while local residents there reported dozens of American C-130 military cargo flights. Were the Americans gun running? When O'Shea's colleagues from the monitoring mission tried to investigate Brac airport, they were intercepted by a group of Croatian 'special police' forces. What makes this book so valuable is that it combines detail of the local Balkan struggle with a clinical – and cynical – understanding of the role the major world powers chose for themselves towards the end of the Bosnian war.

Those ECMM reports which I used to read, and sometimes quote from, to the chagrin of their authors, are here in all their clarity as well as their humour. What a wonderful dispatch I could have sent to my paper, the *Independent*, if I had got my hands on this imperishable report from the ECMM's Team Bihac in March of 1995:

> Team patrolled to Grabez, left our vehicle, and patrolled on foot to collect wild flowers. Team patrolled as far as WK744644 and began to attract the unwelcome attentions of BSA (Bosnian Serb Army). However, 5 Corps immediately retaliated with mortars and we were able to return to our vehicle at walking pace, after some undignified running.

European monitors were, of course, deliberately misled or – worse – manipulated by all sides in the Bosnian war. O'Shea records a sharp rebuke from a senior official who had to remind his men that they had to uphold international humanitarian law for prisoners. I recall another incident, in an area far from O'Shea's area of operations, when European monitors who should have been supervising a body exchange were discovered scoffing calamari with white wine in a local restaurant. And there were times when these men could no longer hide their disgust at the bestialities which they were forced to witness. One of O'Shea's Irish monitor colleagues told me of a Croatian-Serb body exchange which he was forced to supervise near the Bosnian town of Mostar. 'Each side took the bodies out of the bags to identify them,' he told me. 'Several of them had had their heads chopped off. So, to annoy the Croats, the Serbs started playing football with two Croat heads. I took off my European monitor's badge and walked up to the Serbs and told them they made me ashamed to be a soldier.'

O'Shea recounts an equal act of savagery which occurred after two Serb prisoners were handed over to a Croatian officer called Santic, a close chum of President Franjo Tudjman:

He (General Santic) took them to HQ . . . and tortured them and shot one in front of the other to make the other one talk. The Serb who saw his friend shot to death said "I will never tell you anything". Santic immediately shot him dead.

O'Shea includes a chilling verbatim account of the European monitors' attempts to find out from Bosnian General Dudakovic what had happened to Santic:

Q: Do you know where General Santic is?
A: Yes.
Q: Did you have him arrested?
A: No.
Q: Is he safe?
A: No.

In fact, Santic was resting forever in that place where Croatian generals go when they have been murdered.

There was, alas, much interference with the ECMM's work, not only by the local armies but by the European powers as well. Although never formally acknowledged, reports from monitors in Krajina were altered, truncated and sometimes censored out of existence during Germany's presidency of the European Union. When the ECMM recorded events unfavourable to the Croats or favourable to the Serbs, these paragraphs were simply deleted by the Germans. Germany, of course, was Croatia's ally, the first to recognise Croatia's independence in 1991, just as it had been, under somewhat different leadership, in 1941.

But what came over very clearly towards the end of the Bosnian war was the determination of the United States to support first Croatia and then the Bosnian government in the struggle against the Serbs. Galbraith and his colleagues knew in advance of Croatian plans to 'liberate' the UN's Sector West and the Krajina. Galbraith expressed his approval of Croatia's Operation Storm, which ethnically cleansed the 300,000 Serbs out of the Krajina. After the battle, in the company of O'Shea's colleagues and the United Nations in Knin, I toured the area – only to find the usual atrocities. The Croats had burned whole villages to the ground, executed captured Serb soldiers and murdered elderly men and women who had chosen to stay on their land. One woman in her eighties, to whom the UN were supplying food, was dragged from her home, pushed into her battered car and shot through the head. Her brains lay on the driver's seat for more than a week. We heard little from Mr Galbraith about these bestial acts. The Croatians applied for European aid to rebuilt the Serb villages that they themselves had razed to the ground.

O'Shea understands all too well how the burned villages of Kosovo are now replacing the shattered towns of Bihac Pocket. While Bosnia's half-baked 'peace' remains 'a time-bomb primed and ready to explode', the absence of any provision in the Dayton agreement for the Albanian-majority Serb province of Kosovo means that Serbia itself may soon disintegrate. O'Shea talks of Kosovo 'boiling over'. Since he wrote those words, I have been to Kosovo myself and noticed the Europeans and Americans up to their old tricks again. With their demands for a return to their regional autonomy ignored, the Albanians have begun a war of independence from Serbia; and at this very moment, the West – complete with American ambassadors and European monitors – have arrived in Kosovo to tell the Albanians they cannot have autonomy.

O'Shea must observe these events with a heavy heart. So should anyone whose heart is not made of stone. And no doubt the new European monitors in Kosovo will be recording the usual round of meetings with deceitful mayors and lying generals. They too will have the opportunity to write their books in the years to come. But Brendan O'Shea's work is the first of the batch; it is history in the making, a textbook for future research. We journalists should carry it with us in our holdalls – until the monitors of Kosovo provide us with their own books of atrocity and political betrayal.

Robert Fisk
Middle East Correspondent of
the London *Independent*

The Main Protagonists

SERBIA

Slobodan Milosevic — President of Serbia.

CROATIA

Franjo Tudjman — President of Croatia.
Gojko Susak — Minister for Defence.
Mate Granic — Foreign Minister from 1993.
General Janko Bobetko — Chief of the General Staff of the Croatian Army (HV).

THE REPUBLIC OF SRPSKA KRAJINA

Milan Martic — President of the Republic of Srpska Krajina (RSK).
Borislav Mikelic — Prime Minister of RSK.
Milan Babic — Foreign Minister of RSK.
General Milan Celeketic — Chief of Staff of the Army of the RSK.
General Mile Mrksic — Successor to Celeketic in 1995.

BOSNIA-HERCEGOVINA

Alija Izetbegovic — President of Bosnia-Hercegovina.
Ejup Ganic — Deputy President.
Haris Siladzic — Prime Minister.
Muhamed Sacirbey — Ambassador to the UN, latter Foreign Minister.
General Sefer Halilovic — Commander of the Armija of BiH.
General Rasim Delic — Successor to Halilovic.

BIHAC POCKET

Fikret Abdic — Founder of the breakaway Autonomous Province of Western Bosnia (APWB).
General Atif Dudakovic — Commander of Armija's 5th Corps, 1993–8.
Ifran Saracevic — APWB Defence Minister.
Sead Kajtazovic — APWB Camp Leader in Batnoga.
Dzemal Ahmetovic — APWB Camp Leader in Turanj.
Ejup Topic — President of the Bihac Regional Assembly, 1992.
Zlatko Jusic — Prime Minister of the Bihac Regional Government, 1992.
General Razim Drekovic — Commander of Armija's 5th Corps, 1992–3.
General Vlado Santic — Commander of the 101 Brigade HVO in Bihac until his disappearance in 1995.

Colonel Hamdu Abdic	Commander of the 502 Brigade, 5th Corps, confidant of Dudakovic.
Mirsad Veladzic	Minister for coordination between 5th Corps and Sarajevo during the war. Later governor of the Una-Sana Canton.

REPUBLIC OF SRPSKA

Radovan Karadzic	President of Republic of Srpska (RS).
General Ratko Mladic	Commander of the Army of the Republic of Srpska (BSA).
General Manojlo Milovanovic	Chief of Staff of the BSA.
General Boric	Commander of 2nd Krajina Corps BSA.

CROATIAN COMMUNITY OF HERCEG-BOSNA

Mate Boban	President of the Croatian Community of Herceg-Bosna (CRHB); ousted late in 1993.
Krezimir Zubak	A lawyer by profession he replaced Boban and then became President of the Muslim/Croat Federation in 1994.
General Timor Blaskic	Commander of the Bosnian Croat Army (HVO) and indicted for War Crimes in 1995. Appointed to HV General Staff by President Tudjman.

MONTENEGRO

Momir Bulatovic	President of Montenegro and friend of Slobodan Milosevic.

SLOVENIA

Milan Kucan	President of Slovenia.

UN CIVILIAN

Boutros Boutros-Ghali	Secretary General.
Yashushi Akashi	Special Representative of the Secretary General in Former Yugoslavia.

UN MILITARY

General Lewis McKenzie	UN Commander in Sarajevo in 1992.
General Phillipe Morillon	UN Commander in Bosnia in 1993.
General Sir Michael Rose	UN Commander in Bosnia in 1994.
General Rupert Smith	UN Commander in Bosnia in 1995.
General Bernard Janvier	UNPROFOR Force Commander in 1994/5.

THE EUROPEAN COMMUNITY MONITOR MISSION

Ambassador J.P. von Stulpenagle (GE)	Head of Mission 1/7/94–31/12/94.
Ambassador Albert Turot (FR)	Head of Mission 1/1/95–30/6/95.

Brigadier General Bruno Cailloux (FR)	Deputy Head of Mission 1/7/94–31/12/94.
Klaus Cramer (GE)	Head of Operations Division in 1994.
Jean Michel Happe (FR)	Head of Operations Division in 1995.
Hugh O'Donovan (IRL)	Team Leader in Bihac in 1992.
Francis Bonal (FR)	Team Leader in Bihac in 1994.
Bill Foxton (UK)	Team Leader in Bihac in 1995.

THE MEDIATORS

Lord David Owen	Cyrus Vance
Thorvald Stoltenberg	Vitali Churkin
Charles Redman	Carl Bildt
Richard Holbrooke	Peter Galbraith
Anthony Lake	Former President Jimmy Carter

Groupings and Abbreviations

MILITARY

Armija	Bosnian Muslim Army.
BSA	Bosnian Serb Army.
HV	Croatian Army.
HVO	Bosnian Croat Army.
JNA	The old Yugoslav National Army.
SARSK/ARSK	Serbian Army of the Republic of Srpska Krajina.

POLITICAL

HDZ	Croatian Democratic Union; led by Franjo Tudjman in Croatia proper and Mate Boban in Bosnia.
SDA	Party of Democratic Action representing the Bosnian Muslims and led by Alija Izetbegovic.
SDS	Serbian Democratic Party representing the Bosnian Serbs and led by Dr Radovan Karadzic.
APWB	Autonomous Province of Western Bosnia.
RSK	Republic of Srpska Krajina (Croatia).
RS	Republic of Srpska (Bosnia).

INTERNATIONAL

EC	European Community.
ECMM	European Community Monitor Mission.
ECTF	European Community Task Force (Humanitarian).
ICRC	International Committee of the Red Cross.
NATO	North Atlantic Treaty Organization.
NGO	Non-Governmental Agency (Humanitarian).
UN	United Nations.
UNMO	United Nations Military Observer.
UNHCR	United Nations High Commission for Refugees.
UNPROFOR	United Nations Protection Force.

OTHERS

ICFY	International Conference on Former Yugoslavia, based in Geneva.
CGPP	Contact Group Peace Plan.
COHA	Cessation of Hostilities Agreement.
MPRI	Military Professional Resources Incorporated (US).
DMZ	Demilitarized Zone.

Author's Note

During the autumn/winter of 1994 a place called Bihac Pocket, in north-west Bosnia-Hercegovina, became for a time the focus of international media attention when several commentators began predicting the demise of the 5th Corps of the Bosnian Muslim Army at the hands of a combined force of Krajina and Bosnian Serbs, and renegade Muslims loyal to their local political leader, Fikret Abdic. Graphic images via Sky and CNN, of Serb artillery shells ploughing into beleaguered towns and villages, conveyed a very clear message that the citizens of Bihac Pocket were under siege – and so they were. Several monitoring agencies working in the region, with probably the sole exception of the European Community Monitor Mission(ECMM), became convinced that the encircled Muslims could not survive in the face of a concentrated and coordinated Serb/Abdic onslaught, but survive they did, against all the odds.

Thereafter, fighting in other parts of the country became more newsworthy and the commission of several savage atrocities ensured that the plight of the citizens of Bihac would fade to the back pages. But there was much more to the story of the war in Bihac Pocket and this book attempts to explain, perhaps for the very first time, what actually happened there, and how all the main players in the overall Yugoslav conflict either became directly involved or alternatively chose to persistently interfere. Accordingly it becomes essential to understand from the outset that decisions made and actions taken in Sarajevo, Belgrade and Zagreb had a profound impact also in Bihac, where regional considerations always influenced the judgement of the Pocket's many and varied political and military leaders.

It is equally important to understand that this book does not represent another attempt to re-tell the whole story of the modern Yugoslav conflict but rather is focused primarily on the hitherto untold story of the conflict in Bihac and other significant events which had a direct impact on what happened there. For example, I have not attempted to recount the harrowing story of the Bosnian Serb invasion of Srebrenica, albeit that the enclave was also a UN safe area, nor do I attempt to deal with the complex events leading up to the signing of the Dayton/Paris Peace Accords or the ongoing struggle for autonomy by the ethnic Albanians in Kosovo. Instead, I have attempted to maintain a narrower focus in order to provide an insight into the plight of the ordinary people of Bihac Pocket, as their military and political overlords plunged them into three years of living hell. The Carter Initiative, the demise of Western Slavonia and the fall of the Krajina combine with other events cited to provide the context in which the Bihac story unfolded.

Acknowledgements

By the time this manuscript finally appears in print over three years will have elapsed since I first began a re-examination of the recent tragic events in Bihac and elsewhere throughout Former Yugoslavia. I could not have embarked on this project in the first instance had I not been fortunate enough to have worked in the region with ECMM, and accordingly my first vote of thanks must go to those Monitors who, down through the years, took the painstaking trouble to compile detailed reports and assessments of the ever-changing military and political situation. Equally but for the encouragement of Klaus Cramer, Jean-Michel Happe and Pearse McCorley I might never have had the opportunity to pursue my interest in what was 'really happening' in Bihac Pocket, and in this regard I was ably assisted on several occasions by Lennart Leschley, Arne Nyberg, Jos Gannes, Patrick Brook, Andre Lejolly, Philip Wakins and Tim Clifton, who proved themselves loyal and trusted colleagues. I was also fortunate to have had the best of team mates in Olaf Boersma, Rui Fererria, Julien Neil, Guilliano D'Anastasio and Arturo Vinuesa, and between us we learned a great deal as we went about monitoring the situation on the ground. However, it is to all those who worked in Bihac and took the risks that I am most grateful, for without their commitment to remain in the Pocket under fire and to report daily what they saw and heard, there would of course be no story to tell now. Accordingly I remain indebted to each and every one of them but particularly to Hugh O'Donovan, Mark Etherington, Anders Malsten, Henrik Markus, Francis Bonal, Luc Vermeulen and last but not least a remarkable Englishman called Bill Foxton.

I am also mindful of the support I received from the small Irish contingent in Zagreb during the winter of 1994, namely Mick Cleary, Joe Mulligan, Dave Galvin, Gerry Swan, Aidan O'Leary, Susan Lyne, Liam Jenkinson, Tom Hodson, Eugene Field and later on Jim Fitzgibbon. Each in their own way have helped enormously along the way.

My thanks also go to Renaud Theunens and Roddy de Normann who at various points read the script and offered valuable advice on where and how to improve it. Neither would probably admit it but their combined contribution, comment, criticism and advice have proved to be of crucial importance. Similarly I am very grateful to Tim Ripley for pointing me in a number of important directions as the project neared completion and for sharing information with me which he might more profitably have reserved for his own work. Equally Philippe Graton made a huge effort to retrieve some of his excellent photographs which were taken on his visit to Turanj in 1994. I am delighted that we have been able to include some of them because they vividly illustrate the story.

I can also never adequately acknowledge the role played by Robert Fisk in this project. Many months ago he willingly agreed to write the foreword and true to form has kept his promise, but if the truth be told it was probably his continued infectious enthusiasm which was responsible for keeping me going, at times when the easier option by far was to abandon the whole thing. In this regard I must also acknowledge the latitude afforded to me by Dr Geoff Roberts at University College, Cork, which allowed me to concentrate on completing this work when time was at a premium.

At Sutton Publishing I wish to express my sincere thanks to my ever-patient editor Sarah Bragginton, and to Mike Komarnyckyj, who produced such excellent maps. However, in the final analysis, it was Jonathan Falconer's courage which proved the determining factor in bringing this project to fruition and nothing written here could ever adequately explain or appreciate that fact.

Finally I wish to thank my parents Martin and Mary for their continued encouragement throughout, Kevin for his unshakable belief in my ability to see this through, and Clare, and Martin and Katie, for tolerating the amount of time I spent sitting before a computer when there were many other more valuable and pressing things to do.

To everyone mentioned above, and countless others too numerous to mention, I am indebted to you all.

Brendan O'Shea
4 June 1998

CHAPTER ONE

Bihac Pocket

The area known as Bihac Pocket, in the north-west corner of Bosnia-Hercegovina, can claim 738 years of history, with 1260 generally being accepted as the year of the first recorded settlement in the area.[1] In the late sixteenth century it came under Turkish rule and in common with several other places throughout Bosnia, the Slav population converted to Islam in order to preserve their social status and retain their property. This conversion was in most cases simply a matter of convenience, with the people retaining their secular lifestyle, habits and customs. As time went on, it became inevitable that some religious conversion would also take place and it was this adjustment which, in the longer term, would serve to differentiate between the citizens of Bihac and their Catholic/Croat and Orthodox/Serb neighbours. Austro-Hungary eventually reasserted its authority here as the Ottoman influence declined from 1521 onwards, and for a time the area became known as the 'Cazinska Krajina' as it linked up with the 'Vojna Krajina', the military frontier that had until then just surrounded it.[2]

With the inclusion of Bihac in the newly created 'Kingdom of Serbs, Croats and Slovenes' in the aftermath of the First World War, the people of the region consistently supported the concept of a multi-ethnic, multi-cultural society. Their ability to co-habit peacefully with both Serbs and Croats had always been a feature of the area in the past. It was because of this ethnic homogeneity that Josip Broz Tito decided to move his Partisan headquarters to Bihac in order to hold the first meeting of his Anti-Fascist Council for the National Liberation of Yugoslavia there on 26 November 1942.[3] In the spring of 1954 all three groups banded together again in pursuit of their economic interests and revolted against Tito's Communist regime in what would turn out to be Europe's only post-war peasant rebellion; the severity with which this was crushed served only to unite them all even further.[4] Contrary to popular mythology there was no history of ethnic hatred in this part of Bosnia but with the advent of the 1990s all this changed and the region was plunged into needless suffering and senseless bloodshed. Under threat from all sides the situation in Bihac Pocket became exacerbated by an internal power struggle within the Muslim leadership. In turn, this forced the ordinary people living there to take sides in a vicious inter-Muslim civil war in which all the main players in the overall Yugoslav

1

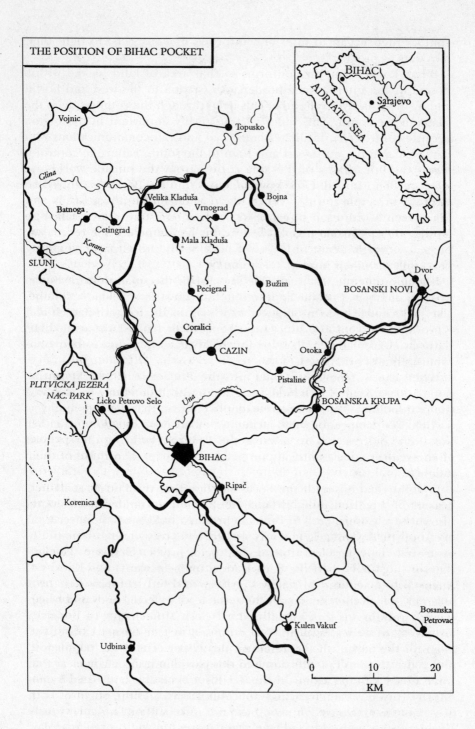

THE POSITION OF BIHAC POCKET

Vojnic
Topusko

Glina

Velika Kladuša
Vrnograd
Bojna

Batnoga
Cetingrad
Korana
Mala Kladuša

SLUNJ

Pecigrad
Bužim

Coralici

CAZIN
Otoka

Pistaline

PLITVICKA JEZERA
NAC. PARK
Licko Petrovo Selo
Una
BOSANSKA KRUPA

BIHAC

Ripač

Korenica

Kulen Vakuf

Udbina

Dvor
BOSANSKI NOVI

BIHAC
ADRIATIC SEA
Sarajevo

Bosanska
Petrovac

0   10   20
KM

conflict then began to interfere, in order, one suspects, to fight their own wars by proxy.

Bihac Pocket roughly conforms to that area of land locked within Bosnia by the international border with Croatia to the west and north, and by the Una river valley that cuts deep through the countryside to the east and the south. This valley is strategically important in the region because control of it facilitates both road and rail communications with Banja Luka in the north-east and Knin to the south. Failure to control it leaves the inhabitants of the area cut off from the outside world and effectively imprisoned. Local government within the Pocket is centred on the four principle towns – Velika Kladusa, Cazin, Bosanska Krupa and Bihac itself – with each surrounded by an administrative area called an Opstina. Over 250,000 people lived in this region before the recent war began, with significant numbers of both Serbs and Croats co-existing peacefully with their Muslim neighbours.[5]

Islamic influence was negligible save for in the small town of Buzim where a number of people appeared to follow a stricter religious routine. The majority of the area's pre-war trade was conducted with Zagreb and Karlovac in Croatia as distinct from Sarajevo or Banja Luka, something that was continually emphasized by the Muslims to indicate their non-fundamentalist orientation.[6]

When the war began to spill into the Pocket in 1992 'the entire population appeared to be well integrated, with little ethnic friction and the civil, political, and religious leaders were firm that the community as a whole was homogenous, and facing its new adversity as a group. Neither was there any resentment towards the 1,500 Serbs living there whose circumstances were essentially no better, or worse, than those of their neighbours.'[7]

Equally, relations with the Serbs surrounding the Pocket remained reasonably civilized until 21 April 1992 when, in tandem with events elsewhere in Bosnia, Serb forces launched an attack across the River Una: the town of Bosanska Krupa was shelled incessantly and systematically destroyed. This senseless violence had been predictable since the early days of July 1991 when the Serb leaders in the town, Gojko Klièkovic, Miroslav Drljaèa and Miroslav Vjestica, decided to form their own assembly, which then sat in parallel to the legally elected body and began passing resolutions that established the Serb Municipality of Bosanska Krupa. Maps were drawn up that proposed to take 60 per cent of the town for the Serbs, who represented just 27 per cent of the population, and if the Muslims failed to agree to this partition it was made clear that force would be used against them. To this end all able-bodied Serb men began wearing paramilitary and police uniforms, and the plight of both Muslims and Croats quickly became untenable. This previously homogenous community had begun its descent into hell.

The last days before war finally broke out are well recorded by a European Community Monitoring Mission (ECCM) Team who went to the area in what eventually turned out to be a pointless attempt to get all sides to settle their differences peacefully. On 13 April 1992 Hugh O'Donovan (IRL), and his team-mates Michel Ducheyne (BE) and Thiery Rousseau-Dumarcet (FR), went to meet Milan Voynovic, the President of the Serb community in the town, but were unable to effect any change in the Serbs' attitude. Instead Voynovic told the Monitors about the situation in the nearby village of Perna, a small hamlet of some sixty houses with a Serb population of about 150 people. Apparently the village had now become completely surrounded by armed Muslims who had begun digging trenches, patrolling the streets and setting up roadblocks. As if this was not bad enough, the Muslims, he said, had begun cutting down trees in the forest which were the property of Serbs and had fired shots at Serbs who had tried to stop them. For Voynovic the theft of these 'Serb trees' had become the last straw.

The following day the Monitor Team went to see the Muslim Mayor of Cazin and his Chief of Police who, after a while, agreed that the digging of trenches around Perna probably constituted a provocation and as a compromise they would just position wooden barriers on the roads. However, they felt that no matter what they did Bosanska Krupa was going to be attacked by the Yugoslav National Army (JNA) within a few days, in order to open up a new front line to the north-west of the country. Serb women and children had already been evacuated from Bosanska Krupa, they said, and this was in keeping with the type of preparation that had preceded attacks on other towns in eastern Bosnia. They were also adamant that the JNA had used helicopters to re-supply the citizens of Perna with mortars and anti-tank weapons, although they could produce no evidence that this had taken place. The best suggestion they could make was that the United Nations (UN) take over administrative control of the whole area and expel the JNA, but realistically there were two chances of that happening – slim and none.

As O'Donovan sat down that night to file his daily report to ECMM HQ in Zagreb he wrote in his diary, 'I feel that our efforts [here] may be pointless'.[8] The next few days would prove him right but as he hit the 'send' button on his Capsat[9] that night he had no idea just how quickly the situation would slide into war. On 17 April the Monitors did actually manage to get all parties around a table in Bosanska Krupa but nothing tangible was achieved. Complaints were made, grievances were aired by all parties and the tension was palpable but no one was prepared to compromise lest it be interpreted as a sign of weakness. Three days later another ECMM team reported small arms fire in the Muslim village of Arapusa to the east of Bosanska Krupa[10] and from here there was to be no turning back.

April 20, 1992 was the last market day before the war came to Bosanska Krupa. On that peaceful Monday there were a lot of people about and the selection of produce was good. The buyers were Serbs. They did not even ask the prices. Did they know or foresee anything? Grandpa Ahmet came from Pistaline. He suspected something, too. Never before has so many cattle been taken towards Grme. 'Something ain't right here. I smell a rat. Well, we'll see!' he thought out loud. The following day there were no early risers on the streets of Bosanska Krupa with its half empty buses, closed shops, and only the usual black market operating in front of the 'Stari Grad'. Thirty Serbs left the hotel lobby and headed toward the city limits. What was going on? At one o'clock armed members of the Serb Territorial Defence surrounded the Health Centre and prevented the departure of trucks filled with equipment, medicine and sanitation materials.[11]

Certain now that the situation was spiralling out of control, O'Donovan and his team went back to Bosanska Krupa on 21 April, arriving there at about 1630 hrs. The situation had now become critical. Large-scale troop movements had been observed in the hills overlooking the town to the east and the Serb leadership had apparently disappeared.

When we arrived the town was deserted. We travelled to the Town Hall where the local leaders were gravely concerned about the situation. During our discussions General Spiro Nikovic (Commander 10 Corps JNA) arrived, spoke to the Mayor, and then departed to speak to the other side. The Territorial Defence (Muslim), who were positioned around the Town Hall, were now becoming increasingly excited and nervous. At 1750 hrs, without warning, continuous small arms and machine-gun fire erupted in the hills around Bosanska Krupa and began impacting in the area of the Town Hall.[12]

As the Monitors beat a hasty retreat all they could do was impress upon General Nikovic the absolute necessity of having the fighting stopped, but as the General was actually taking refuge in the back of an ECMM Landrover at the time, and effectively relying on the EU Monitors for his own protection, there appeared to be little prospect of him instigating any immediate solution.[13] For the present there was nothing more to be done except count the shells impacting all around and plot the location of a new front line on the overall map of Bosnia. The ordinary citizens of Bosanska Krupa did not have the option to jump into a white Landrover and head for the relative safety of Bihac town. These poor souls would have to stay and deal with the hail of death that was now beginning to rain down on them.

It began violently and surprisingly, and for those who had never seen something like this before, it seemed almost unreal. Just after 1700 hrs on 21 April, the first explosion from a shell fired near Vranjska was heard and was followed by rounds from machine-gun and assault riffles. A state of panic occurred and everybody fled from the right to the left bank of the Una river. In a mere hour and a half the town was drowned in a rain of shells and bullets. At the same time, from six Chetnik strongholds, fellow-workers, friends and neighbours were being fired upon. Many buildings were hit and flames engulfed the beautiful building of the Trade Centre. Irfan Kadic, a taxi driver, right by his own house, was the first civilian casualty. Terrible news of dozens of wounded and dead came from Mahala and Ustikolina. Nero Tatarevic was killed and his brother was wounded, while a piece of shrapnel hit and injured Zlatan Aliddanovic. Mujaga Mesic was badly wounded, Emin Kabiljagic was killed and Husein Sabic was massacred. Ibro Mesic was killed by his neighbour Stevo Strbac on his own doorstep. Sharp-shooters brought death from all major locations. Bosanska Krupa was continually shelled for the next few days and over 1,000 Muslims who could not make it out were forced to remain in the town. On Saturday 25 April the Chetniks began the 'cleansing' of the town. The disobedient ones were killed on the spot while others were taken away to prison camps through Jasenica and on towards Sanski Most, Prijedor or Banja Luka. This was how the right bank was taken from its inhabitants – the Muslims. Those in other villages who did not manage to escape became easy targets for the unleashed Chetnik bands. Approximately 3,000 civilians, mostly senior citizens, women and children, who were physically beaten after being interrogated at the 'courts-martial', were then deported to Bihac and Kamengrad from the concentration camps at Arapusa, Petar Koèic Elementary School and Jasenica. During the attack and 'cleansing' thirty-five civilians were killed and, according to witnesses, three prisoners at the Bosanska Krupa Jail were executed, while one young girl was raped. Other prisoners from Krupa were used for forced labour, mostly for clearing rubble and corpses, as well as for general repairs. Most of the houses were looted, burned and destroyed after the final occupation of the part of the city on the east bank of the Una river.[14]

As the Muslim population either fled or were herded into detention centres Bosanska Krupa became divided between the opposing Serb and Muslim forces. Both sides settled into entrenched positions with the big guns positioned high on the plateaux east of the Una valley. The Bosnian Serbs then began constructing fortified positions all along 'their' bank of the river, from Otoka right around to Bihac town, as sniping, indiscriminate shelling and the occasional limited offensive became the norm. To compound matters further the Muslims were barely able to defend themselves because of a deliberate policy that the JNA had implemented as they withdrew from the area earlier that month. While they handed over huge quantities of arms and equipment to both the Krajina and Bosnian Serbs, the Muslims and Croats were given nothing. From then on the local Serb militias were at liberty to use tanks, artillery, mortars, anti-aircraft guns and helicopters more or less at will, leaving the beleaguered Muslims in the unenviable position of trying to hold the line with just a handful of rusty muskets, an assortment of shooting rifles and whatever bits and pieces they had managed to pilfer from the JNA before they withdrew.

Recognizing this imbalance and the opportunities it presented, more Serb troops were moved forward into new positions overlooking the river, and on 12 June over 1,000 shells were fired in an attempt to 'soften up' the Muslim positions for an infantry attack. Amazingly it did not work, and with resistance proving much more determined than expected the confrontation line remained more or less where it was. As a result of this, both sides adopted 'stand-off' positions, with the Serbs regularly shelling into the Pocket and mounting the occasional probing raid. By November these tactics had left 200 dead and 1,600 wounded; the Muslims took most of the casualties.[15]

Identifying that this had now become a battle for survival, the Sarajevo government ordered the establishment of a new District Assembly, whose first task was to marshal all available forces into an organized unit.[16] Within a short time the Bosnian army's 5th Corps[17] came into being under the command of General Ramiz Drekovic, a professional officer from Sandzak,[18] who had only left the JNA in September 1991, and who was still wanted for alleged war crimes by the Croatian government.[19] By the autumn of 1992 this restructuring was complete and Drekovic was ready to defend Bihac Pocket against the Serbs. His new corps had been organized into seven brigades but the strength of each of these was probably no more than 800 men, while the few pieces of heavy equipment that remained in the Pocket – a few field guns, the odd tank and a handful of light mortars – were also put under corps control. Additionally there was a Bosnian Croat (HVO) brigade located in the mountains to the south-west of Bihac town, which went by the colourful name of the '27th of July Brigade'. About 600 strong, this Croat brigade was initially led by a Colonel Sedic who was also appointed Deputy Commander of the 5th Corps, thus bringing everyone theoretically within the one chain of command. Later Sedic would be replaced by a colourful character called Vlado Santic but for the moment the HVO coexisted comfortably enough with Drekovic. Supporting these full-time soldiers was a reorganized version of the old Territorial Defence Force

(TDF) and, although poorly equipped, these people could operate reasonably well as a local defence unit in each of the Pocket's municipalities.

Having spent the summer reorganizing his forces, Drekovic's efforts were greatly undermined by the failure of several local politicians and officials to fully support him. This was especially so in the north of the Pocket around the town of Velika Kladusa, where a thriving black market had been established. If one could deal in hard currency, goods were readily available from both Croatia and Serbia, and regular meetings were taking place between local officials from Velika Kladusa and the Serb authorities in the Krajina. A complete range of 'agreements' had been entered into involving the importation of a huge variety of domestic and industrial goods; the exportation of a limited number of dairy products; the purchase of safe passage from the Pocket to Croatia for around 1,000 Deutschmarks per person; and the importation, distribution and sale of humanitarian aid. At the time ECMM correctly reported that 'this has created tension between Bihac [town] and Velika Kladusa, and the start of a possible North/South divide'.[20] Within twelve months this division would become a reality as the municipal authorities in Velika Kladusa, led by Fikret Abdic, would decide to go their own way. In the longer term this would prove to be a very costly mistake.

Throughout November the Bosnian Serbs[21] received more infantry reinforcements from the nearby towns of Drvar and Kljuic, as well as a detachment of Krajina Serb special police from Knin. They also obtained 15 T55 and M84 tanks, 6 artillery batteries (24 guns) and 10 Multiple Launch Rocket systems (MLRs). Using the tanks as mobile artillery, and with the field guns firing between 800 and 1,200 shells per day,[22] the 'First Battle for Bihac' began on the morning of 1 December 1992. The Serb objective was to gain control of the Grabez plateau in the south-east from where they could dominate Bihac town and control the road and rail network in the Una valley. After seven days of intense shelling and hand-to-hand fighting, the 511th Brigade, supported by other elements of the 5th Corps, still clung ferociously to 60 per cent of the plateau, despite taking very heavy casualties.

In the south-west Sedic's HVO had also come under attack from the Krajina Serb's Lika Corps based across the border in Croatia. This was the first indication that from now on Drekovic would have to deal with a combined Serb offensive, and EU Monitors on the ground were quick to point out the wider implications this would have. 'This alleged involvement of the ARSK [Krajina Serbs] is not likely to be tolerated by the HV [Croatian army] and it could be used as a platform or excuse for greater involvement by Croatian forces which could eventually lead to a renewal of the conflict in the Krajina itself.'[23] This assessment, which was first made by EU Monitor Norman Tremblay in December 1992, proved to be absolutely correct. An excuse had indeed been found for long term Croatian involvement in the internal affairs of Bosnia-Hercegovina, and this same pretext would ultimately provide President Tudjman with the ammunition he needed to justify overrunning the Krajina two and a half years later. For the moment, however, Sedic and Drekovic managed to hold the line in the face of incessant shelling, and the 'First Battle of Bihac' ended in stalemate. The 5th Corps survived intact to fight another day but the ordinary people of the Pocket had been condemned to a very different lifestyle. For the next two-and-a-half years they would have to come to terms with living under siege.

As the conflict deepened other factors also came into play. Industries which up to that point had not been war damaged were now unable to continue in production as the supply of raw materials dried up. Initially many of these plants could have been restarted reasonably quickly but as time went on, and with little or no maintenance being carried out, this option soon evaporated. Those that struggled on intermittently soon fell silent as the economic infrastructure collapsed. Regular communication with the outside world quickly disappeared as the external mail service stopped and the telephone service soon followed suit. A few satellite phones continued to operate but these were not available to the general public, and became the exclusive property of senior politicians and the military. No external newspapers were delivered and the local ones only appeared weekly at best – sometimes not at all. Small radio stations continued to operate in Bihac, Cazin and Velika Kladusa, but their range was limited and they could only broadcast for a few hours at a time.

Bihac TV could only operate for a few hours each day and while stations in Zagreb and Banja Luka could be picked up this depended on whether or not the electricity supply was functioning, or if there was enough fuel to run a generator. Prior to the war, Bihac had been serviced by an extensive Federal power grid, which took no account of Republican boundaries. Now, however, access to the grid had been cut by the Serbs leaving the whole region dependant on one small and unreliable hydroelectric station on the Una river. However, it was still possible to buy electricity from the Serbs, despite the fact that a war was going on, and when the impoverished Muslims were able to scrape together a few thousand Deutschmarks, the grid could be reconnected in Banja Luka. Unfortunately this did not last long as the money soon ran out or was needed for more important things like food, so over 250,000 encircled people resorted to tearing down the forests and using the wood for heat and cooking. Their TVs, radios, fridges and cookers stood useless in their homes as a stark reminder of better times.

With the framework of society collapsing it was inevitable that before long the medical services would begin to crumble too. The main hospital was located in the south-western suburbs of Bihac town and had 700 beds.

Smaller facilities were available in Cazin and Velika Kladusa but there was already a shortage of specialist equipment and, in spite of the best efforts of the Red Cross, supplies of conventional medicines were running out.[24] Medical evacuations to Zagreb had initially been allowed to pass through the Krajina at the rate of eight per week, so long as they were authorized by ICRC officials,[25] however, in January 1993 this facility was suspended by the Krajina Serbs. This resulted in the beginning of a 'medivac black market', where huge sums of money were handed over to acquire safe passage to Croatia. Those who could not afford to pay just stayed at home and died. Yet again in the Balkans war was war, but business was still business.

By now food had also become a luxury with UNHCR[26] estimating that 3,000 tons of provisions per month were required to support the basic needs of the people. Unfortunately only 2,400 tons were being delivered as the humanitarian effort strained to keep pace with increasing demands from all over Former Yugoslavia. The cost of the European Union's Humanitarian Aid programme had spiralled from 13 million ECU in 1991 to 276 million ECU in 1992,[27] and represented almost 70 per cent of all humanitarian aid ploughed into the region, but it still fell well short of what was required.[28] Bihac, like several other places across the Balkans, was at that point already operating well below UNHCR's planning figures, and the situation got progressively worse when the Krajina Serbs refused permission for aid convoys to cross their borders. When the occasional convoy was allowed through, a large percentage of the cargo would end up confiscated as a transit tax. Food and humanitarian aid had now become weapons in a very dirty war. It is a comment in itself that EU Monitors on the ground saw fit to report as significant that, 'the region was quite proud of the fact that no one died of starvation during the winter of 92/3'.[29] Life had now become very black and white for the embattled citizens of Bihac Pocket as they looked into the uncertainty of another new year.

Political authority in the Pocket had traditionally been exercised by the mayors and their Opstina Councils but as an emergency war measure a District Assembly was established on 8 May 1992, which was approved in August 1992 by the national government.[30] This was a clear attempt by Sarajevo to retain political and military control and thereby ensure that the Pocket remained loyal to the concept of a united Bosnia, or at the very least refused to yield one square inch of land to the Serbs. It was not surprising, therefore, to discover that the President of the District Assembly was a Dr Ljubijankic, who also happened to be the local president of Alija Izetbegovic's Party of Democratic Action – the SDA.[31] A medical doctor who had previously worked in Zagreb, Sarajevo and Belgrade, Ljubijankic was quite popular at that time but after it was discovered that he had sent his family to live in Zagreb when the war broke out this mood began to change.

In the aftermath of the pre-Christmas Serb military offensive another attempt was made to tidy up the political structures within the Pocket and to closely supervise political activity in the four Opstinas – up to that point, the local mayors had enjoyed virtual autonomy. It was also designed to clarify the relationship between the military and political leaderships in the Pocket, and to impose a modicum of law and order on an ever-deteriorating social and humanitarian situation. It worked, and for a while all were of one voice, but as the overall situation deteriorated further and the plight of the ordinary people got worse, it became inevitable that frustration with the political leadership would grow. In March 1993 a power struggle developed between Dr Ljublijankic and a group who had until then been regarded as political moderates.

It quickly emerged that the first casualty here would be Ljublijankic himself, and his resignation was quickly followed by those of several other senior figures – coincidentally all friends of his. The main reason this purge succeeded was the existence of corruption at all levels of officialdom and the common perception that the District President and his associates were condoning it.[32] Whatever the reality, there was no denying that things were getting out of control and the slide to chaos had to be arrested by someone – and soon. With this in the background Ejub Topic became President of the Regional Assembly and Zlatko Jusic took on the role of Prime Minister of the Regional Government. They immediately set about introducing a programme of reform, which included the establishment of new governmental structures. By the end of April they had produced a provisional constitution for the Regional Assembly and shortly afterwards it was published and circulated. They also set about reforming the police, including the removal of several officers and the indictment of others on corruption charges. Customs inspectors were appointed and began clamping down on the black market while, in return for implementing these changes, the Opstina Councils were offered discussions on a system of 'political power-sharing'.

The new regime was adamant that they were following the direction and general guidelines of the Sarajevo government but the feeling on the ground – in part privately confirmed by senior figures – was that they were really charting a course for independence. The leadership also stated openly that they were trying to develop a framework for provincial government as envisaged in the Vance-Owen peace plan for Bosnia as a whole and that they hoped to show the rest of the country just what could be achieved once their plan became operative. But when Vance-Owen collapsed due to the intransigence of the Bosnian Serbs the Bihac Assembly was effectively left without a long term objective to focus on and not for the first time found itself thrown into political limbo. It was from this vacuum that a man called Fikret Abdic began to resurrect his

11

political career and once again propel himself to the forefront of Bosnian politics. He could not have known in 1993 just how pivotal his role was about to become nor could anyone else have predicted that the political and military backwater of Bihac Pocket would ultimately serve to bring the whole Serb house of cards crashing to the ground.

NOTES

1. ECMM Background Report, 11/7/93, para. 2.
2. ECMM Report/Info. Cell, November 1992.
3. Stevan K. Pavlowitch, *Tito: A Reassessment* (C. Hurst & Co., p. 38).
4. Misha Glenny, *The Fall of Yugoslavia*, p. 152–3.
5. 1991 census.
6. ECMM Report/Info. Cell, November 1992.
7. ECMM Background Report: 11/7/93, para. 8.
8. Taken from Comdt Hugh O'Donovan's personal diary of 1992.
9. Capsat is a satellite communications system which all ECMM teams used to make their daily reports to ECMM HQ in Zagreb. It is not a secure system but it is totally reliable and allows ECMM to put monitors into remote places and still remain in contact with them.
10. ECMM Team Bihac daily report: 20/4/92.
11. Senudin F. Jasarevic, *Aggression on the Bihac Region*, (1994).
12. ECMM Team Bihac daily report: 21/4/92.
13. ECMM Team Bihac daily report: 22/4/92.
14. From Jasarevic, *Aggression on the Bihac Region* (1994).
15. ECMM Report/Info. Cell, November 1992.
16. Mark Etherington, 'The Political and Military Situation in Bihac', ECMM Papers (1995).
17. The Bosnian army, also known as the Armija, was the army of the Republic of Bosnia-Hercegovina and 98 per cent Muslim.
18. Sandzak is a predominantly Muslim region in south-west Serbia that borders both Kosovo and Montenegro.
19. Bill Foxton, 'Bihac Pocket, A Tactical Appreciation', ECMM Papers (1995).
20. ECMM Report/Info. Cell, November 1992.
21. The 2nd Krajina Corps of the Bosnian Serb army was the formation deployed to the east and south of the Pocket.
22. Mark Etherington, 'The Political and Military Situation in Bihac', ECMM Papers (1995).
23. ECMM Report/Info. Cell: 12/12/92.
24. ECMM Report/Info. Cell: 10/3/95.
25. ICRC: International Committee of the Red Cross.
26. UNHCR: United Nations High Commissioner for Refugees.
27. 1 ECU = $1.30 US (1992 average value).

28. Humanitarian Aid Annual Report, 1992.
29. ECMM Background Report: 11/7/93, para. 47.
30. ECMM Report/Info. Cell, November 1992.
31. Dr Ljubijankic would later become the Foreign Minister of Bosnia-Hercegovina. While serving in this appointment he was killed when his helicopter was shot down by the Krajina Serbs in 1995. He was succeeded as Foreign Minister by Mohammed Sacirbey.
32. ECMM Report/Info. Cell, November 1992.

CHAPTER TWO

Enter Fikret Abdic

Fikret Abdic was born in 1939 in the small village of Donja Vidovska near Velika Kladusa, the third child of a large family, and when he left school he began working for the local agricultural cooperative which at the time employed twenty-six people. Twenty-five years later he had transformed this small 'Co-Op' into an agricultural food-processing industry called Agrokomerc with 13,500 people on the payroll, 430 farms operating in 50 villages, and 52 factories churning out a variety of food products but with a clear monopoly on the chicken and turkey market. Abdic had become a man of considerable influence and having joined the League of Communists in 1959, managed to get himself elected as a Deputy in 1963. By 1967 he had become a member of Bosnia's Communist Party Central Committee and was an emerging national figure and a very powerful man in the Bihac region where, directly or indirectly, his influence touched the lives of thousands of people. Later that year he received Bosnia-Hercegovina's highest recognition when he was conferred with the King Faisel Award for his success with Agrokomerc.

In 1987, however, things began to go wrong for Abdic when he was charged on several counts of corruption surrounding the acquisition of lucrative contracts for Agrokomerc, and he was held in investigative detention for over two years. It was alleged that Agrokomerc had been effectively printing money for itself by abusing the Yugoslav 'bank bond' system on a huge scale, and as a consequence the entire economy of north-west Bosnia was threatened with collapse.[1] When no indictments were proffered against him at the end of this period Abdic set about re-establishing himself and quickly recovered from the scandal. He resumed his place within the party and the presidency, and succeeded in becoming a delegate to the Assembly of Yugoslav Republics. He also managed to save his company thanks to his skill as a political negotiator and thereby succeeded in keeping his trade corridor to Croatia open, by doing several deals with the Krajina Serbs.

In 1991, at Bosnia-Hercegovina's first multi-party elections, Abdic emerged as the main threat to Izetbegovic both within the SDA and also as a potential new President of the country. When the votes were counted he emerged over 200,000 votes ahead of Izetbegovic but almost immediately announced that he was not interested in the top job and was prepared only to continue as a member of the Presidential Council. In the light of subsequent events some commentators began to blame Abdic for 'abdicating' his responsibilities, allowing Izetbegovic to take control, and ultimately leading the country into the war that followed. This is not a particularly fair assessment because, notwithstanding that he had polled so well, Abdic never had the backing of the SDA heavyweights in Sarajevo, nor did he have the support of the Bosnian Serb members of the Presidency. The only casualty of an attempt to force the issue would have been Abdic himself and in an interview in 1994 he was quite clear on this subject: 'it is true that I, of all the members of the Presidency, received the most votes in the recent elections; Croats, Muslims, and Serbs voted for me. But that is not important because the SDA, in whose ranks I received the most votes, had the right to decide whom it would recommend to be the President of the Presidency of Bosnia-Hercegovina. The leaders of the party decided on Izetbegovic and recommended him as President. Nikolai Koljevic, in the name of the Serbian Democratic Party, also said that they supported Izetbegovic. According to an internal agreement of the Presidency members received various tasks and responsibilities so I asked to be involved in economic matters because that was where I thought I could do the most good.'[2] While this all sounded very magnanimous Abdic conveniently omitted to mention another squence of events which took place in early May 1992 and which tended to offer a better explanation of his relationship with Izetbegovic.

Returning from another failed peace conference, this time in Lisbon, Izetbegovic flew into Sarajevo on the night of 2 May, oblivious to the fact that all hell had broken loose in his absence following an attempt by the Bosnian Serbs to divide the city in two. He was also unaware that General Milutin Kukanjac, the officer commanding the JNA's Second Military District in Sarajevo, together with his headquarter's staff, was now trapped in their barracks to the east of the city, and that Sefer Halilovic was demanding their immediate surrender and a handover of all weapons. Expecting to be met on the tarmac by UNPROFOR vehicles which would escort him back to the Presidency Building, he instead found himself surrounded by thirty members of the JNA with orders from Kukanjac to arrest him and take his party to the Lukavica Barracks in a Serb-controlled village on the southern edge of the city. Once there it was Kukanjac's intention to initiate a procedure whereby Izetbegovic would be released once he had successfully negotiated safe passage for his own personnel out of the area which was now held by government troops.[3]

However, when Izetbegovic arrived in Lukavica, he managed to gain access to a telephone and made contact, via one of the very few serviceable P&T lines in Sarajevo, with the city's TV station whereupon he confirmed that he had in fact been arrested by the JNA. He went on to nominate Ejup Ganic as acting president in his absence and then the two of them began a discussion of the situation live on air. While the conversation was taking place another twist to the story unfolded when Fikret Abdic unexpectantly walked into the TV studio enquiring about the President's well-being. Initial surprise at his presence soon gave way to total disbelief when it emerged that earlier in the evening he had successfully made his way from Bihac, by travelling first to Split on the coast and thereafter through Mostar, Zenica, Kiseljac and Visoko before eventually arriving in Sarajevo. He had managed to make his way through several Muslim, Croat and Serb checkpoints, apparently without any difficulty whatever, a feat which was at that time considered totally impossible. When this emerged Ganic immediately became suspicious and decided that an attempt was in hand, probably orchestrated by Abdic, to actually depose Izetbegovic. A meeting of the government was called at once and convened in the Presidency building where the Interior minister, Alija Delimustafic, opened proceedings by advocating the selection of a new president who might be better equipped and disposed to do a deal with Kukanjac and the JNA. While this suggestion certainly contained a great deal of merit Ganic rounded on the minister and the proposal was summarily quashed. What he singularly failed to eradicate however was the lingering suspicion that Abdic had been in league with Belgrade, the JNA high command, and a number of cabinet ministers in an attempt to remove Izetbegovic and assume control himself. There is of course no direct evidence that this was Abdic's intention but thereafter his political career in Sarajevo proved to be irreparably damaged, and when Izetbegovic was exchanged for Kukanjac the following day in the course of a botched operation in which six JNA officers were killed, it became quite clear to him that the hardliners in the SDA were firmly in control.[4]

Within a short period Alija Delimustafic gave up on politics in Sarajevo too and went to live in Austria while it became quite clear to Abdic that the longer he remained in Sarajevo the more marginalized he would become. His talents might be far more appreciated in Bihac where with a bit of luck he would be able to keep Agrokomerc in production and prevent his people from starving. Accordingly, in mid-September 1992, he returned to Bihac and assumed an advisory role in the District Assembly. Within a short time Abdic had once again regained his influence. The demise of Ljubijankic in March was almost certainly executed with his approval and indeed Topic's reform package appeared to have 'Abdic philosophy' stamped all over it. The main problem was clearly going to be trying to keep Bihac out of a war that was engulfing the rest of the country. This was brought home very dramatically to Abdic on 27 April 1993 when an attack was launched by the Krajina Serbs in which they managed to capture a large swathe of land in the north-east corner of the Pocket, around the town of Bosanska Bojna.

The local Serb commanders were adamant that this was only a 'limited local offensive' by troops who had previously been expelled from the area by 'uncontrolled elements', and that all they were doing was reclaiming their own land. At face value this was plausible but when one delved a little deeper it emerged that the attack was very much coordinated, employing infantry, armour and artillery drawn from three Serb brigades in the area. When the 5th Corps counter-attacked they found themselves repulsed in a very controlled and orderly fashion, which lead them to the conclusion that this was not an ad hoc incursion by a handful of frustrated displaced Serbs. In fact it was widely believed that the whole thing was strictly coordinated with the Bosnian Serbs in order to force Drekovic to re-deploy some of his troops away from the front line in the south. When it later emerged that senior Krajina and Bosnian Serb commanders had met the previous day; that the field commander for the attack was in fact a member of the Bosnian Serb Army's 1st Corps in Banja Luka; and that both the Bosnian and Krajina Serb artillery had opened fire at exactly the same time, all the pieces of the jigsaw fell into place.[5]

The message here for Abdic was very clear. If Bihac was to survive, and the people were to be spared the brutality of all-out conflict, then he would have to take the initiative himself. No confidence could be derived from the UN announcement that declared Bihac town a 'safe area' because there were no means to enforce it, and even if by some quirk of fate the Serbs respected this declaration for a while there was nothing to stop them pursuing their campaign elsewhere in the Pocket later on. Furthermore it was now blatantly obvious that the 5th Corps could not be expected to initiate any significant operations and could not even be depended upon to hold the line in the face of a concerted and coordinated attack. There was nothing for it but to negotiate with the Serbs and attempt to establish some criteria acceptable to everyone. The first phase of this policy came into play more or less immediately when UNPROFOR suggested a demilitarization of the disputed area around Bosanska Bojna. The plan involved the placement of French UN troops between the warring parties, policing the area with civil police (UNCIVPOL), and the re-settlement of the original inhabitants who were now living elsewhere. The last part of this was extremely ambitious – and everyone knew it – but agreement was obtained and the situation settled down for a while.[6]

As the overall situation throughout Bosnia continued to deteriorate, and the Vance-Owen peace plan effectively came to nothing, matters were not helped by a decision in Sarajevo to reject the new set of proposals, which were to become known as the Joint Action Programme (JAP).[7] This was an attempt by the United States, France, Spain and Russia to try and find a basis for what they called 'common action' by the International Community in Bosnia, and it set out a series of measures that they hoped to implement. These included a cessation of all hostilities; confirmation of UN Resolution 824, which promised to increase the strength of UNPROFOR; deployment of Monitors along the border between Serbia and Bosnia; employment of economic sanctions against Croatia if they continued supporting the activities of the HVO; and increasing international pressure to resolve the ethnic problems in both Kosovo and Macedonia.

It must be admitted that there was nothing essentially wrong with any of this (as, in many respects, it represented little more than a re-worked Vance-Owen Peace Plan) and could have served at least as a basis for further discussions. Radovan Karadzic, the leader of the Bosnian Serbs, had no sooner accepted the plan and indicated his willingness to start talking than Izetbegovic came out and rejected it, appealing instead to his people 'to continue the fight for the preservation of the sovereignty and territorial integrity of Bosnia'. The reality was that Izetbegovic had rejected the initiative purely because the Serbs had accepted it and Abdic, now openly appalled at what was happening, saw the gulf between Izetbegovic and himself widening by the day. It got worse when a row erupted during a meeting of the Presidential Council on 23 June over a proposal to effectively partition the country into three ethnic provinces as part of a negotiated settlement, rather than continue the fighting that was resolving nothing.

Abdic had no difficulty supporting this suggestion because he believed that partition was already a reality on the ground anyway, but Ejup Ganic vehemently opposed him, advocating that the fight, such as it was, must go on. Izetbegovic was equally dogmatic and went so far as to propose that government representatives should boycott the peace talks in Geneva if partition remained on the table as an option to resolve the conflict.[8] The remainder of the collective Presidency overruled this absurd approach but neither Izetbegovic nor Ganic would participate further, leaving Abdic and the others to wheel and deal among themselves. When Abdic went to the conference table in Geneva a few days later he knew exactly where he stood. He could effectively agree to whatever he wished but if that did not subsequently meet with Izetbegovic's approval then all his efforts would be in vain. He was supposedly negotiating on behalf of the Presidency of his country but he could not deliver on any issue while Ganic and Izetbegovic held a veto at home.

By July Abdic was unable to endure this situation any longer and he took the unprecedented step of writing a public letter to Izetbegovic and the other members of the Presidency, in which he set out his assessment of the situation and what he believed they were doing wrong. Whether this was inspired by a genuine concern for the people or by economic ulterior motives will probably never be known, but either way it is quite clear that he certainly understood that militarily the Muslims were never going to win the war. What he said turned out to be prophetic but like many prophets before him he would not be accepted by all his own people. He was never going to be admitted to the inner sanctum of the SDA and consequently a great deal of bitterness is to be found in what he wrote. Nevertheless the letter provides a unique insight into SDA politics at the time and one is led to the inescapable conclusion that perhaps there was, after all, another way to deal with the situation, had Izetbegovic been prepared to take it.

> No presidency, or any negotiating body, can or should be allowed to suspend the will of the people, who will in any case have the final say on the future organization of the state of Bosnia-Hercegovina. . . . I am confident that you are now aware of the ruinous futility regarding the belittling and negating of the right of the Presidency to be the collective head of state, regarding negotiations, and regarding the continual insistence that only you and the inner circle of your like-minded associates have the authority to render decisions and, moreover, that you are finally liable to abandon these sterile policies. The affirmation of the Presidency as the collective representative and legal state institution, and your choosing to take your rightful seat as 'first among equals' can only serve to advance the peace process and establish a pluralistic Bosnian policy, as opposed to a monopolization of the decision-making process by two or three individuals. . . . The situation in Bosnia-Hercegovina leaves no room for the luxury that allows for the politically ill-considered caprice of one party, even if it be the President, to push the nation into further catastrophe. Before our country takes on the fate of a still-born child, and the Muslim people are forced on to reservations and condemned to slow death, we have to turn the situation to our advantage and finally become seasoned partners, mature enough to deal with the historic cataclysm which we now face.

With all his cards on the table, and finding himself in a minority of one, Abdic was convinced that Izetbegovic had no intention of entering into any form of negotiated settlement that might involve the concession of jurisdiction over their own territory to the Serbs. Whenever it looked as if a settlement might be possible, Izetbegovic usually found an excuse to walk away and as far as Abdic was concerned, he had put up with enough. Taken in the context of trying to survive in Bihac, isolated yet surrounded and over 350 km from Sarajevo, Abdic was now forced to identify how best the Pocket could survive in both political and economic terms. Quickly he came to the conclusion that there was no point waiting for guidance from Sarajevo and that it would be better for the citizens of Bihac if they decided to fend for themselves. The events of August 1993 played right into his hands.

In the wider context, attempts to resolve the conflict in both Croatia and Bosnia had by this time moved to the headquarters of the International Conference on Former Yugoslavia in Geneva. On 15 July the so-called 'Erdut Agreement' was signed, which allowed the Maslenica bridge, Zemunik airport and the Peruca dam to be placed under UNPROFOR control, with the establishment of an UNCIVPOL presence in certain villages within the Krajina. Three days later President Tudjman was busy performing opening ceremonies at Maslenica and Zemunik, so officially everyone was happy, and it was as a counterpoint to this that Lord Owen and Thorvald Stoltenberg began a series of bilateral talks on Bosnia,[9] which resulted in the announcement on the 28th that Karadzic, Boban and Izetbegovic had agreed to issue instructions to their respective forces for a cease-fire. However, by the time they had all re-convened six days later, a section of the Maslenica bridge lay submerged in water following several Serb bombardments. The signs were not good, and they deteriorated further on 10 August when all talking came to a halt following the re-imposition of the blockade of Sarajevo by Serb forces on the ground. On the 16th, just when the conference appeared to be getting back on track, Izetbegovic sent a letter to Owen and Stoltenberg in which he refused to have bilateral discussions with Mate Boban until the Croats complied with the terms of the Makarska Agreement[10] and gave full freedom of movement to all the humanitarian agencies. This would allow them access to Muslim communities in places like Mostar. Then, having overcome that problem, Izetbegovic walked out of the next meeting on the 19th, accusing the co-chairmen of having decided on a plan to divide Sarajevo that would give half to the Serbs, when nothing of the sort was the case.

At this point the process was clearly going nowhere: the best Izetbegovi could agree to was a 'conditional' acceptance of the plan, contingent upon the immediate return of all Muslim land now held by either the Serbs or Croats. While the parliament in Sarajevo was mandating Izetbegovic to this effect, by sixty-one votes to eleven,[11] President Tudjman was meeting Fikret Abdic on the island of Brijuni.[12] It was very surprising to find this man, who by now had become completely marginalized in Bosnia, advising the President of Croatia on how to proceed at the next round of international peace talks, but it was nothing short of amazing to discover the extent of Abdic's influence. This was there for all to see in President Tudjman's address to the combined session two days later. 'We were talking about the solution to the crisis in Bosnia and Hercegovina, about the acceptance or non-acceptance of the package proposed by the Co-chairmen . . . the Serbian and Croatian sides do accept it, but the Muslim side has remarks,[13] which set back the conference by a great deal, if not to the very beginning.'[14] Nobody was prepared to acede to Izetbegovic's conditions so the Muslims did not sign and the following day Tudjman went on the offensive again, declaring to anyone who would listen that the conference had broken down because of Muslim intransigence.

Fortified by the support that was now coming from Tudjman, and anxious to ensure that his economic links with Croatia remained intact, Abdic, in the course of an interview on Bihac TV, announced that as far as he was concerned the future of the Pocket lay in the peoples' own hands and not in slavishly following the dictates currently emanating from Sarajevo. Gathering together a group of like-minded associates, he held a meeting at the Agrokomerc offices in Velika Kladusa on 7 September and a committee was formed to promote what was called an 'Initiative for the establishment of the Autonomous Province of Western Bosnia within the Republic of Bosnia and the Union of Republics of Bosnia-Hercegovina'.[15] In three days 17,238 people from all over the Pocket had put their names to the Initiative proposals and the President of the Initiative Committee, Professor Asim Dizdarevic, wrote to the District Assembly inviting all the Municipal Councils within the Pocket to declare their position on the matter.[16] The letter concluded with a warning that 'Until competent authorities declare themselves and form suitable bodies, the Initiative committee will continue with its work, bearing in mind that they do not have the right to ignore the plebisicitary request of the citizens in any issue'.

In response an extraordinary session of the Bihac District Assembly was held the following day. It was decided that if Articles 47 and 84 of the Constitution of Bosnia-Hercegovina were to be complied with, the people were indeed entitled to express their opinion on the matter and the municipalities of Bihac Town, Bosanska Krupa, Cazin and Velika Kladusa were instructed to immediately ascertain the views of the other 230,000 citizens of the Pocket.[17] Ejub Topic appeared to be almost in favour of the proposals himself at this point. However, within three days, all that had changed when the response from the municipalities indicated that there was no evidence of *any* overwhelming support for the Initiative. Instead it transpired that the only people in favour were all connected to Agrokomerc and not representative of the population as a whole. But the seeds of conflict had been sown and a 'war within a war' was in the offing.

The Initiative committee was now faced with political isolation unless it took the matter a stage further. After prompting by Abdic an assembly was established in Velika Kladusa on 27 September, which proclaimed the existence of the 'Autonomous Province of Western Bosnia' (APWB), an area equating roughly to the northern half of Bihac Pocket and where Agrokomerc was most influential. For the ordinary people in this part of Bosnia life had become simply a matter of survival – if there was the remotest chance that their conditions and prospects were going to improve by throwing their lot in with Abdic, then they were quite prepared to do so. Equally those members of the 5th Corps and the

Territorial Defence Forces (TDF), who were originally from Velika Kladusa and its environs, had no qualms about supporting the new political set-up: they fully understood that they stood a far better chance of receiving payment for their services from the coffers of Agrokomerc than they did from the Sarajevo government. So, within a very short period of time, the Pocket had become politically and militarily polarized; in effect, divided in two. Skirmishing began almost immediately[18] but, undeterred, Abdic announced the creation of his new political party, the Muslim Democratic Party (MDS),[19] and his disciples began settling into a new pattern of existence as towns and villages were fought over, changed hands, and then sometimes changed back again. Mediation attempts by UNPROFOR's General Briquemont proved unsuccessful[20] and the fighting escalated, especially in Cazin, which became the first town to experience the new conflict.

The town initially fell to Abdic forces on 15 October but returned to 5th Corps control the following day after much skirmishing.[21] In order to ensure that the only threat to APWB came from Sarajevo, Abdic quickly moved to sign non-aggression pacts with the other Bosnian leaders and on 21 October he travelled to Zagreb to conclude a deal with Mate Boban, representing the Bosnian Croats and, more specifically, the HVO within the Pocket. The following day he moved on to Belgrade and entered into a similar arrangement with Radovan Karadzic.[22] To complete the picture he also entered a rapprochement with the Krajina Serbs on 28 October, which included a non-aggression pact and the demilitarization of the disputed Bosanska Bojna area in the north-east. With all external relations resolved Abdic believed he was now in a position to pursue his own objectives within the Pocket. This, however, would prove more difficult than even he had bargained for. An ECMM team, led by Mark Etherington, spent five days in the Bihac area around this time and their observations were interesting.

> The root causes of Abdic's declaration of autonomy lie in local factors. For many years the Bihac region has regarded itself as having a separate identity. But Abdic's action is motivated by an intense personal rivalry towards Izetbegovic and deep-seated disagreements over the Bosnian Presidency's attitude towards the peace process . . . Abdic claims he has 80% of popular support but 50% is a more accurate estimate. Sympathy for him is balanced by concern for his methods . . . Abdic will remain a potent political force for as long as Izetbegovic continues to encourage Moslem Bosnians that the war must continue. An early rapprochement between Abdic and Izetbegovic may prove elusive and the present uneasy stand-off between Bihac and Velika Kladusa will therefore continue.[23]

The Sarajevo government's problems were not confined exclusively to Bihac. Several other parts of the country also began to think about organizing their own affairs, not least among them the municipality of Tuzla in north-central Bosnian, where the notion of autonomy was being seriously considered. In response to this perceived disintegration, and the failure of the 5th Corps to deal satisfactorily with Abdic and his supporters, General Drekovic was moved sideways to take command of the 4th Corps while his deputy, Colonel Atif Dudakovic, was promoted to Major General at thirty-nine years of age, and took over command in Bihac. This was a shrewd move by Sarajevo: it gave the impression of radical reorganization but at the same time retained a high degree of continuity within the Corps. Dudakovic relished his new appointment and was ready to take the fight to Abdic in a way that Drekovic never would.

Born in Bosanska Dubica in 1954 Dudakovic was very familiar with the terrain over which he would now operate and this former JNA officer, whose last posting had been in Zadar, Croatia, in 1991, immediately began a reorganization of his forces. He introduced a corps tactical headquarters that he could deploy rapidly to any flashpoint, on any of his front lines, at any time. It must have struck Dudakovic as somewhat ironic that having spent many years in the JNA becoming an expert on the use of artillery, he now found himself in Bihac with only a few badly constructed mortars to call upon while all his enemies appeared to have little difficulty raining a whole range of calibres down on top of him. This would force him to improvise, something which in time would allow him to turn the tables completely on those who in the summer of 1993 seemed almost invincible.

Elsewhere in Bosnia other battles were also being fought and on 3 November the Armija High Command launched a large scale offensive on the Croat town of Vares on 3 November.[24] Faced with elements from both the Armija's 2nd and 3rd Corps the local HVO brigade abandoned their checkpoints and quickly withdrew south-eastwards across Serb-held territory to the village of Dastansko. Here, with the help of some Serb mercenaries, they dug in and managed to hold their positions. The capture of Vares, however, gave a much needed shot in the arm to the Presidency of Izetbegovic and tactically linked up four Armija Corps – the 2nd in Tuzla, the 3rd in Zenica, the 6th in Konjic and the 4th in Mostar. Politically it also vindicated the President's faith in the Armija General Staff, who had been so influential in having the Geneva Peace Plan rejected on the basis that they could, if given the opportunity, reclaim all Muslim lands that had been lost by use of force. Few observers gave this claim much credibility as the Armija's military capability consisted largely of badly armed infantry with a few light mortars, a few pieces of captured light artillery and a handful of armoured vehicles – but things did appear to be getting better. This conviction was reinforced by the fact that for the very first time ammunition had become available for live fire training exercises with all of their limited range of weapons.[25] A pertinent question here might well have been where was all this ammunition coming from, but somewhat surprisingly, nobody asked. In any event this euphoria, such as it was, turned out to be short-lived because, on 9 November, after very heavy shelling by the HVO, the old Turkish bridge in Mostar, which had spanned the Neretva river for four centuries and survived many wars and floods, was blasted into pieces and sent crashing into the waters below.

This was a poignant moment for Muslims and Croats alike, and while this senseless vandalism made it obvious to everyone that the values of the past were now well and truly gone, it also triggered a reaction from the politicians who were at least theoretically supposed to be in control of their military. Within three days Mate Boban had fired his top general, Slobodan Praljak, replacing him with the more moderate Ante Rosso, and in Sarajevo the Croatian Foreign Minister Mate Granic met with the Turkish Foreign Minister Hikmet Cetin and together with Haris Silajdzic they signed a common declaration on an immediate cease-fire between the Armija and the HVO.[26] Five days later in Geneva Sadako Ogata of UNHCR succeeded in extracting another signed declaration from the political representatives of all three sides, which purported to guarantee the free passage and security of all humanitarian convoys operating in Bosnia.[27] When the Armija and HVO came on board on 24 November it began to look as if a major breakthrough might have been achieved.

As the year drew to a close the overall situation on the ground, while remaining totally unresolved, nevertheless appeared to be quietening down. This was, however, as attributable to the winter weather as much as anything else, and all the parties remained focused on their own objectives and aspirations. Karadzic was still ready to discuss any proposals that might lead to the ultimate partition of the country, while his military commanders continued to provide local support to both the HVO and Armija in different places along the confrontation line, in the hope that they would inflict more damage on one another and thereby allow the Serbs to benefit from the fallout. For their part, the Bosnian Croats became embroiled in an internal political row as their pockets of territory in central Bosnia became even more isolated than before and could only now be re-supplied by air, courtesy of helicopters on loan from the HV in Zagreb.

Further HV support for the HVO was to be found in Gornji Vakuf, where fighting continued unrelentingly, while in Kiseljak assistance to the HVO was being provided by the nearby BSA unit who were more than willing to drive their tanks across the confrontation line, fire a few rounds at the Muslims, and then withdraw from whence they came. The only consideration regulating the frequency of this kind of cooperation was the ability of the HVO to provide adequate compensation, which could range from direct cash payments in hard currency, to the provision of food and fuel, to turning a blind eye to Serb incursions into Croat territory in order to launch their own raids against Armija positions. Like everything else in the Balkans, if the price was right, anything was possible.

Within the Muslim community, it had now become clear – following the rejection of the Geneva Peace Plan – that for the moment at least the military held sway over the politicians, and Abdic's declaration of autonomy in Bihac served only to push the SDA leadership into a concentrated effort to ensure that similar problems did not spring up elsewhere. They were also acutely aware that Abdic was now 'doing business' with all of their sworn enemies and following a meeting on 7 November with Vladimir Lukic and Jadranko Prilic, the prime ministers of the Republic of Srpska and CRHB respectively, it was now apparent that Abdic had entered into a whole range of political and economic programmes. Izetbegovic began travelling extensively throughout the country, attending a wide range of meetings in a gesture of solidarity with his long-suffering supporters who, by now, were barely eking out an existence in the hundreds of battle-damaged towns and villages. Harris Silajdzic remained behind in Sarajevo to look after international matters and between the two of them, while they certainly did not resolve the situation, they did manage to stabilize it for a while. In this context what they least needed was more trouble in Bihac – but that was exactly what they got.

On 4 December Abdic forces launched a ground attack into the area of Izacic in the west of the Pocket, using a force of around 1,000 troops. What made this manoeuvre different was that these people had earlier managed to disengage from the confrontation line within the Pocket and withdraw northwards through the town of Velika Kladusa into the Krajina; they then transited – apparently unhindered – to the south, through territory controlled by the Kordun Corps of the Krajina Serb army. Finally they advanced in an easterly direction from the village of Licko Petrovo Selo to re-enter the Pocket in a deliberate flanking attack on 5th Corps positions. While all of this was going on the remainder of Abdic's forces increased the pressure all along the confrontation line, escalating the overall conflict significantly. This, of course, had been predictable since mid-November, when the mobilization of all adult males in APWB had been ordered and UNHCR convoys had for a time been denied access through Velika Kladusa, on the pretext that they were supposedly supplying food to the 5th Corps. ECMM personnel were also accused of spying and were arrested, while Abdic was reported to have sanctioned the detention of forty people from the south of the Pocket to be used as hostages or bargaining tools if the situation required.[28]

In a meeting with an UNMO team in Cazin on 4 December General Dudakovic was scathing in his condemnation of the RSK authorities for permitting Abdic unrestricted transit through their territory, and for re-supplying his forward troops. While this was probably warranted, Dudakovic's criticism of UNPROFOR for failing to curtail these activities most certainly was not. As on previous occasions all any of the UN troops on the ground could do was watch and wait as the conflict raged around them, and later on help pick up the bodies and ferry the wounded to hospital. This was precisely the situation in which they found themselves during the early days of December: all they were able to do was set up dressing stations near the scene of the fighting and transport the wounded back to Vojnic hospital, and onwards to Karlovac in Croatia if necessary.[29]

By 8 December, although the situation had stabilized with little gain to the APWB forces, Abdic had succeeded in forcing Dudakovic to commit troops to several new positions. This in turn made Dudakovic very vulnerable to attack from the Bosnian Serbs all along the southern confrontation line and presented him with a problem he could well have done without as he began reorganizing his now depleted and over-extended Corps. However he did manage to contain the situation in spite of increased shelling by the Serbs to the south of Bihac town and in Bosanska Krupa itself.

On 23 December units from the 5th Corps managed to remove Abdic troops from the Skokovi Pass with little loss of life, thanks largely to the fact that the area was sparsely populated. By Christmas morning they had also succeeded in evicting them from Pecigrad but Dudakovic was well aware that this was really as far as he could push the matter without over-extending himself completely. Both sides had suffered many casualties, with over 300 dead and 1,000 wounded and the willingness of the Krajina Serbs to come to Abdic's assistance had added a new dimension to the problem.[30]

He was also acutely aware that Abdic had somehow managed to marshal his forces into a formation of six brigades[31] which appeared to have a functioning chain of command, and had recently acquired new light mortars and heavy machine-guns, purchased from the Krajina Serbs. EU Monitors on the ground remained active, suggesting to all sides that their best option lay in an immediate cease-fire and Dudakovic eventually decided to run with this, not because he was interested in doing business with the APWB, but because he badly needed time to re-group, re-organize and prepare for the next phase of the struggle that would undoubtedly come.[32] Mr Kabiljagic, the President of the Bihac Regional Assembly, also came out in favour of a cease-fire, if only to evacuate twenty-seven families who had unwittingly become trapped along the internal confrontation line and had been unable to move to one side or the other. Senior figures within APWB were anxious to give matters a rest too.[33] Accordingly ECMM continued to shuttle between both camps, dodging incoming Bosnian Serb artillery, which was clearly designed to keep the conflict going, and as the year drew to a close some kind of breakthrough looked to be probable.

In the middle of all this an amazing request was made to the ECMM team in Bihac town on Wednesday 29 December, when Dudakovic asked them to set up a meeting between himself and the Commander of the Krajina Serbs' Licka Corps, who were bordering the Pocket to the south-west and through whose area all black-market goods flowed. War might well have been going on but business was still business and neither commander had any difficulty accepting this situation and working through it. However, the more significant development by far was the realization that the RSK forces were not operating under a unified command structure but were functioning instead as independent units, very much doing their own thing and following their own agendas. Banija Corps to the north-east of the Pocket had chosen to remain neutral *vis à vis* the internal conflict following the demilitarization of Bosanska Bonja in agreement with Abdic. Kordun Corps to the north and north-west of Velika Kladusa were now in active collaboration with Abdic and, provided the price was right, were supplying him with whatever he needed. Licka Corps, as just mentioned, were passively supporting Dudakovic against both Abdic and the Kordun Corps by allowing the black market to flourish. To further complicate matters the same black-market goods were originating not in the RSK but in Croatia, and were in turn transiting through areas patrolled and controlled by the Croatian army and police, both of whom were, *de facto* and *de jure*, at war with the Krajina Serbs. And if all of that were not complicated enough, it later emerged in the course of a UN investigation that a relative of Gojko Susak, the Croatian Defence Minister, was also supplying Abdic with a variety of weapons, the ammunition for which was being donated by the Bosnian Serbs.[34]

Elsewhere throughout Former Yugoslavia there was little room for optimism as the new year approached. Heavy fighting continued in central Bosnia in spite of a Christmas cease-fire that had been agreed and signed. Armija troops launched a major attack on the Croat Vitez Pocket on 22 December while simultaneously shelling Zepce, Visoko and Kiseljak. But, after six days of fighting, no significant territory had changed hands. In Tuzla, while the situation was generally quiet, tension remained very high in anticipation of the next BSA attack; the Serbs had taken to firing Frog/Orkan Rockets and SA-2 surface-to-air missiles against ground targets in the town itself.[35]

The confrontation line in Croatia also remained comparatively quiet and the seasonal truce was generally respected by both sides – with the

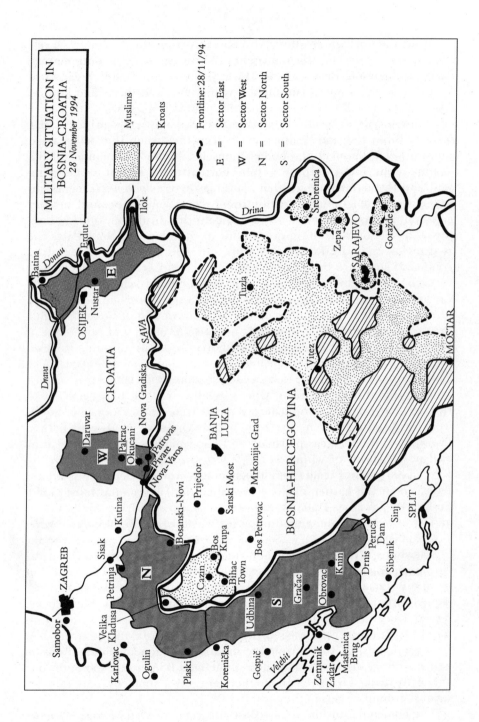

MILITARY SITUATION IN
BOSNIA-CROATIA
28 November 1994

Muslims

Kroats

Frontline: 28/11/94

E = Sector East
W = Sector West
N = Sector North
S = Sector South

exception of Colonel Bosonac. He was the local Krajina Serb Commander in the south-western part of Sector South, and continued his own programme of daily shelling which had no tactical objective and was designed solely to intimidate the Croatians who lived there, and anyone else who ventured into the area. Additionally, results from the recent elections in the Krajina, while admittedly incomplete, indicated that though some of the main personalities were going to change appointments, little else was likely to emerge. As the last seconds of 1993 died away there was nothing to indicate that the new year would bring any great improvement to the lives of these Yugoslav people. It seemed to matter little which God any of them worshipped because nobody appeared to listen to their prayers – let alone answer them.

NOTES

1. Misha Glenny, *The Fall of Yugoslavia*, p. 152. See also Woodward, Susan, *In the Eye of the Storm* and Dyker and Vejvoda, *In Yugoslavia and After*, Longman, 1996, p. 162.
2. Vanjska Politika, Srijeda, Aleksandar Milosevic, 2 Veljace 1994.
3. MacKenzie, Lewis, *Peacekeeper – The Road to Sarajevo*, Douglas and McIntyre (Toronto), 1993, p. 165.
4. Silber and Little, *The Death of Yugoslavia*, Penguin/BBC 1995, p. 262.
5. ECMM Report/Info. Cell, 11/5/93.
6. ECMM Report, 11/7/93. Abdic had no difficulty signing: for him it was the only way forward.
7. 23/5/93. See Lord Owen, *Balkan Odyssey*, Indigo, 1996, p. 184.
8. 28/6/93.
9. Talks began on 27 July 1993 with Karadzic, Boban and Izetbegovic, and also involved the participation of Presidents Tudjman and Milosevic, with Bulatovic as appropriate.
10. 10/7/93. Signed at Makarska, Croatia, in the presence of representatives from all international humanitarian agencies, this was an agreement on the delivery of humanitarian aid to the whole area of Bosnia-Hercegovina under the control of the Croat and Muslim forces.
11. ECMM Weekly Mil./Pol. Summary: 29/9/93.
12. 29/8/93. ECMM Sequence of Events, p. 115.
13. 'Remarks' in this context mean conditions.
14. 31/8/93, Geneva. ECMM Sequence of Events, p. 115.
15. Taken from the letter of the President of the Initiative Committee, Professor Asim Dizdarevic, to the President of the Bihac District Assembly Ejub Topic on 11/9/93.
16. 11/9/93.
17. Minutes of the Meeting of the District Assembly on 12/9/93, signed by Ejub Topic.

18. 2/10/93. The first skirmishes were reported near the village of Skokovi.
19. 3/10/93: the founding of MDS.
20. 6/10/93.
21. 16/10/93.
22. 22/10/93.
23. ECMM Weekly Consolidated Report: 29/10/93.
24. The attack on Vares was directly linked to atrocities carried out by the HVO in the village of Stupni Do on 22 October. Bosnian Croat forces entered the village at 0800 hrs and systematically burned fifty-two houses to the ground, killing thirty-six Muslims in the process. It later transpired that the villagers had been told to leave a few days previously by the HVO but had decided to stay in the hope that the tension would dissipate. They were wrong.
25. ECMM Weekly Report: 11/11/93.
26. 12/11/93.
27. 18/11/93.
28. ECMM Weekly Mil./Pol. Summary: 9/12/93.
29. RC Zagreb Daily Reports: 4–5/12/93.
30. Abdic had written a letter of protest to the Croatian Prime Minister, Nikica Valentic, on 28 November in which he denied that APWB was supplying equipment to the Krajina Serbs. This was most probably true – he had barely enough for his own troops. What became clear a few days later was the willingness of the Serbs to assist Abdic, provided, as usual, the price was right.
31. A brigade in this context probably constitutes no more than 850 troops and should be equated with a conventional battalion. An UNMO report, quoted by RC Zagreb on 4/12/93, indicated that a company commander from Abdic forces, now a POW, had revealed that an APWB brigade consisted of 6 companies, with 120 troops in each, giving a total of 720.
32. ECMM Re-Assessment/Bill Foxton: 30/5/95.
33. RC Zagreb Daily Report: 21/12/93.
34. UN/G2 Assessment Review: April 1994.
35. ECMM Weekly Mil./Pol. Summary: 30/12/93.

CHAPTER THREE

The 5th Corps Fights
for Survival

While Mate Granic and Haris Silajdzic were busy trying to iron out their political differences in Vienna in order to bring the slaughter in central Bosnia to an end,[1] EU Monitors in Bihac Pocket continued their search for a solution to the internal conflict. Their efforts were eventually rewarded with an announcement that a cease-fire had been agreed, which both sides were willing to formalize by having it witnessed by the French UN Battalion Commander, Colonel Legrier. On 18 January Asim Delic and Irfan Saracevic for APWB, and General Dudakovic on behalf of the 5th Corps, put their names to a cease-fire agreement that left several matters unresolved but nonetheless provided a much needed respite for everyone involved. In the weeks that followed meetings took place on an almost daily basis but the pity of it was – as on so many other occasions – that both sides were operating to totally different agendas. Dudakovic was intent on bringing all armed elements in the Pocket under 5th Corps control before any discussions took place on new political structures, while Abdic wanted all prisoners exchanged as a precondition to discussing anything else. In this impasse it was obvious that the cease-fire would not last and when the Bosnian Serbs renewed their offensive in the south on 6 February the whole thing fell apart, leaving Dudakovic to concentrate on more immediate matters – his survival.

In the meantime Abdic had given an illuminating interview to *Vanjska Politika* from the comfort of the Agrokomerc offices in the Croatian port of Rijeka. Far removed from the operations he was conducting on the ground, he set out his objectives and explained current policies.[2] The essence of his argument remained, that when the war began in Bosnia he had advocated a negotiated settlement with both Croats and Serbs, while Izetbegovic, allegedly prompted by foreign advisors, had opted for a continuation of the war and remained steadfast in that position. The creation of APWB was not a secession from Bosnia-Hercegovina *per se* but rather an attempt to save a part of the country from destruction and death, and to preserve some kind of economy so that the people might not starve. Abdic's assessment of the situation as of 2 February 1994 was that it was 'not too bad within APWB although it could of course be much better'.

Convoys of civilians and weapons[3] were now constantly coming and going through the RSK, to and from Croatia, as part of Agrokomerc was still in production. In relation to the ongoing fighting with the 5th Corps Abdic again blamed Izetbegovic for ordering Dudakovic to 'break the secession' and while a cease-fire had been agreed on 18 January, no political discussion followed it. The reason for this, he believed, was that while a delegation from the Bosnian Presidency had been scheduled to enter negotiations, Ejup Ganic, Izetbegovic's deputy, had scuttled the plan, presumably on the grounds that the Sarajevo government was really only prepared to talk to APWB looking down the barrel of a gun. Despite this regrettable situation Abdic believed that, thanks to his leadership, the people in the northern half of the Pocket were enjoying a far better standard of living than their counterparts in the south. A bag of flour, for example, cost 7 Deutschmarks in Velika Kladusa while the same product cost over 70 Deutschmarks in Cazin, Bosanska Krupa and Bihac town, if, of course, one could get it at all. When asked about the ongoing Croat–Muslim conflict in central Bosnia Abdic was again critical of Izetbegovic and Ganic for making demands that could never be realized. A case in point here was Sarajevo's demand to have unrestricted access to the Adriatic at either Neum[4] or Ploce, when both ports were well within Bosnian Croat territory and virtually guaranteed to remain so. A far better option as far as Abdic was concerned would have been to explore the possibility of developing duty-free facilities at Ploce and Rijeka (where, coincidentally, Abdic just happened to have his offices), and to recognize the fact that Bosnia-Hercegovina was dependent on Croatia economically and geographically. He concluded by saying that in his opinion good relations between Croats and Muslims could be achieved and that as the war drew to an end this cooperation could become even better. These would ultimately prove to be prophetic words.

By 16 February, however, having been snubbed by Sarajevo, and knowing that Colonel Legrier had been unable to extract any clear explanation of what constituted the 'safe area of Bihac' from either UNPROFOR HQ in Zagreb, or from UN HQ in New York, Abdic rejected more ECMM proposals for political discussions and launched his forces on a new series of offensives which successfully managed to punch a hole almost 2 km deep into 5th Corps' positions.[5] This was no sooner complete than representatives from all sides again managed to make their way back to the negotiating table, and agreed to implement yet another cease-fire and to exchange some recently captured prisoners of war.[6] Unfortunately this message never made its way to those manning the front-line trenches and widespread fighting continued with EU Monitors on the ground predicting for the first time that the 5th Corps was about to collapse.

As the number of casualties arriving at Bihac hospital increased significantly,[7] Dudakovic's position got progressively more uncomfortable over the next few days, especially when General Boric's 2nd Krajina Corps of the BSA began to pound front-line positions all along the Una river with artillery and Abdic's troops continued their push from both the north and the west. The situation appeared to be deteriorating so quickly that several agencies, including ECMM, advised Dudakovic to contact Sarajevo immediately in the hope that Izetbegovic might relent and begin negotiating some kind of deal with Karadzic for the whole Bihac region.[8] To compound matters further a journalist working for VIP News in Belgrade filed a report on 22 February which indicated that General Ratko Mladic, the BSA Supreme Commander, had begun coordinating a combined APWB/RSK/BSA attack on the Pocket, pursuant to a new agreement between Abdic and Karadzic. This had allegedly been signed in the presence of Slobodan Milosevic and the new RSK President Milan Martic in Belgrade.[9] Whether or not any of this was actually true made very little difference because the mere suggestion of such collusion was sufficient to generate wholesale paranoia among the besieged community, who had long since come to the conclusion that the whole world was ranged against them anyway. The best estimate of the situation by far was produced by Klaus Cramer of ECMM, who, following hours of detailed discussion with Generals Dudakovic and Mirsad Veladzic, the minister responsible for liaison with Sarajevo, and Colonel Djakovic, the Deputy Commander of the RSK's Lika Corps, as well as several ordinary citizens of the Pocket, came to the following conclusions:

The situation in Bihac becomes more and more critical for the 5th Corps as they have to fight on two fronts. Abdic forces do not take advantage of their critical position in the south but they do not respect the cease-fire agreement of 17th Feb. Accordingly the 5th Corps is forced to keep several Brigades on the internal confrontation line when these troops are urgently needed to reinforce the units fighting the BSA in the south. The tremendous superiority of the BSA heavy weapons (tanks, artillery, mortars), and the very real possibility of the 5th Corps having its resupply routes cut, creates a desperate situation for the Corps. It is hard to predict how long General Dudakovic will be able hold off these attacks but his troops will all fight to the last man. RC Zagreb estimates that the aim of the BSA is to capture and control the road and rail lines along the Una river valley and the Kostel power station as well.[10] Secondary objectives may be Bihac city and its airfield but for the moment the attack seems to be limited. Should the Bosnian Serbs take control of the whole Pocket they might then allow Abdic to run the area as a dependant of the RSK and/or the Republic Srpska.[11]

As Klaus set off to meet with Fikret Abdic and General Boric in the hope of arranging yet another cease-fire, the overall situation remained critical. As usual the bulk of suffering was being sustained by women, children and the elderly, who were forced to come to terms with a whole new way of life in order to survive. They were now effectively trapped – crammed into cold dark cellars beneath their badly constructed red brick houses – and surviving on whatever humanitarian aid was available. In the southern part of the Pocket this had now decreased to just a trickle and any prospect of improvement was miniscule. That said, no matter how bad things were in Bihac they were worse in Sarajevo where another act of unprecedented savagery took place on the morning of Saturday 5 February. As the ordinary citizens went about their business in the hope of acquiring a morsel or two to eat, a 120-mm mortar shell smacked into the central market square, which was packed with people at the time.

> When the ambulances arrived they found bodies – and pieces of bodies – scattered everywhere. Several had been decapitated by shards of flying steel. Eight were so badly mangled it was impossible to tell if they had been men or women. The dead were loaded into cars and pickups and even a dump truck was hastily transformed into a hearse. By Saturday night the death toll had reached 66 and estimates of the number wounded exceeded 200.[12]

The reason for this unprovoked attack remains completely unclear. Some commentators suggested that it was all an unfortunate mistake and had to do with a local cease-fire arrangement that the Serbs thought had expired and the Muslims believed had not. Other more suspicious observers seriously wondered if the shell had been fired by the Armija in order to allow government officials to walk away yet again from ongoing negotiations with the Serbs, because strangely enough this is precisely what followed. Whatever the truth of the matter, this terrible incident allowed the UN to again threaten large scale NATO airstrikes if the Serbs refused to withdraw their heavy calibre weapons from around the city. This time the threat was serious – and the Serbs knew it. Within a few days the ultimatum was complied with and resulted in what became known as the 'Sarajevo Cease-fire of the 9th of February'. Both sides agreed to stop fighting and to withdraw their heavy weapons 20 km outside the city, or put them into UN designated and controlled weapons storage sites.[13] And then, as if to prove that NATO was indeed serious in its intentions, an attack by six Bosnian Serb aircraft on the Armija's munitions factory in Novi Travnik in central Bosnia resulted in four of the planes being shot out of the sky for breaching the UN No Fly Zone over Bosnia. This was a staggering response and was clearly designed to show the Serbs that a new 'get tough' policy was in place. If one did not know better this might have been mistaken for progress.

NOTES

1. 4/1/94.
2. Fikret Abdic interviewed by Aleksander Milosevic in *Vanjska Politika*: 2/2/94.
3. The weapons that arrived at the time were allegedly supplied by a relative of Croatia's Defence Minister, Gojko Susak.
4. Neum could never have been converted into the type of deep water port they had in mind.
5. RC Zagreb Daily Report: 17/2/94.
6. Cease-fire agreement: 17/2/94.
7. RC Zagreb Daily Report: 19/2/94.
8. RC Zagreb Daily Report: 21/2/94.
9. RC Belgrade Daily Report: 23/2/94.
10. General Manojlo Milovanovic, Chief of Staff of the BSA, who subsequently took control of all Serb forces attacking Bihac, consistently maintained that the only objective the Serbs ever had in the region was to gain control of the railway between Banja Luka with Knin. This is consistent with ECMM assessments but probably still only accounts for some of the story.
11. Special Report, HRC Zagreb: 3/3/94.
12. *Time Magazine*: 14/2/94.
13. Central to Serb acceptance of the agreement was the deployment of Russian UN troops around Sarajevo which had the twin objectives of, on the one hand, allowing Karadzic to 'save some face' and, on the other, presenting Boris Yeltsin as a Superpower leader, something which, by now, he clearly no longer was.

CHAPTER FOUR

The Advent of Bosnia's Muslim/Croat Federation

On the political front some movement was evident when on 23 February Ante Rosso, Commander of the HVO, and Rasim Delic, Commander of the Armija, turned up together in Zagreb and signed a cease-fire agreement. Three weeks later, Tudjman, Izetbegovic, Silajdzic and Krezimir Zubak, representing CRHB, all made their way to the United States and ended up signing what became known as the Washington Agreement. This established for the first time a political federation between Croats and Muslims in central Bosnia and a confederation between this new body and Croatia proper.[1] It was the speed with which this new arrangement was unveiled that took most people by surprise, especially since the only previous achievements had been to polarize the situation to such an extent that Croats and Serbs had more in common with each other than either of them had with the Muslims. In fact the Croatian Republic of Herceg-Bosna (CRHB), and the Republic of Srpska (RS), had by now evolved into two distinct geo-political entities and despised the Sarajevo government equally, which they both believed to have lost all legitimacy as it represented only Muslim interests.

The big question then is what happened in February 1994 to make the Croats and Muslims embrace each other. The answer is that this had more to do with the regional interests of the United States and Germany, and President Tudjman's long-term ambitions for the creation of Greater Croatia[2] than anything else. This federation did not develop indigenously but was imposed from outside and, not surprisingly, left both partners looking for different things from the outset of the new arrangement. For the Bosnian Croats the main inducement was the promise of formal Confederal links with Croatia proper which in turn would provide a useful excuse for the large number of Croatian troops (HV) already operating within the borders of Bosnia-Hercegovina.[3] It would also allow for closer political and cultural links with Zagreb, and provide a stepping-stone to wider Croatian objectives. From the Muslim perspective joining the Federation at least brought the struggle with the HVO to an end and this would allow the Armija to redirect their attentions to their real enemies, the BSA.

On a more practical level both Izetbegovic and the rest of the SDA leadership were well aware that they had arrived at a point where they risked losing international support for their position unless they agreed to something soon, and entering a vague and as yet ill-defined Federation fulfilled that criteria very nicely. The agreement also envisaged the creation of a Federal Assembly with its own budget, army and police force, which would guarantee the safety of all displaced persons as they returned to their homes. What was not envisaged was that both sides would just pay lip service to the process as they continued to pursue their own long-term objectives. Only time would tell if the Federation would develop into anything more than a glorified cease-fire, but as far as the Croatian government were concerned their complicity in the whole thing was rewarded with a 128 million US dollar loan from the World Bank. Having shown their willingness to cooperate with the Americans they could now look forward to increased support for their claim to reintegrate the Krajina, or to integrate it in the first place, depending on the perspective.[4]

From the American point of view bringing both sides together represented the culmination of a process that Charles Redman, President Clinton's special mediator, and Peter Galbraith, the US Ambassador to Croatia, had been working on behind the scenes for months. But, at the end of the day, they had literally to threaten the Croats into signing. The bottom line was very simple. If Croatia wanted any help in regaining the Krajina then they were to get their army out of Bosnia, put their ambitions for 'Greater Croatia' on hold, and release their stranglehold on the Bosnian Muslims, allowing them to get on with the business of fighting everyone's real enemy – the Serbs.[5] If they failed to agree then it was made quite clear that recent US investigations into detention centres run by the Bosnian Croats, and more importantly what was taking place within them, might be made public with a view to prosecutions being recommended to the International War Crimes Tribunal. Apparently the prospect of being prosecuted, sanctioned and isolated, or in other words to be considered no better than the Serbs, was what finally convinced the Croatians to come on board.

Also of critical importance was the US commitment to deploy an American group called Military Professional Resources Incorporated (MPRI) in Zagreb. This was a US State Department approved agency which employed both the former US Army Chief of Staff, General Carl Vuono, and the former head of the US Army in Europe, General C. 'Butch' Saint. Providing training and technical support to Croatia's armed forces, and believed to have connections with the weapons brokerage firm Cypress International, MPRI's expertise would prove invaluable and would also assure American support for Tudjman's long-term objectives.[6] That this amounted to a clear violation of the UN embargo on the transfer of defence goods and services to all the republics of Former Yugoslavia seemed to bother no one, and so for several reasons which had little to do with peaceful coexistence, Croats and Muslims were prevailed upon to stop killing one another in Bosnia.[7]

In tandem with all of this another series of negotiations was taking place behind closed doors at the Embassy of the Russian Federation in Zagreb, and which resulted in another signed agreement on 29 March between the Croatian government and the Krajina Serbs. Both sides agreed to an immediate cessation of hostilities, a freezing of the military situation on the ground and the establishment of an exclusion zone for infantry, and 10 km and 20 km exclusion zones on both sides of the cease-fire line from which all mortars, tanks and artillery would be removed. Where for one reason or another it was deemed impossible to remove these weapons the required distance, then they could be retained within the exclusion zones but had to be stored in specially designated 'weapons storage sites' which were to be controlled and monitored by UNPROFOR. When the separation zone was established it would come under the exclusive control of UNPROFOR and no military, paramilitary, militia or police personnel from either side would be permitted to operate within the area. The cease-fire itself would be monitored jointly by both ECMM and UNPROFOR, who would use the mechanics of the Joint Commission system to iron out any points of conflict that were guaranteed to arise between the parties.

Signed by Messrs Sarinic and Rakic on behalf of the parties, and witnessed by Ambassadors Eide and Aherns on behalf of the UN and EU, and in the presence of the UN Force Commander General De Lapresle,[8] the 'Cease-fire Agreement of the 29th of March' was a major step forward. Taken together with the Washington Agreement it did look briefly as if the prospects for some short-term stability right across Croatia and Bosnia appeared to be reasonably good.[9] But then, as always in the Balkans, just when it looked as if a settlement might be in the offing, the Bosnian Serbs took it upon themselves to divert attention away from the peace process and on to another obscure battlefield. This time the focus was on a place called Gorazde.

NOTES

1. Washington Agreement: 18/3/94.
2. HQ ECMM Special Report: 21/9/94.
3. Boutros Boutros-Ghali had also threatened to impose sanctions against Croatia if they continued their involvement in Bosnia, and with the HVO suffering several defeats during the winter months it was in the best interests of all Croats to take a break.

4. This is a moot point and revolves around the Krajina Serbs' claim that they were never part of an independent Croatian state. For them the question of reintegration never arose. I recall a heated debate on this very subject taking place at HQ ECMM early in February 1995 with Lennart Leschley, Arne Nyberg and myself forming the opinion that, perhaps legally, the Serbs did indeed have a point.

5. Tudjman's primary goal always remained the recovery of the Krajina. *Time Magazine*, 14 March 1994, unwittingly got it right when it said, 'In return for his co-operation in this marriage, Croatian President Tudjman was promised western financial aid and unspecified help in recovering the Krajina region from the Serbs who had controlled it for more than two years'. This 'unspecified help' would come in the shape of US military personnel, both serving and retired (MPRI), and the decision by the US and Germany to ignore the fact that the Croats were busily arming themselves with whatever hardware they could buy, in clear violation of the UN Arms Embargo, Security Council Resolution 713 of 25/9/91, which was supposed to apply equally to all republics of Former Yugoslavia.

6. Defense and Foreign Affairs Strategic Policy: 31/10/95.

7. One of the main casualties of this process was the hard-liner, Mate Boban, who drifted out of the picture at the end of 1993. He was replaced by two pragmatic and moderate politicians, Ivo Komsic and Kesimir Zubak, who were gradually forming the opinion that the ongoing violence was leading nowhere. All these two needed was a little push, which they got in due course from the US.

8. The influence of Peter Galbraith should not be underestimated in securing this agreement. Fresh from his success in Washington it was now vital from the American perspective that some settlement be arrived at with the Krajina Serbs, which would allow the Croatian army to withdraw its major units from the front line and begin training and preparing for the forthcoming military campaign that they had been promised. It must be considered somewhat ironic that this deal was hammered out with the assistance of Vitali Churkin, who clearly did not realize just what the hidden agenda contained.

9. The 'Cease-fire Agreement of the 29th March 1994', which came into effect at 0900 hrs on 4 April, envisaged three steps on the way to a settlement: (a) cease-fire; (b) economic agreement to re-open the Zagreb–Belgrade highway and reactivate the oil pipeline from Sector East to Croatia proper; and (c) negotiate a political solution to the reintegration of the Serb occupied areas. This worked reasonably well until the Croatian government decided it no longer had any relevance for them and unilaterally breached it, launching an unprovoked offensive on the area known as Western Slavonia, or in UN parlance, Sector West, on 2 May 1995.

CHAPTER FIVE

The Safe Area of Gorazde

The pretext for the Serb attack on Gorazde in April 1994 was provided by the Armija themselves. They had continually used the enclave as a springboard from which to launch raids on Serb construction workers nearby, who were attempting to build a by-pass around the area to provide better communications between Trebijne and the Posavina corridor. These raids had been going on for some time and while in real terms they amounted to little more than what had become a normal level of irritation, they continued to occur in blatant disregard for the status of Gorazde as a UN 'safe area'. It had been clear for a long time that if this continued it would only be a matter of time before the Serbs struck back – and eventually they did. The only real surprise was the scale of the attack because it turned out to be more vicious and sustained than anything that had gone before, but there were reasons for this too.

General Mladic, who had been away from Bosnia on compassionate leave following the death of his daughter in Belgrade,[1] believed that with the prospect of an overall solution about to be imposed on all the parties there remained very little time to tidy up outstanding matters, and the pacification of Gorazde was for him an important outstanding matter. For a long time this enclave with its 60,000 Muslim inhabitants had remained a thorn in his side and, amazingly, had managed to survive, in spite of being surrounded and cut off from the rest of Bosnia for over a year and a half.[2] When Mladic's troops began tightening their grip on Gorazde in the first week of April 1994 it looked as if a repeat performance of what had happened in Srebrenica the year before was about to occur. Thousands of people from outlying villages had again begun to run for their lives before a creeping artillery barrage, which indiscriminately flattened everything before it, but this time the stakes were different. This time Mladic had decided to attack a designated UN 'safe area', with the intention of securing its systematic destruction. With no electricity, gas or water, and the situation getting worse by the minute, surely the world was not about to stand idly by – again.

For General Sir Michael Rose, the new UN Commander in Bosnia, this development represented the first major threat to his personal authority in the region and while he clearly wanted to respond, the use of airstrikes was very much a last option he rather hoped he would never need to use. He genuinely believed the use of air power to be inconsistent with the concept of peace-keeping and was acutely aware of how the Americans had got it so completely wrong in Somalia when they attempted to enforce peace. 'You cannot fight a war from the backs of white painted vehicles', he would frequently remark, and he was determined not to step across the 'Mogadishu Line', which would turn peace-keeping into peace-enforcement and serve only to put his own troops at risk when they could barely defend themselves.[3] The UN troops on the ground were very fortunate that Sir Michael had fully grasped what the UN could and, more importantly, could not do in Bosnia. A weaker personality might have been pushed or tempted to take the war to the Serbs, especially since Western public opinion, influenced significantly by calls from Madeline Albright at the UN in New York and Admiral Leighton Smith at NATO's base in Naples, had turned into an incessant demand for aggressive action. To have intervened in this way would, however, have sacrificed the UNPROFOR's neutrality in the conflict and thereafter, from the Serb perspective, every UN soldier would have become a legitimate target. The UN was very fortunate to have had the leadership of a remarkable soldier at what turned out to be a pivotal time in the history of the whole Yugoslav conflict. Sir Michael's understanding of his mission was what saved him.

> Once a military force has deployed in a humanitarian aid role it is precluded by its rules of engagement from acting as an occupying power, which can dictate its own political and military agenda to the parties in the conflict. For if it is to carry out its humanitarian function successfully, such a mission will inevitably become a hostage of the situation itself. It is consequently only able to operate with the consent of those elements who control the territory and therefore it must remain non-combatant, neutral and impartial. Nor will the act of adding military fire-power at a later date change this basic rule, for all who engage in such missions have to act within the limits prescribed for the use of force in any peace-keeping mission. The clear lesson of Somalia and Bosnia is that to confuse the strategic goals of war-fighting and peace-keeping will risk the success of the mission and also the very lives of the peace-keepers and aid workers themselves. A peace-keeping force designed to assist the delivery of humanitarian aid simply cannot be used to alter the military balance of force in a civil war, modify political goals of one party or another, or even attempt to enforce the passage of a convoy – for these are pure acts of war.[4]

It was hardly surprising then that when news of the Serb advance on Gorazde began to filter through, the General and his staff in Sarajevo attempted to play down the significance of what was happening on the ground rather than overreact to an 'as yet' unclear situation. Bosnian government officials led by Haris Silajdzic took a different view of the matter, however, and courtesy of CNN and Sky News began to peddle the line that the Muslim population of the enclave was on the verge of annihilation as UNPROFOR stood by and did nothing. However, on 8 April, when Mladic launched a three-pronged attack and bombarded the city centre with tank, artillery and mortar fire, it was quite clear that if General Rose failed to do something the enclave was going to fall.

At 1625 hrs he asked Yasushi Akashi, a man who also saw no merit in crossing the 'Mogadishu Line', for permission to call in close air support, and fifty minutes later it was granted. Then, at 1825 hrs, two American F-16Cs arrived overhead and in four minutes dropped six 250-kg bombs, which obliterated a Serb command and control bunker. Mladic was not impressed. The Serb attack continued and the city centre was shelled again. The following day two US Marine Corps F/A 18A Hornets,[5] operating out of Aviano, Italy, were directed on to further targets by British SAS personnel on the ground who were working in the enclave as forward air controllers (FACs), among other things.[6] Using six Mk 82 bombs the strike successfully destroyed two armoured personnel carriers and one tank, but bad weather prevented an attack on some other tanks that were on the original 'shopping list'.[7] The official justification for the strikes was to protect the fifteen UN personnel who were operating within the enclave but the real reason was to send a clear message to Mladic. He was not amused and immediately ordered his troops to take UN personnel hostage against further air intervention. Very quickly over 150 UN personnel in Bosnia were taken into Serb captivity and Tuzla city was shelled as the attack on Gorazde continued.

On 15 April the final push began and with his own personnel now at risk Rose decided to call once more for close air support. Again he needed Akashi's permission but was unable to contact him because he had gone to lunch with Dr Karadzic in Pale. A farcical situation then developed as Rose asked Akashi for permission while Karadzic listened in on the conversation. The Serb leader then picked up a second phone and spoke directly to Mladic on the battlefield, who accused the UN in Gorazde of being in the wrong place and indicated that as far as he was concerned they deserved whatever they got. Karazdic then rounded on Akashi – 'they were on the front line, what were they doing on the front line, they are not supposed to be there' – and in danger of being taken hostage himself if he went ahead and called in another airstrike, Akashi declined to give permission. Mladic then continued his advance as the Muslim defences to the north of Gorazde collapsed and two British Forward Air controllers were wounded when the Serbs overran their positions. One of them later died from his wounds.

Back in Pale, Karadzic and Akashi finished their dinner without further interruption. The next day the Serbs announced to the media that they held all the key terrain around Gorazde and were continuing to push forward. Faced now with another 'Srebrenica', General Rose pleaded with Akashi once more for air support and in the afternoon he reluctantly agreed. However, by the time the planes arrived overhead, the weather had closed in and their only achievement was to have a British Harrier shot down, hit by a surface-to-air missile. Alarmed at how the situation was escalating, Vitali Churkin, the Russian Special Envoy, made his way to Pale only to discover that Karadzic, seemingly oblivious to the possibility of massive air retaliation, had gone off to Banja Luka for a series of political meetings. Undeterred, Churkin contacted Akashi, who was still in Sarajevo, and informed him that he had brokered a deal with Momcilo Krajisnik, the President of the Bosnian Serb parliament, whereby in return for a cancellation of the airstrikes the Serbs would stop shelling Gorazde, withdraw 3 km from their current positions and release the 150 UN hostages. Needless to say none of this happened, and when Karadzic and Akashi returned to Pale the following morning for discussions they found Churkin in a rage and so severely embarrassed that he eventually stormed out of the meeting.

Ever the diplomat Akashi pleaded with Karadzic for some morsel of good news with which to feed the media and eventually they came up with the following statement: 'President Karadzic and I agreed that all sides should restrain themselves to the maximum from all offensive activities. In the meantime we shall review the talks and try to sign an agreement as soon as possible in order to stabilize the situation. President Karadzic has agreed to an urgent evacuation of humanitarian personnel and population from Gorazde. UNPROFOR is ready to do so tomorrow morning at 0800 hrs.'[8] All this amounted to nothing more than an empty promise, and everybody knew it. The following day the military push on the ground continued and the shelling resumed where it had momentarily left off the day before. While the politicians grasped at one straw after another, people were dying on the streets of Gorazde. As Izetbegovic said in a letter to Boutros Boutros-Ghali, 'the so-called safe area has become the most unsafe place in the world'.

While the international community dithered and NATO failed to find a common position on what to do next, the Bosnian Serbs continued to take advantage of the situation. On 19 April they raided the weapons collection point at Lukavica Barracks in Sarajevo and made off with a variety of weapons in clear breach of the Sarajevo cease-fire of 9 February, as the death toll continued to rise in Gorazde.[9] The next day NATO finally managed to issue an ultimatum, in spite of clear policy differences between the Americans and the British, which threatened punitive airstrikes if three conditions were not met by the Serbs: an immediate cease-fire, the withdrawal of troops 3 km from the centre of Gorazde by first light on 23 April, and the withdrawal of heavy weapons 20 km from the centre of the town by the evening of the 26th. Mladic chose to ignore these demands and continued to shell Gorazde. When nothing had happened by 23 April Admiral Leighton Smith from his base in Naples contacted Akashi, who was in Belgrade, and asked for permission to begin the airstrikes on the basis that the first condition – the establishment of an immediate cease-fire – had not been met. Akashi refused because he said he believed the Serbs were withdrawing some of their heavy weapons. Instead he told General Rose to deploy 247 UN troops[10] to Gorazde and when these were inserted under cover of darkness on the night of 24/5 April, any further airstrike programmes that NATO might have been contemplating were effectively scuttled. Manfred Woerner, NATO's General Secretary, was outraged but there was little he could do. Akashi had identified gestures of goodwill from the Serbs and for now that was deemed adequate. What followed on was a carbon copy of the attempt to demilitarize Srebrenica the year before.

The Serbs withdrew, burning houses and destroying the water pumping station as they left. The Armijia handed over a small number of rusty muskets as British and Ukrainian troops were interpositioned between the opposing forces and a cease-fire was then established, to be monitored by a variety of agencies. But without doubt the most significant outcome was that the Serbs were left in control of all the high ground overlooking the town and retained the potential to shell it whenever they wanted to. Haris Silajdzic lost no time in pointing this out and complained bitterly that some Serb artillery remained within the 20 km exclusion zone. Unfortunately this issue was never dealt with properly at the time, largely because a row broke out between the Sarajevo government and General Rose over what he supposedly said when he went to the enclave to visit his conglomerate force there. In the course of a tactical appreciation of the conflict he observed that the Armijia appeared to have abandoned their defensive positions too quickly and expected the UN to fight their battles for them. Once again, in Bosnia, a large group of Muslims had been left living in what amounted to one large concentration camp, isolated and surrounded, and right smack in the middle of Serb-held territory.

While the enclave might not have fallen Mladic had in effect still won, although politically Karadzic was left carrying the can and appeared to have become even more detached from Belgrade, if that was possible. Lord Owen believed that 'Relations between Karadzic and Milosevic were never the same after Gorazde. They [the Bosnian Serbs] were shown up to be bare-faced liars, all the time saying they weren't after Gorazde when they were. They lost the support of the Russians for quite a while after that. Which they deserved. It was outrageous what happened over Gorazde.'[11] This is probably too simplistic an explanation. A better evaluation might take account of the fact that Milosevic had all but washed his hands off the Bosnian Serb politicians after the collapse of the Vance-Owen Plan and this latest episode was really only more of the same thing. Equally the whole Gorazde operation, the same as Srebrenica the year before, was strictly directed by Mladic, with the politicians having little or no influence. Karadzic could and should have distanced himself totally from what had happened but not for the first time he took the wrong option, and rather than admit his impotence he ended up being photographed playing chess with Mladic near the front line, while the enclave burned in the background. He was never in a position to call Mladic to heel and this powerlessness may well have accounted for his absence from Pale when Vitali Churkin came to see him. Rather than admit the truth, he chose to abscond, leaving Momcilo Krajisnik behind to give undertakings which he knew would never be honoured.

Karadzic was only ever really in control when Mladic decided to go along with him. When Mladic initially arrived to take command of the Bosnian Serb army following his exploits in Croatia, he demanded that the political leadership in Pale immediately and unconditionally yield all control to him and that they refrain from making any political decision without the approval of his military command. Later on he took it upon himself to threaten the commencement of a terrorist campaign against London and Washington which, on 17 March 1993, forced Karadzic into open conflict with his general when he publicly denounced the statement as 'idiotic, irresponsible and unauthorized'.[12] It is one thing to simply blame Karadzic for everything that happened in the name of the Bosnian Serbs but it is altogether another to determine whether he ever really had the power to influence the conduct of any given military operation. As time went on his relationship with Mladic would deteriorate even further, culminating at a point where he was forced to form his own 'praetorian guard' to ensure his personal safety, and later again he would make several unsuccessful attempts to sack Mladic.

Instead of concentrating on the growing void between Milosevic and Karadzic, which was indisputable, it might have been far more interesting to examine the relationship between Milosevic and Mladic and attempt to discover why the Serbian President never condemned the ex-JNA officer, even during the worst excesses of the Bosnian Serb's military campaign. If one accepts that Milosevic never abandoned his dream of Greater Serbia then what better double-cross than to publicly vilify Karadzic on the one hand while simultaneously encouraging Mladic to continue the struggle on the other? In that scenario the only relevant question was which of the remaining 'UN safe areas' would next receive the General's undivided attention.

NOTES

1. Mladic's daughter was believed to have committed suicide, apparently because she could no longer cope with the barrage of criticism the other students threw at her in relation to the way in which her father was conducting military operations in Bosnia.
2. A human mule train travelled most nights across the mountains, through Serb lines, in order to bring in supplies of everything, from food to medicines and ammunition.
3. Silber and Little, *The Death of Yugoslavia*, p. 362.
4. General Sir Michael Rose, 'A Year in Bosnia', *The RUSI Journal*, June 1995.
5. 512 Fighter Squadron, based in Ramstein Germany and operating from Aviano, Italy.
6. Prior to this call for close air support (CAS), the UN was represented in Gorazde by just a small number of unarmed observers (UNMOs). The forward air controllers (FACs) were only inserted just before the CAS request was put to Akashi.
7. 'The Rules of Engagement for these strikes required the Forward Air Controllers (FACs) to have the target in their line of sight, simultaneous two-way radio communication with the attacking aircraft, and a valid expectation of causing limited collateral damage before the final instructions could be given to the pilots from the ground.' Barbara Starr, *Jane's Defence Weekly*, 16/4/94. An inability to fulfil all three criteria was primarily why, on several other occasions, the FACs could not convey the final instructions to pilots who were on their final approach to target.
8. Silber and Little, *The Death of Yugoslavia*, p. 368.
9. Aid workers put the figure at over 300 dead and over 1,000 wounded since the attack began. Bosnian government figures were considerably larger but as usual were a distortion of the truth.
10. 247 peace-keepers: 117 UK, 20 RUS, 48 UKR, 5 FR, 51 EGY, 51 NOR. This number was later increased to 474.
11. Silber and Little, *The Death of Yugoslavia*, p. 371–2.
12. Gaja Petkovic, 'Guarantees of the Almighty', *NIN Magazine*, 11/3/94.

CHAPTER SIX

The Contact Group Plan

While Mladic was attempting to flatten Gorazde, international efforts to underpin the Washington Agreement continued in Vienna where, on 8 May, Krezimir Zubak and Haris Silajdzic signed what became known as the Vienna Agreement. In reality the new Federation still amounted to little more than a glorified cease-fire but for the international politicians who were singing its praises it could be whatever they wanted it to be – a new political departure, a victory for Western diplomacy, or indeed a convenient way around the arms embargo. Andre Lejoly, a Belgian EU Monitor who carried out a detailed study on the implementation of both the Washington and Vienna Agreements, was absolutely correct when he observed that as time went on the Federation became nothing more than 'a reflection of the vested political interests in Bosnia-Hercegovina'.[1] But the circus moved on and the next performance took place on 25 May, in the town of Talloires at the foot of the French Alps. Here for the first time Krezimir Zubak and Haris Silajdzic, both representing the Federation, and Momcilo Krajisnik representing the Serbs, were introduced to something called the 'Contact Group', a new body that the International Community had determined would begin resolving the remainder of Bosnia's problems now that the Muslims and Croats had stopped killing one another.

The Contact Group was in many ways the logical successor to the work of Owen and Stoltenberg. However, it differed from this because it represented, almost for the first time, a clear attempt to broaden the negotiating base by actively involving the United States and Russia in a formal structured manner. Having these two countries continually on the periphery had never made any sense and Lord Owen's assessment was correct: 'You had to find a way where the Americans were involved in the nitty gritty of negotiations, and in dirtying their hands in a settlement which they then had to go out and support.'[2] Within a short time Charles Redman and Vitali Churkin began to drive the process forward and a new plan for Bosnia began to emerge. The country would be preserved within its internationally recognized borders but be composed of two subordinate political entities; one Serbian with 49 per cent of the territory, and the other a Muslim/Croat Federation with 51 per cent. Once presented to the parties they would have two weeks to accept it or reject it. There would be no negotiation. Like Vance/Owen the year

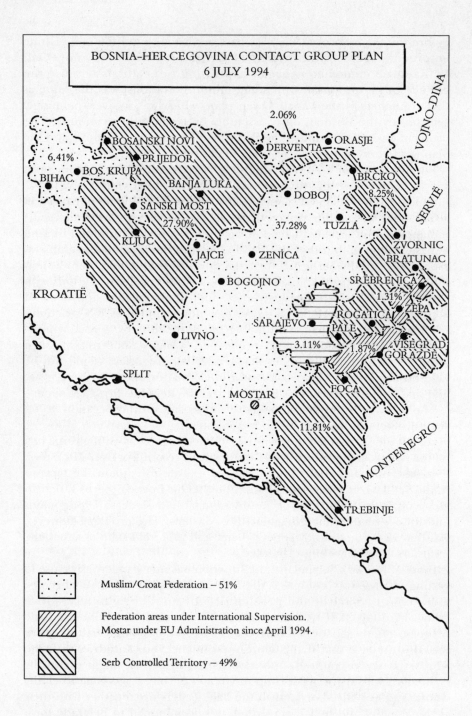

BOSNIA-HERCEGOVINA CONTACT GROUP PLAN
6 JULY 1994

VOJNO-DINA

2.06%

BOSANSKI NOVI
DERVENTA
ORASJE

6.41%
PRIJEDOR
BRCKO
SERVIË
BIHAC.
BOS. KRUPA
8.25%

BANJA LUKA
DOBOJ

SANSKI MOST
27.90%
37.28%
TUZLA

ZVORNIC
KLJUC
JAJCE
ZENICA
BRATUNAC

KROATIË
BOGOJNO
SREBRENICA
1.31%
ZEPA
ROGATICA
SARAJEVO
PALE
3.11%
LIVNO
1.87%
VISEGRAD
GORAZDE

SPLIT
FOCA
MOSTAR
Ø

11.81%

MONTENEGRO

TREBINJE

Muslim/Croat Federation – 51%

Federation areas under International Supervision.
Mostar under EU Administration since April 1994.

Serb Controlled Territory – 49%

before the theory proved the easy part but it took until the end of June before the maps outlining the detailed proposals were unveiled. Dr Karadzic immediately began expressing reservations because the essence of the proposal, with some minor alterations, was the same as that contained in the Vance/Owen plan, which was so overwhelmingly rejected by the Bosnian Serb Assembly twelve months previously. The problem was still the same – the Serbs held 73 per cent of Bosnia and the plan would only allow them to keep 49 per cent.

For the likes of General Mladic this represented surrender, and surrender was out of the question. Karadzic dismissed the maps as humiliating and designed to ensure that the Serbs would be portrayed in a bad light when they rejected them. The Sarajevo government was unhappy too, especially in relation to the proposed distribution of land in eastern Bosnia, but they decided to live with the plan for the moment, especially since the Serbs had turned it down.[3] The question now was how Milosevic would react and on 6 July the answer was given. Furious with the Pale leadership because they had ignored his approval of Vance/Owen, and with Serbia's economy now crippled by UN sanctions, for many months he had been telling the Bosnian Serbs to compromise. Zoran Lilic, the President of what remained of Yugoslavia, had also issued a public warning to the effect that ten million Yugoslavs would not be held hostage to any leader in Yugoslavia, no matter where he came from, and that included the Republic Srpska and the Republic Srpska Krajina.[4]

The message from Belgrade was very clear but on this occasion, as on several others in the past, nobody was listening in Pale. When Milosevic accepted the Plan[5] it looked as if the Contact Group was on the verge of a major breakthrough and the British and French Foreign Ministers, Douglas Hurd and Alain Juppe, rushed to Pale to explain the facts to Karadzic. The message was very simple: if the Bosnian Serbs failed to come on board then Europe would reluctantly accede to US demands and lift the arms embargo against the Muslims. The problem, however, was that Karadzic did not believe them, and in a mild state of shock the ministers went home empty handed.

From Milosevic's perspective the situation was now dangerously close to getting totally out of control as the Bosnian Serbs had effectively become a law unto themselves and were apparently unwillingly to take advice from any quarter. If he failed to rectify this position there was little prospect of any sanctions being lifted and to compound matters there was also the risk that if this continued unchecked, Karadzic, with the support of several radical opposition parties in Serbia, might eventually challenge him for the leadership of Greater Serbia. It was time to clarify who was calling the shots and so the Pale leadership, together with their senior military and police personnel, were summoned to Belgrade for a lecture. Once again they were faced with a combined approach from

Milosevic and Bulatovic who left them in no doubt what was required, and having spent long hours and many days closeted away in the Dobanovici military base, trying to find a formula of words that the Contact Group would accept, Karadzic and his colleagues returned to Bosnia in defiant mood. As had become the norm, an assembly meeting was held behind closed doors and, aware that the Muslims and Croats had by now reluctantly accepted the plan, and of Belgrade's insistence that at the very least the plan should be endorsed as a basis for further negotiation, the Bosnian Serbs wrote their decision on a sheet of paper and then placed it in a pink envelope to be opened in Geneva at the next round of talks. It quickly became apparent that the contents of the envelope amounted to a rejection of the plan and that the Vance/Owen situation was occuring again. The Muslims went on the offensive immediately and the following day, at an afternoon press conference in Sarajevo, Izetbegovic announced that he was withdrawing the Sarajevo government's previous unconditional approval and acceptance of the plan, saying that as the Bosnian Serbs had refused to accept it he now wished to add a few new conditions of his own.

With the media's attention focused firmly on Sarajevo and Geneva President Tudjman's visit to Mostar almost went unnoticed. With a frozen smile on his face and protected by a hoard of EU officials he went for the first time across the Neretva river and ventured on to the streets of Mostar east. As the German Foreign Minister Klaus Kinkel began outlining what the new EU administration could do for both parts of Mostar, Tudjman and his Defence Minister Gojko Susak got a unique opportunity to see for themselves just how effective Croat artillery had been in flattening the old city, killing thousands of civilians, and forcing those who remained to move underground to live in dank musty cellars. That the pair of them were not taken away and lynched when the people discovered who they were must surely remain one of the great mysteries of the entire conflict.

Back on the diplomatic front a last ditch attempt to salvage the peace talks was being made by Vitali Churkin and the Russian Defence Minister Pavel Grachev, who first went to Belgrade[6] where reportedly they had an explosive meeting with Mladic. They then moved on to Pale but their only achievement there was apparently to convince Karadzic that the Russian army would come to his aid if Western forces attacked him, something that Grachev never intended to convey and was in no position to deliver anyway. A second assembly meeting was called following this visit but the response remained exactly the same. 'Acceptance of an unfinished and unknown peace plan would be the beginning of the end for the Serb people on their centuries-old territories and a prelude to national suicide,' Momcilo Krajisnik said in a letter written jointly to Milosevic and Russian President Boris Yeltsin. 'Only a sovereign Serb state with compact territory and inviolable borders, with Russian, Serbian and Yugoslav guarantees, can provide for the survival of the Serbs west of the Drina.'

International reaction was predictable and in Washington, Secretary of State Warren Christopher called for the world to act against the Bosnian Serbs, notwithstanding that a split within the Contact Group was becoming more and more apparent. Testifying before Congress, Christopher reiterated the US position that lifting the arms embargo against Bosnian Muslims would remain an option if the Serbs persisted in rejecting the peace plan. A far better evaluation of the situation was made that day by John Steinbruner of the Brookings Institute in New York but unfortunately received very little attention. His prediction of how events were about to unfold would prove to be far more astute than anything the Secretary of State had to offer. His argument ran that Serb rejection of the peace plan would finally force the West to face up to the 'reality' of the war in Bosnia and its long-term consequences.

> The international community will have to go in on the ground in sufficient numbers to impose or induce a settlement by taking the military option away from all the militias and this will not occur until the United States joins the enterprise. This is face-the-music time. We're not going to control this situation until we act more assertively. The Clinton administration cannot avoid either taking the initiative or suffering the consequences of leaving the Bosnians to continue their struggle. Walking away from Bosnia is even riskier [than getting involved] because of the conflict's potential to spread to Macedonia and other places, unleashing more fighting and massive refugee flows that could undermine the vulnerable governments of such major European countries as Italy, Germany and Russia.[7]

It would take another year and a half for this 'decisive action' to be taken and many more would die in the interim, but at this point the foreign ministers of the Contact Group met in Geneva over the weekend of 30/31 July and adopted a number of measures following Pale's rejection of the plan, which included further tightening of the existing sanctions against Serbia and Montenegro and a 'beefing up' of the safe areas within Bosnia. The option to remove the arms embargo was also discussed but Russia, Britain and France remained steadfastly opposed to such a move.[8]

Unable to contain his anger and frustration any longer Milosevic launched into a public vilification of Karadzic and his colleagues and warned them that 'Nobody has the right to reject peace in the name of the Serbian people'. In a letter to the Pale Assembly he warned the members that if they rejected the plan they were on their way to committing a crime against their own people. 'You do not have the right to the lives of the citizens of Yugoslavia', he told them, and while one further assembly meeting was held the result remained predictably the same. On the night of 3 August, at yet another assembly meeting, the plan was rejected for the third time and a referendum was called for 27/28 August to put the matter before the people for confirmation. There was little doubt in anyone's mind what the outcome of that particular exercise was going to be as both the army and those Serbs living in land designated for the Federation were guaranteed to reject it.

That night Milosevic rang Bulatovic in Herceg-Novi. 'Unfortunately they rejected the plan, we must put into force that decision to close the border. Do you agree?' Bulatovic said he did. 'They made their decision,' said Milosevic, 'our decision takes effect tomorrow.'[10] The following day Yugoslavia's border with the Republic Srpska was closed along the Drina river:[11] after several threats to abandon them Milosevic had finally cut the Bosnian Serbs adrift. The dream of Greater Serbia that he had spawned and nourished since the early 1980s seemed to have finally been abandoned at the altar of economic and political expediency on 4 August 1994. All that remained to be done was to sell this policy at home, and Milosevic and Lilic launched into a vicious propaganda campaign against their Bosnian cousins. The gospel according to Belgrade had changed. Karadzic and his followers were now the root of all Yugoslavia's ills and to be regarded as nothing more than a gang of intransigent bloodthirsty criminals, who were only interested in holding the remainder of the Serb nation to ransom. And then, as if to prove this very point, Bosnian Serb troops snatched some heavy weapons, including a tank, from the UN weapons collection point at Ilidiza in the Serb suburb of Sarajevo, and while making their escape fired on a UN helicopter that was following them.[13]

Totally disillusioned with the situation, Sir Michael Rose looked for an airstrike and got it. That afternoon NATO jets attacked and destroyed an armoured personnel carrier that was operating within the exclusion zone and almost immediately the Serbs offered to return the weapons they had taken that morning.[14] Momcilo Krajisnik then began a damage limitation exercise and rang up Serge Viera De Mello, the Head of UN Civil Affairs in Sarajevo, and apologized for what happened. But it was more important to ask why the incident was allowed to happen in the first place.[15] If the Bosnian Serbs had tried to pick a more inopportune moment to behave like a crowd of thugs it is hard to believe they could have done so, which in turn surely begs the question, what was going on? Officially the answer was that uncontrolled elements had acted on their own but that is a less than satisfactory explanation. Within the Bosnian Serb military very few people 'acted on their own', unless they harboured a death wish and wanted to be personally disposed of by Ratko Mladic. The one thing that has always differentiated the BSA from both the Armija and the HVO was discipline, and nothing ever happened by accident. To put it more succinctly, nothing much happened at all if

Mladic did not know about it. So what had Mladic to say about all of this? Amazingly he was nowhere to be found and had been unavailable for comment since the CGPP had first been rejected in Pale. Not for the first time the politicians in Pale ended up apologizing for the independent adventures of their military people, over whom it was quite obvious they had little or no control. It remains very difficult not to conclude that Mladic was yet again taking his instructions from Milosevic, who, after all, was the man who had given him his job in the first place, continued to pay his wages, and to whom he could ultimately look for another appointment if things went seriously wrong in Bosnia in the future.

A quick examination of NATO's increased involvement in the conflict would have confirmed for Mladic that things were indeed beginning to change. That the airstrikes called against his forces that Friday marked the fourth occasion the Alliance had attacked in Bosnia would not have been lost on him either. Neither would the fact that all the targets had to date been Bosnian Serb. NATO's involvement began in July 1992 when it was decided to employ a naval force in the Adriatic to monitor compliance with UN sanctions imposed against Serbia and Montenegro, and the following year it was given greater powers, enabling it to enforce the sanctions. By October of that year surveillance aircraft began monitoring the UN-declared No Fly Zone for military flights over Bosnia. In April 1993 this was increased to combat patrolling with fighter aircraft to enforce it and became known as Operation Deny Flight. By June 1993 NATO was offering close air support (CAS) to UN troops on the ground if they came under attack, and in August airstrikes were threatened against Bosnian Serb positions if they continued to shell Sarajevo. At a summit meeting in Brussels in January 1994 all of these previous measures were confirmed and a decision was made to use airstrikes to reopen Tuzla airport for humanitarian aid flights if so required. In February 1994 the Serbs were given ten days to withdraw their heavy weapons from around Sarajevo, hand them over to the UN or face airstrikes. The Serbs complied. However, US fighters found Serb light attack aircraft violating the No Fly Zone and shot four of them down. This was NATO's first combat action since it was founded in 1949, and in April Alliance aircraft made their first attack on ground targets when two airstrikes were launched against Serb positions around Gorazde in order to protect UN personnel in the enclave. Later in April NATO announced that airstrikes would be used to protect all six UN designated 'safe areas' in Bosnia, and Mladic was given a deadline to withdraw his troops from around Gorazde. He complied. On 5 August NATO planes attacked an armoured personnel carrier that was violating the total exclusion zone around Sarajevo, and in retaliation for the removal of heavy weapons from the UN weapons collection point at Ilidiza that morning.

The following day reaction to the airstrike was unanimous – the Bosnian

Serbs had got what they deserved. Moscow just stopped short of endorsing the airstrike, blaming the Serbs for bringing it upon themselves, Warren Christopher thought it was a positive step forward, and in Brussels it was presented as an affirmation of EU/UN/NATO resolve to impose their will on the situation once and for all. In Belgrade all state media services launched a concerted attack on the Bosnian Serbs and it quickly emerged that Milosevic intended to use this opportunity to topple Karadzic as well. State-controlled television interviewed a range of political figures who all advocated acceptance of the CGPP and denounced the Bosnian Serbs for rejecting it. For the first time in the history of the conflict Belgrade acknowledged the suffering of civilians in Sarajevo from BSA shelling and specifically blamed Karadzic for it. 'Once peace comes, the people cannot be led by the men who bombarded civilians in Sarajevo and those who, to the world's revulsion, promote their poetry over Sarajevo while the city is burning.'[16] And then, almost as if it were pre-planned, the Bosnian Serb military managed to get themselves even more bad press when reports began to filter through of their latest activities in the north-eastern town of Bijeljina.

Apparently another 64 Muslims – 47 women, 8 elderly people and 9 children – had been evicted from their homes in the middle of the night, and having been stripped of their clothing, relieved of their possessions, and forced to sign away all legal rights to their properties, they were then released into a minefield from which they were allowed to commence a lonely treacherous trek to the relative safety of Tuzla. The men had been separated and taken away to begin a programme of forced labour. This was nothing new; this type of ethnic cleansing had been going on now for two years, especially in Bijeljina, but the timing of the latest episode was nothing short of incredible. The last thing Karadzic needed at that particular moment was for new evidence to appear which would indicate that his agents had not abandoned their obscene policies, and that heinous atrocities were still being committed in the name of the Bosnian Serbs. This he did not need – but this was exactly what he got. It takes very little imagination to suggest that whoever ordered this latest outrage did so with the expressed intention of further discrediting Karadzic and his associates, thereby making their position untenable in the face of mounting attacks from Serbia and elsewhere. Although not confirmed officially the inside track here suggests that Mladic was most definitely behind it.

When Karadzic eventually emerged to face the international media the best he could do was remain defiant and state that his people were prepared to fight on alone if necessary.

It seems to us that we have to grow up to be separate from our mother, and to be older and adult we have to fight. Now we are totally, totally alone, only God is with us. Sanctions are unacceptable and unbelievable. We do understand that Yugoslavia cannot support us any longer and cannot follow us in our fight for freedom and our own state, but we cannot understand the measures [imposed by Milosevic] which are even tougher and stronger than those the International Community has imposed against Serbia and Montenegro. It is an unprecedented blockade. We cannot understand these bad words told to us by Yugoslavia. All our enemies are encouraged now. Muslims and Croats have launched new offensives and NATO found it easier to shoot at us.[18]

The following day Aleksa Buha, Pale's Foreign Minister, was equally defiant. 'We don't have any choice,' he said, 'we have to survive, even in this isolation.'[19]

There was, however, one thing in Karadzic's remarks which was not the product of paranoia and that was his assertion that a new Muslim-Croat offensive had begun.[20] In keeping with the well-known Balkan tradition of never losing an opportunity to exploit the opponent's discomfort, the Armija had indeed launched a fairly large scale offensive from the town of Vares and had succeeded in retaking over 20 square km from the Serbs.[21] Intent on securing the road that had previously connected Sarajevo with Tuzla, and having successfully captured the important town of Brugle, local HVO units now joined in with their Federation partners in order to exploit the situation even further. And as the Serbs lost more ground, and Mladic remained conspicuously absent, a palpable feeling of 'serves them right' became identifiable in several quarters. Nobody asked where the Muslims had got all their new equipment from, given that the arms embargo was still supposed to be in force, and there was no response at all from the Contact Group; this can only lead one to presume that they saw this latest military operation as in some way contributing to the prospect of an overall settlement in the region. In the light of what was about to unfold it might have been better if somebody had asked, 'What exactly was going on?'

With the eastern access routes into Republic Srpska now closed the economic blockade began to have an immediate impact. The price of basic foodstuffs, which had never been in plentiful supply, now soared. Crowds began queuing outside shops in Pale and Banja Luka, hoping to purchase small quantities of cooking oil, sugar, processed meat and canned food, as deliveries from Serbia and Montenegro had now stopped. Border guards in Serbia were so intent on complying with their new orders that UNHCR relief convoys bound for Pale were turned back, in spite of the fact that it was permissible to allow humanitarian supplies of food and medicine through. In response to what was now approaching a crisis situation, Karadzic ordered all municipal authorities to mobilize a compulsory work force in order to generate the best possible yield from the harvest, and as a morale booster pictures were transmitted on Bosnian Serb TV of Karadzic working in the fields. All holidays, such as they existed, were cancelled, and a ten-hour working day was introduced.[22] Life was becoming very difficult in Pale as Karadzic did his best to hold the whole thing together but Mladic was certainly not helping matters as artillery battles raged between Serb troops and the Armija in and around the 20 km Sarajevo exclusion zone. In fact the situation was deteriorating so quickly that General Rose was once again forced to threaten further airstrikes, Akashi's calls for mediation fell on very deaf ears, and the Serb military continued to operate more or less independently.

Karadzic was certainly not conducting operations. Instead he was involved in serious discussions with Patriarch Pavel, head of the Serbian Orthodox Church, and several other bishops who had come to Pale to condemn the blockade and to express their solidarity with the Bosnian Serbs in their quest for a 'just peace'.[23] This support was critical to Karadzic for a number of reasons but primarily because with the church on his side he could retain popular support in Serbia, in spite of Milosevic's attempts to drive him into the political wilderness.

Later on that day the Bosnian Serbs received another boost when a US State Department official announced that it would be some time before any international action would be taken against them. Basically the Contact Group members were unable to agree on a course of action.[24] Further evidence of this confusion was evident the following day when, in a letter to Congress, President Clinton stated that if the Bosnian Serbs had not accepted the CGPP by 15 October he would introduce and formally support a resolution at the UN Security Council to lift the arms embargo, within two weeks of that date. Translated this read that there would be no substantive action taken by the International Community for at least three months, and then only if the Security Council agreed to it. So, yet again, by just saying 'no' the Bosnian Serbs had bought themselves some time. In the normal run of events it was reasonable to expect that by November another plan with another set of maps would appear on the table and then the whole process could begin all over again. In some ways it was hard to blame the Serbs for the way in which they behaved considering the subliminal messages the West continued to send them.

From the Serb perspective there was never a valid reason to part with one square inch of territory because it was blatantly obvious there was no one prepared to actually go and take it from them. In the same vein it had become unmistakably clear that UNPROFOR was involved in little more than a holding operation and was barely able to protect itself. And even if a decision was taken on the ground to flex some military muscle it was virtually guaranteed that their political masters would overrule it. On the odd occasion when people got very angry an airstrike might be called, but the Serbs could live with that. It was after all a relatively small price to pay for continually getting your own way. As if to confirm this hypothesis Michael Williams, UNPROFOR's spokesman in Zagreb, began saying that if the US went ahead with their plan to lift the arms embargo it would be difficult to see how the peace-keeping troops could remain in place.[25] Then the whole focus of attention switched to the doomsday scenario of extracting all these personnel if the Muslims and Croats refused to let them go and the International Community launched into another intellectual debate.

Meanwhile, back in Sarajevo, General Rose and his staff continued their efforts to make the best of a bad job and appeared to have convinced both Muslims and Serbs to abide by an 'Anti-Sniping Agreement', which was to come into effect on Monday 15 August. Serbs and Muslims both pledged to patrol high-risk areas with UN personnel and to flush out and prosecute as criminals any snipers who disobeyed these new orders. The threat of NATO airstrikes had more or less halted the shelling of the city since February, but these well-hidden gunmen had maimed and killed dozens of civilians and defied UN anti-sniping teams that were set up specifically to fire back. General Rose was optimistic. 'We're looking at joint measures for the detection and final suppression of snipers who may be about in buildings,' he said. 'It's a very important step towards returning the city back to normality.' He was absolutely right, it was an important step, but it could only be implemented if both sides continued to respect the agreement. There was no way in the world that the UN could enforce it and therein lay the source of the whole problem. With 20,000 troops in Bosnia, and a huge civil administration supporting them, all UNPROFOR could do was *ask* the warring parties to behave themselves.

NOTES

1. 'Federation Building in Bosnia-Hercegovina', Andre Lejoly: ECMM SR: 30/11/94. Lejoly's assessments were absolutely correct.
2. Silber and Little, *The Death of Yugoslavia*, p. 374.
3. It has frequently been suggested since that the only reason the Federation, and especially the Muslims, accepted the plan was because they knew the Serbs never would. There is probably more than a small grain of truth in this assessment.
4. 7/6/94.
5. 6/7/94.
6. Reuters Sarajevo: 26/7/94.
7. Reuters: 28/7/94.

8. ECMM Weekly Information Analysis Summary: 29/7–4/8/94.

9. Silber and Little, *The Death of Yugoslavia*, p. 380.

10. Ibid., p. 380.

11. Renaud Theunens once heard from an ICFY Monitor, who was stationed on the border between Serbia and the RS, that 'No Smoking' signs had been erected on the roads near the border because of the clandestine trade in fuel. On the other hand Comdt Mick Duffy who worked in Serbia for ICFY at that time was adamant that the border was securely closed. The truth was probably somewhere in between.

12. Unofficial estimates of Milosevic's support for the Bosnian Serbs in 1994 ranged as high as 20 per cent as of Serbia's GNP.

13. Friday 5/8/94.

14. Reuters Sarajevo: 5/8/94.

15. Reuters Zagreb: 5/8/94.

16. Reuters Belgrade/Politika: 5/8/94. This attack stopped just short of calling Karadzic a war criminal. Interestingly enough Ratko Mladic was spared any vilification, which gave further credibility to the theory that he was operating hand in glove with Milosevic all the time.

17. Report from Peter Kessler, UNHCR, Tuzla.

18. Reuters Pale: 7/8/94.

19. Reuters Sarajevo: 7/8/94.

20. This was what General Rasim Delic announced in June 1994 as the 'Liberation War' in which the Muslims set out to recover all territories where prior to the conflict there had been a Muslim majority.

21. ECMM Daily Monitoring Activity Report.

22. Beta News/Reuters Pale: 9/8/94.

23. Tanjug News/Reuters Belgrade: 10/8/94.

24 Mike McCurry announced that there was no agreement on tightening sanctions or a timetable for lifting the arms embargo against the Muslims/Reuters Washington.

25. The French were first off the mark to announce that if the arms embargo was lifted they would withdraw their troops from UNPROFOR. Defence Minister Francois Leotard announced on French TV-TF1 that he had already informed the US Administration of this decision.

CHAPTER SEVEN

Bihac Under Siege

Back in Bihac the situation remained equally unresolved with Abdic continuing to hold the northern one-third of the Pocket. Dudakovic, for his part, juggled his limited resources in an attempt to keep the internal confrontation line quiet while simultaneously resisting a combination of harassment shelling and regular low intensity offensives by the Bosnian Serbs.[1] In mid-February the ECMM team located in Bihac town began a very determined effort to bring all sides to the table for discussions, and for a while it appeared as if some progress was being made. It also appeared that a split was emerging between Abdic and other leading members of APWB. Prime Minister Jusic, for example, was certainly inclined at this time to seek out a political accommodation with the 5th Corps but the whole thing became academic on 16 February when APWB forces launched several attacks against 5th Corps positions and succeeded in moving the confrontation line 2 km to the south.[2] Not for the first time observers on the ground were left wondering just how long this could go on, as Dudakovic, now under fire from all sides and with dwindling stocks of ammunition, appeared to be on the verge of a total collapse.[3]

The following day, as shells rained in on top of them, over 1,000 people gathered in front of the gates of the French UN Battalion's Headquarters in Coralici and demanded that UNPROFOR intervene and protect them from the Serb attacks. The French, however, had no mandate to do this and the matter of what constituted the 'safe area of Bihac town' had still not been resolved. All they could do was facilitate yet another meeting between representatives of the 5th Corps and APWB in the hope that this time they might come to their senses and implement the cease-fire that they had been talking about for over a month.[4] To the south of the Pocket the ongoing snowfalls made little difference to the Serbs, and now, augmented by Special Forces from Prijedor, the 2nd Krajina Corps of the Bosnian Serb army began to pulverize 5th Corps positions all along the Una river valley.[5]

As each day passed the situation became progressively worse with thousands of shells impacting on all front-line positions. The 5th Corps were quickly forced to withdraw to their previously constructed second and third line defensive positions; miraculously they were able to extricate themselves without too many casualties. Clearly Dudakovic saw nothing wrong with 'running away to fight another day', provided his troops knew where they were running to and what exactly they were expected to do when they got there.

Even so it became impossible not to wonder how much longer this last ditch defence could be sustained. After eighteen days of relentless Serb aggression, and having acted almost as an intermediary between Dudakovic and the outside world, Canadian EU Monitor Bill Boswick, the Operations Officer in the Regional Centre at Zagreb, wrote in his daily report on 23 February, 'RC Zagreb has been regularly reporting the events taking place in Bihac Pocket and has passed the many formal protests from the commander of 5th Corps to HQ ECMM. If the fighting continues on two fronts, and if the previously reported BSA reinforcements are deployed, we have to face a collapse of the 5th Corps in the very near future . . .'. The situation had become very volatile and the news emanating from Belgrade indicated that it was about to get worse.

VIP News ran a story on 22 February that General Mladic had now taken command of all Serb forces attacking Bihac. His objective, it was alleged, was not to capture the town but rather to assist Abdic by fixing large numbers of the 5th Corps in position along the Una river and thereby denying Dudakovic the capability to manoeuvre them.[6] To compound matters further it emerged that Abdic had recently met with Radovan Karadzic in Belgrade and, in the presence of Milosevic and Milan Martic, had signed what they called a 'peace agreement'. When it was then announced in Knin that General Milan Celeketic was taking command of all Krajina Serb forces it did seem as if Dudakovic's days were numbered.[7] The last thing he needed was an organized coordinated Serb alliance operating in tandem with Abdic. The best estimate of the Danish UN Battalion, which was stationed just north of the Pocket, indicated that the 5th Corps would collapse within two weeks and all other monitoring agencies on the ground agreed with them.[8]

The Bosnian Serbs continued to launch one attack after another across the Una river and were supported by rockets, artillery fire and helicopters. To the south-west of Bihac town the 101 Brigade HVO also found themselves in trouble as elements of the Krajina Serbs' Lika Corps began to penetrate into the Pocket for the first time, using heavy mortars to soften up the HVO positions. On the internal confrontation line Abdic forces continued to exchange fire but without making any real progress.[9] The following day the Bosnian Serbs shelled the main industrial part of Bihac town and also targeted the Kostel power station. In the village of Pokoj a French UN armoured personnel carrier was sniped at, probably by elements from the 5th Corps, but unable to verify the matter the best response the UN could muster was to have two NATO Mirage F-1 jets buzz both BSA and 5th Corps positions. This achieved nothing and deterred neither side from continuing their war of attrition where minor pieces of land were lost and won, and then lost again, as the confrontation line remained more or less in the same place.

A similar picture also emerged along the internal line which allowed commentators to report that the situation had become 'stable'. This comparative tranquillity then provided an opportunity for the rumour factory to begin production; almost immediately stories of Dudakovic's sacking began to circulate. He had supposedly been replaced by the more hard-line Brigadier Nanic who, up to that point, had been holding the internal line with the 505 Brigade in Buzim. On the Bosnian Serb side General Boric was also supposed to have been replaced, and rumours abounded that the 503 and 504 Brigades of the 5th Corps had defected to Abdic. As things turned out, none of this was true. Taken together with a programme of night-time operations which all sides engaged in tensions continued to run high and everyone remained on edge. The French UN troops on the ground also felt the brunt of this anxiety and on several occasions were fired upon by the 5th Corps. Fortunately no one was injured. The relative calm was also used by several UNMO teams to organize body and prisoner exchanges. At one point APWB were holding 136 prisoners while the 5th Corps had 83, and effecting these exchanges generally served as a calming influence.[11] However, this good work was no sooner complete than another incident happened.

On 7 March, the twenty-eighth day of the BSA's siege, shells fired from three M-84 tanks smashed into the post office building in Bihac town, killing three people and wounding several more. The physical damage was quite significant and communication with the outside world, which was never great in the first place, now effectively vanished altogether. All General Dudakovic could do was visit the ECMM office in the town and hand over yet another protest for transmission to Zagreb and onwards. For the past month shells had been raining down on both his troops and the civilians that he was supposed to be protecting at the rate of 107 per day.[12] There was nothing he could do about it except continue surviving on his wits and pray that one day soon the boot would be on the other foot. While the political leadership in the Pocket struggled to understand why living in a UN declared 'safe area' was turning out to be so hazardous, Fikret Abdic continued to have meetings with President Tudjman in Zagreb where he was still regarded as a legitimate representative of the Bosnian Presidency.[13] This said more about the state of relations between Sarajevo and Zagreb than anything else but for the moment Abdic was still in favour with his economic allies, and that was all that worried him. Nobody seemed to be too concerned about the fate of UN troops, who were still trying to interpose between all parties in the Pocket and on 11 March Bosnian Serb snipers saw fit to take the life of a French peace-keeper, who was doing nothing more than simply manning an observation post near the town of Otoka. He was shot twice in the back.[14]

By the end of March life in the region had settled into a predictable but none the less dangerous routine, and daily reporting conveyed the message that no matter how ugly life becomes humankind can come to accept practically anything: 'At 1700 hrs 3 artillery/mortar shells landed in the centre of Bihac town hitting the only open coffee shop/pizzeria. Eight people were badly wounded'[15] or 'A relatively calm day with only three shells and one civilian killed.'[16] Fighting continued wherever the opposing forces were in contact with one another, while the French UN Commander again looked to New York for a definition of the term 'safe area'.[17] In keeping with the aforementioned Balkan principle that 'while war may be war, business is still business', the 5th Corps and APWB still managed to organize crossing points in the front line on Mondays, Wednesdays and Fridays, where civilians could cross and re-cross in order to buy food and trade in cigarettes and other items. A formal meeting was also organized on 23 March to discuss a large-scale purchase of food from APWB by the 5th Corps themselves, and while this may seem incredible it was nothing more that normal practice at this time.[18]

In response to letters sent to Yasushi Akashi by the political leadership in Bihac, a Commission chaired by the Chief of Staff of UNPROFOR's BH Command[19] arrived in the region on 24 March to resolve the problems of both the internal and external confrontation lines. Their solution involved three separate cease-fire agreements: one between the 5th Corps and APWB; a second between the 5th Corps and the BSA; and a third between the 5th Corps and the Krajina Serbs. Once these were in place the next phase would be to demilitarize the Una river valley and patrol it with French troops. The zone of separation between the forces would then be increased and weapons storage sites established to house all heavy weapons which would be administered and controlled by UNMOs. Once all this had been achieved the railway line between Banja Luka and Knin was to be reopened and in order to reinforce the cease-fire within the Pocket, UNPROFOR BH Command in Kiseljak would put pressure on Izetbegovic to negotiate directly with Abdic. In theory all of this was fine but in reality it ignored three specific problems.

Firstly, the French had no authority to go patrolling a DMZ between two warring parties. The UN was in Bosnia to support the distribution of humanitarian aid and nothing else. Secondly, the 5th Corps would never tolerate the free passage of Serbs along the railway. Thirdly, and perhaps most importantly, Izetbegovic had long since abandoned any intention of negotiating with Fikret Abdic ever again. So what had just been witnessed was yet another well-intentioned group of people failing totally to grasp the real issues involved and the bitterness of those concerned. These proposals, like everything that went before them, were destined only for the scrap heap.[20]

The pointlessness of international involvement in the Pocket at this time was well articulated by Colonel Legrier, the Commander of the French UN Battalion, when, in an interview with World-Wide Television News (WTN), he made a number of telling points. Firstly, he said his battalion had been sent to Bihac to protect convoys distributing humanitarian aid, although the mandate had 'probably' changed with the declaration of Bihac as a 'safe area'. The situation was now unclear as the exact delineation of the 'safe area' had yet to be established, in spite of several requests to have the matter resolved. Secondly, there was the matter of 'opening fire' or, more colloquially, rules of engagement, and it transpired that his troops could only fire back if someone had fired directly at them in the first instance. They were not empowered to take pre-emptive action in order to protect the 'safe area of Bihac' – whatever that was. Thirdly, he concluded that as far as he was concerned the Serbs were not totally responsible for all that had happened – both sides were to blame. His troops, he said, had become 'the machines of peace in the logic of war'.[21]

With the confrontation lines comparatively quiet, international efforts to resolve the conflict were redoubled in the political arena and an avalanche of officials descended on the Pocket, not least among them the head of UN Civil Affairs, Mr Vieira de Mello.[22] After days of fruitless discussion they discovered what ECMM had been reporting all along; essentially, no solution was negotiable until both groups of Muslims started talking to one another, and thereafter made some attempt to sort out their relationships with the Serbs. Abdic was, of course, quite willing to negotiate with anyone, but Sarajevo had no intention of doing business with him.[23] Equally Izetbegovic's government was not interested in doing deals of any kind with the Serbs and all of this left General Dudakovic taking instructions from his political masters to maintain two active front lines. As a result of this he became the recipient of a barrage of criticism from the monitoring agencies, who mistakenly believed it was his own decision to continue with the fighting.[24] Once Dudakovic decided to obey these orders the die was cast but from time to time, when it became militarily expedient to take a break, it was also possible to arrange the occasional spontaneous cease-fire.

On 31 March, for no obvious reason, Dudakovic met with General Boric, his BSA counterpart in the 2nd Krajina Corps, and produced a draft cease-fire agreement that apparently established an actual line on the ground, across which both sides agreed not to step. Overseen by General Van Baal, Chief of Staff UN BH Command in Kiseljak, there appeared to be every chance that this might hold, even though ECMM's assessment at the time suggested that this might have had more to do with providing an opportunity to exchange prisoners of war than anything else.[25] This supposition proved incorrect and was confirmed a few days later when General Rose visited the Pocket and chaired a tense meeting, attended by both commanders.[26] Boric remained willing to cooperate but expressed reservations about Dudakovic's ability to sign an agreement that appeared to be in direct conflict with his own government's expressed position. Boric was right but this was part of a new strategy by the 5th Corps and had far more to do with Dudakovic's long-term strategy for dealing with Abdic. If the internal situation was ever to be resolved he had no option but to temporarily close down the external confrontation line and re-deploy some of his forces to the north. With several new UNMO teams crawling all over the Una valley, and both sides apparently out of direct contact with one another, a relative calm descended on the south and east of the Pocket for the first time since 21 August 1992. It would last all of two days, until another twelve tank rounds landed in Bihac town on the morning of 7 April. When asked why they were breaking the agreement Serb officers informed the UNMOs that they were only applying their standard rule, which was to return ten rounds for every single shell the 5th Corps fired at them. Other than that they were quite happy to respect the agreement and from their perspective they were satisfied that they were.[27]

On the same day that General Rose met with Dudakovic and Boric in the south he also attended another meeting, this time at Colonel Legrier's headquarters in Coralici.[28] In attendance were Legrier, Dudakovic and Jusic, Cicel, and Saracevic representing APWB. Very significantly, the Deputy President of Bosnia, Ejup Ganic, had also made his way from Sarajevo and it looked like a comprehensive cease-fire agreement on the internal line was imminent – until it emerged that Fikret Abdic was not going to turn up. The meeting broke up without any consensus and everyone, including the three APWB representatives, were aware that this had been a wasted opportunity. It also left both Ganic and Dudakovic under no illusions as to what would now be required to pacify the north of the Pocket. Abdic had missed his last chance. From now on there would be no more talking until it was over.

In keeping with Abdic's apparent contempt for the recent attempts to resolve the situation, intelligence reports began to emerge which indicated that the BSA and APWB were planning a new offensive against the 5th Corps. With their movement totally restricted, and Serb shells coming down on top of them in Buzim and Otoka, the UNMOs in the Pocket went to 'alert state red' on 11 April, in anticipation of an imminent coordinated attack.[29] On the 13th their worst fears were confirmed when APWB infantry attacked along the internal confrontation line and, supported by both Krajina and Bosnian Serb artillery, managed to push forward about 1 km into an area just south of the village of Todorova.[30] However, just as quickly as it started, the offensive ground to a halt leaving the local radio stations to engage in a propaganda war instead. Radio Bihac alleged large-scale cooperation between the Serbs and the APWB but the reality probably amounted to no more than the usual artillery support bought and paid for by Abdic. A second report, no doubt designed to whip up further hysteria among the people, proved in the longer term to have been quite correct. It revolved around the existence of a chicken farm near Velika Kladusa, which had been turned into a prison camp where intellectuals, dissenters and prisoners were now detained. The radio station alleged that 2,000 people were detained there. Although this was a gross exaggeration, a camp did exist, and it was later discovered by British journalist Robert Fisk in the course of his investigations in the region. It was called Dubrava and located just north of Velika Kladusa where up to 450 members of the 5th Corps and others had been detained over a long period of time. Some of these prisoners were used to clear mines by crawling through minefields on their hands and knees. Others, like Fikret Nadarevic and Edep Murtic, both aged thirty, would die there, with nothing but a badly made wooden cross to identify where they lay.[31]

As news of Dubrava and similar places spread throughout the Pocket the ever-increasing tension got worse. The UN Secretary General's report of 16 March, on the application of the 'safe area' principles to Bihac, did nothing to reassure the population and served only to confirm their worst fears and suspicions. This policy, if one could even call it that, had now become completely unworkable. As far as the UNSG was concerned it was 'unclear' whether UNPROFOR had any mandate to deter attacks on the safe area from outside the borders of Bosnia-Hercegovina, i.e., the Krajina. It was also considered 'unclear' whether any attempt could be made to intervene in the internal conflict if one or other of the parties decided to attack. No consolation was brought to the people either when the Secretary General ruled that air power could only be used within Bosnia-Hercegovina, effectively declaring that UNPROFOR could not call for NATO close air support against the Krajina Serbs, no matter how many shells they lobbed into Bihac town and elsewhere. The whole thing had become one big mess but one from which Abdic could profit nicely if he got his act together.

As April drew to a close all sides in the conflict set about seriously consolidating their positions, with each responding to their own particular circumstances. The HVO, to everyone's surprise, decided that they needed to be 'formally' established and duly held a parade in Bihac to show off some heavy weapons that they had recently acquired.[32] In Velika Kladusa the APWB police set about rounding up people who, for one reason or another, were refusing to fight.[33] This was probably linked to reports that in the course of recent fighting the APWB's 1st Home Guard Brigade had actually refused to attack the 5th Corp's 505 Brigade in the area of Buzim.[34] While this scenario obviously presented a major problem for the APWB leadership it was also very understandable; all these people knew one another very well and had until recently been peasant farmers and artisans sharing the same community. The BSA on the other hand issued a statement on behalf of their Chief of Staff, Manojlo Milovanovic, in which he said that his priorities were now in the Posavina corridor in north-central Bosnia.[35] Somewhat amazingly an anti-war demonstration even happened on 20 April when over 1,000 people assembled in Bihac town to protest against the UN's handling of events around Gorazde. The District Assembly began preparations for municipal elections scheduled for 27 April while the Krajina Serbs appointed a new government to preside over their non-existent economy, and the seventeen new ministers elected Borislav Mikelic as Prime Minister.[36]

This was good news for Abdic because Mikelic had been a friend of his when he ran a meat processing plant in Petrinja in better times. It was generally believed, however, that the connection was much closer and that each had shares in the other's business, which may well have been the case, but at the very least they could safely be considered kindred spirits. If nothing else could be guaranteed it was a safe bet that Mikelic's appointment would assure the continued safe passage of all kinds of goods from Croatia through the Krajina to Velika Kladusa. It also virtually insured continued Serb military support for the APWB in their ongoing campaign against Dudakovic.

Taking advantage of this comparative calm EU monitors managed to visit the site of the heaviest recent fighting on the Grabez plateau and adjoining areas to the south and south-east of Bihac town. In a rare interview with Colonel Sarganovic, the Brigade Commander of the 5th Corps' 501st Brigade, they learned a number of interesting things about the Bosnian Serbs and their intentions.[37] From a tactical perspective they learned that the BSA appeared to have several brigades in reserve but rather than commit any one unit, they preferred instead to use elements from all of them simultaneously.[38]

Apparently, the idea here was to dilute the effect of battlefield losses and thereby maintain the integrity and morale of the overall force – but it must have made for a dreadful chain of command. Sarganovic estimated that BSA losses currently stood in the region of 15–20 per cent but admitted that his own casualty figures were very similar. He believed that the main Serb tactic to date had been to attack strategic points along the front line and with this approach they had captured several small villages. He felt that this pattern would continue as it attracted little enough international attention and that with new problems in the Posavina corridor, Milovanovic would resist making any fundamental alterations to the overall structure of his army. The continuing major headache for the 5th Corps was going to be the threat from Serb artillery and tank fire. Neither Sarganovic nor any of his fellow brigade commanders were in a position to counter this situation, which allowed the Serbs to remain safely in their defensive positions and then shell the pocket with impunity. Four days after the monitor's visit it was business as usual on the Grabez plateau when the level of Serb shelling increased once again and on 9 May the internal line flared up too, with APWB troops attacking along the western border in an attempt to cut the Cazin–Trzacka Rastella road. Over the next few days the 5th Corps were forced to give ground in several places as the Krajina Serbs once again supported the attack with artillery.[39]

While all of this was taking place on the ground events elsewhere were about to have a profound impact on how the remainder of the APWB campaign would be conducted. Having signed the Vienna Agreement on 8 May and bowed to US pressure to behave himself in relation to Bosnia, President Tudjman was now faced with the problem of how to deal with Fikret Abdic. He had after all been an ardent supporter of Abdic up to that point and the level of influence which Abdic exerted on the President had been clear for all to see, but the time had now come for another sacrificial offering at the altar of expediency. When questioned by UN Civil Affairs on 13 May, Mr Jusic, APWB's Prime Minister, confirmed that Croatia's support of Abdic was now over.[40] As if that were not bad enough the 5th Corps then regained everything they had lost during the previous week, and personnel within the APWB leadership, Jusic included, were well aware that things were about to change. The first indication of this occurred when UNHCR was prevented from carrying out its work in Velika Kladusa and the ordinary people, who were in dire need of assistance, were coerced into signing an oath of allegiance to Abdic before they got any help. Teachers who refused to sign were dismissed from their schools, which were only barely functioning anyway, and shopkeepers who refused to cooperate had their businesses forcibly closed down by APWB police. All UN vehicles were now being stopped and searched to prevent any 'unlawful' aid distributions that had not been sanctioned by Jusic. The situation was slowly but surely sliding into chaos.[41]

On the night of 2 June the 5th Corps launched a limited infantry attack against the APWB in the area of Liskovac, the first time they had taken the initiative in the internal struggle. This was followed up by another attack on the 3rd in the area of Pecigrad. The French UN troops in the area reported that they believed this was just a rehearsal for something bigger. In fact the UNMOs in the area were so convinced that a new attack was imminent that they suggested all international organizations avoid the area of the Skokovi pass in the centre of the Pocket.[42] The following day fighting continued in several places with the UN again reporting gains for Dudakovic all along the line. They also reported that for the first time the 5th Corps had begun using improvized 137-mm calibre rocket launchers, which were having a nerve-shattering effect on the Abdic troops.[43] As both sides regrouped calm was restored until 0710 hrs on the morning of 10 June when, with artillery support from the Krajina, APWB forces mounted a counter-attack in the area between Pecigrad and Skokovi. After three hours of fighting APWB troops had definitely regained some ground because UNMOs in the area observed a number of 5th Corps platoons withdrawing from their positions.[44]

By now the entire confrontation line had become active and the Mayor of Bihac instructed all international organizations operating in the Pocket to move to the Park Hotel, or their security could not be guaranteed. This was just the usual excuse given to lock up the foreigners while the locals got on with the business of slaughtering one another but strangely no one ever called that particular bluff. The Mayor also said that the 5th Corps had captured the village of Golubivici and pushed forward more than 3 km in that area. When the Liaison Officer Colonel Nurvet Dervisevic later arrived at the hotel he too had the same story, announcing that the offensive had been ordered by Armijia HQ in Sarajevo with a view to concluding the internal struggle by the end of the month.[45] The push continued on 13 June with the EU Monitors reporting that the fighting was 'fierce'. The Commander of the 5th Corps 511 Brigade was killed while visiting his forward troops and UNMOs who managed to get themselves into forward positions confirmed that the 5th Corps was indeed moving forward, supported by their own light and mostly home-made mortars. On the APWB side of the line some reinforcements were actually arriving from the north but this was generally believed to be little more than a holding operation until the civilians living in the area could extricate themselves from the battle, and in order to evacuate the APWB wounded to hospital in the town of Vojnic in the Krajina.[46] It then emerged that the Krajina Serb army was about to actively enter the conflict in support of Abdic if the 5th Corps advance transgressed a line that the ARSK Generals had drawn on the map. The actual location of this line was known only to the Serbs but the UN's Sector North Headquarters in Topusko was informed that they would get two hours' advance notice in order to move their troops to safety.[47]

The reason the Serbs were in a position to do this was because of the huge quantities of tanks, guns, mortars and rockets that were now in position all around the Pocket. What is not generally known or understood, however, is why all this equipment was located where it was. The Serbs put it there deliberately but not specifically to attack Bihac Pocket. This equipment was where it was because the UN insisted that it be put there in order to comply with the terms of the Cease-fire Agreement of the 29th March, between Croatia and the Krajina Serbs, which established specific 10 km and 20 km weapons exclusion zones either side of that separation line. This presented no problem for the Croats but in the Krajina the further the Serbs pulled back from the Croatian front lines the nearer they got to Bihac Pocket. When some of these weapons were not withdrawn the Croatian authorities lost no time complaining to either Akashi or the Force Commander, who in turn demanded from the UNMOs on the ground that they obtain Serb compliance. One such UNMO based near Topusko in Sector North at the time explained the situation as follows:

> We continually demanded that the Serbs, and equally the Croats on the other side of the Separation Zone, either take their heavy weapons outside the exclusion zones or put them into storage sites as per the terms of the Cease-fire Agreement of the 29th of March. The problem here was that for the Serbs to comply with the Agreement they almost had to have some of these weapons back on the Bosnian border, and even when they put them into the storage sites there were still problems. I mean, when is a weapon in storage and when is it not? It was quite possible for a weapon to be in a storage site, at a specifically appointed grid reference, and complying with the terms of the Agreement, but still capable of being brought into action very quickly. I specifically recall seeing a battery of howitzers sitting in a storage site, complete with ammunition, and yet complying fully with the 'exclusion zone' part of the Agreement. When I later spoke with my UNMO counterpart in Bihac Pocket, I discovered that these same guns had recently fired a number of shells which had impacted in the Pocket. The simple mathematics of artillery firing left none of this in doubt.[48]

One can only conclude from this that a more inclusive type of agreement in the first place might have yielded far better dividends. As it was, the whole thing played right into Fikret Abdic's hands and if he was prepared to grease a few palms along the way, then there was little difficulty encouraging some bored Serb officers to make use of these guns and tanks, which in most cases just happened to be sitting there anyway.

Whether or not Dudakovic was aware of the preparations taking place in the Krajina his offensive continued to make steady progress, particularly in the area immediately east of the Velika Kladusa–Cazin road. Radio Bihac also kept up a tirade of propaganda announcing that several villages had been liberated,[49] that 267 former APWB soldiers were now fighting for the 5th Corps, and that an APWB Brigade had that day refused to continue fighting.[50] This latter information was actually correct and referred to the 4th APWB Brigade who had disobeyed their orders and withdrawn from Pecigrad, thereby leaving the town in no man's land. The civilian population had also fled northwards and the town was now completely deserted.[51] The following day Dudakovic paid an unexpected visit to the French Battalion HQ in Coralici and announced his intention to push on to Velika Kladusa but felt he did not have the resources to do it at present. In the meantime he said he intended to continue attacking from east to west and re-establish what he called a 'legal civil service' in the areas he had retaken.[52] 5th Corps casualties in the course of this particular attack were assessed by the French at 70 killed and 240 wounded, with APWB figures unknown. In a campaign such as this these figures were very high and probably had more to do with Dudakovic's decision to stall the operation than any 'shortage of resources'.[53]

A few days later the EU Monitors in Bihac met with Mirsad Veladzic, the Minister for Co-ordination between Sarajevo and Bihac, who, having been appointed by Izetbegovic was in an unique position to articulate the 'official' government position on the ongoing war with Abdic. He began by saying that there was no question of the President or the government being impatient with the authorities in Bihac, or that the 5th Corps was being urged to take action against APWB. The current use of force against Abdic forces, he claimed, was in response to an attack initiated by them on 10 June. The order to attack at this time had, he admitted, been given by General Razim Delic, the Armijia's Supreme Commander, and he did believe that the 5th Corps would now go on and reclaim APWB but would stop at the internationally recognized borders of Bosnia-Hercegovina and refrain from hunting them down within the Krajina. In relation to the possibility of a negotiated cease-fire he believed that Abdic would have to give up the notion of an 'autonomous province', place all his troops under 5th Corps command, and re-establish the legally appointed civil authorities in Velika Kladusa. Thereafter an amnesty for political leaders might be considered. In the immediate future he was adamant that Croatia was developing closer ties with Bosnia and that all trade and support to Abdic was now about to stop.[54] He concluded by insisting that there was no popular support for 'autonomy' within APWB and that ECMM should reflect that in their reports, rather than pretending otherwise. Accordingly, what the Monitors actually said about the meeting is interesting.

> The meeting was difficult but productive. Veladzic firmly rejected the possibility that the idea of autonomy was supported by the public here, an assertion that is plainly false. Veladzic seemed to suppose that anyone who was pro-autonomy was necessarily pro-Abdic, and that anyone who was pro-Abdic was obviously being paid by him. It is alleged by many that Sarajevo is completely out of touch with the wishes of ordinary people; since Veladzic is one of the ministers required to liaise with Sarajevo this is not surprising. It is plain that Sarajevo absolutely rejects Abdic's presence in any political structure and are determined to defeat him. It is possible that the Presidency granted Delic permission to use force against the APWB long ago,

but that the right moment only recently appeared. There are indications that the present offensive was planned: ICRC were encouraged to transfer as many medical cases as possible before the offensive began, probably in order to create more bed-space in Bihac hospital. Bihac seems willing to talk with APWB authorities but the proposed terms are so harsh that it is unlikely that a solution can be reached. Veladzic was prompted to consider amnesty, but is evidently reluctant to offer it. He was angry about RSK military action and stated strongly that UNPROFOR should do more to prevent their support of Abdic. The issue of Croatian support is an interesting one; the Federation/Confederation developments make it increasingly likely that Croatia will cease trading with Abdic and will begin to support Bihac [from now on].[55]

The following day the Monitors met Dudakovic who was agitated that the monitoring agencies, both EU and UN, were concentrating on the internal conflict when he felt they should focus their attentions on the external situation and the activities of the Bosnian Serbs. He said that the 5th Corps were holding their positions although the fighting had been intense, and in some cases the most vicious of the whole war. He admitted that the APWB forces had been tougher than he expected in some areas, while in others it would appear that large formations had simply surrendered. He stated that he now expected Krajina Serb troop intervention but that his biggest single difficulty was logistics. Dudakovic implied that he had received Croatian support but would not elaborate further and while he expressed a willingness to negotiate at any stage with Abdic, he felt there was no discernible platform for discussion at this time. He stressed that the internal conflict should be solved from where it had begun – internally – and that Abdic should negotiate with Kabiljagic and Veladzic. Again the ECMM assessment is interesting:

The impression given was that 5th Corps remain confident about the outcome of this conflict, but are shaken by their losses which exceeded expectation, and are now concerned by logistic difficulties. It is evident that casualties on both sides have been high, though estimates vary wildly. It may be that Abdic hopes to hold out long enough for the central Bosnian cease-fire to expire, in order that the BSA can exert pressure on 5th Corps at the External Confrontation Line. Bihac [authorities] still entertains hope that the APWB will collapse under pressure, and evidently never expected to be forced into military action against them. In this sense they have underestimated Abdic and the APWB. There appeared to be no weakening of 5th Corps' resolve; there is little hope that the two sides would agree to meet, and no real agenda for cease-fire

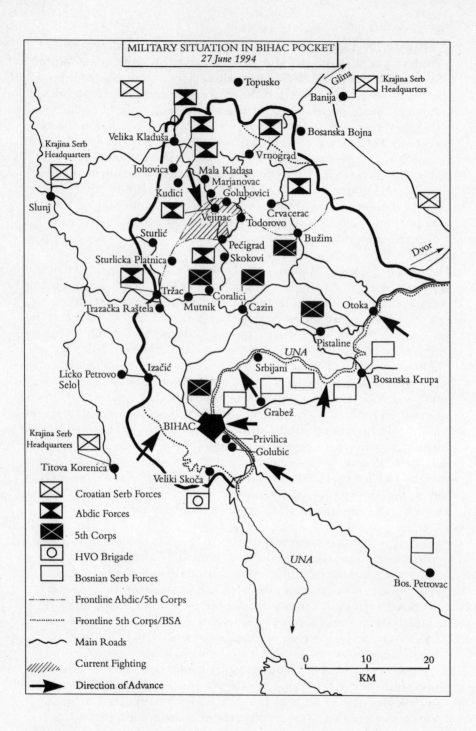

MILITARY SITUATION IN BIHAC POCKET
27 June 1994

Topusko

Glina

Banija

Krajina Serb
Headquarters

Bosanska Bojna

Krajina Serb
Headquarters

Velika Kladuša

Vrnograd

Johovica

Mala Kladaša

Marjanovac

Kudici

Golubovici

Slunj

Vejinac

Crvacerac

Todorovo

Bužim

Dvor

Sturlić

Pećigrad

Skokovi

Sturlicka Platnica

Tržac

Coralici

Trazačka Raštela

Mutnik

Cazin

Otoka

Pistaline

UNA

Srbijani

Bosanska Krupa

Licko Petrovo
Selo

Izačić

Grabež

Krajina Serb
Headquarters

BIHAC

Privilica

Golubic

Titova Korenica

Veliki Skoča

UNA

Bos. Petrovac

	Croatian Serb Forces
	Abdic Forces
	5th Corps
	HVO Brigade
	Bosnian Serb Forces
—·—·—	Frontline Abdic/5th Corps
··········	Frontline 5th Corps/BSA
~~	Main Roads
/////	Current Fighting
➤	Direction of Advance

0   10   20

KM

negotiations suggests itself. We suggested that a public offer of amnesty might provide an alternative route for the APWB leadership and this was apparently taken seriously. It was very clear however that Bihac/Sarajevo are intent on eliminating Abdic and are prepared to continue until that goal is achieved.[56]

Over the next few days all sides began responding to the new situation within the Pocket. The BSA reinforced their positions all along the Una valley although the numbers varied considerably between 1,500 and 3,000.[57] UNMO reports then began to indicate that the 5th Corps might now be in receipt of ammunition re-supply, thanks to nightly helicopter flights into Coralici by the Croatian army/air force. Initially there was no proof of this but within a few days the UNMOs could confirm that this was the case, and identified the aircraft involved as two camouflaged Croatian MI-8 helicopters, with white panels painted with large red crosses. There were also twin machine-guns sticking out the front. These were observed unloading, among other things, tank ammunition for the one tank that the 5th Corps had available to them, and this provided the clearest evidence yet of how the game had changed.[58] There were also reports of Iranian aircraft flying in with a variety of new equipment, fresh troops from elsewhere in Bosnia, and a group of Mudjahadeen fighters, but none of this could be substantiated. In Velika Kladusa Abdic started to come under pressure as it suddenly dawned on the people that, from now on, more of them were going to die if the APWB was to survive.

The situation was not helped either by radio broadcasts from Croatia on 29 June which clearly established that for as long as Abdic remained in collusion with the Krajina Serbs, there would be no trade between Velika Kladusa and Croatia. The house of cards was now beginning to topple and the only question was how long it was going to take. Not even the most optimistic observer expected Abdic to buy his way out of trouble on this occasion. On 1 July Bihac TV reported heavy fighting and shelling in several places, with the 5th Corps holding the general line from Trzac, through the south of Pecigrad, north to Vejnac and then further on in an east/north-east direction. With the 4th APWB Brigade having managed to fight their way back into Pecigrad, Dudakovic proposed a meeting between the Krajina Serbs, Abdic and himself, but Abdic would not participate. He chose instead to pull back what few tanks he had left and a variety of light mortars into the southern suburbs of Velika Kladusa to conduct his last stand.[59] This left his best troops completely vulnerable in Pecigrad and the question must be asked, why, having extracted them at the end of June, he insisted they return to their former positions now. If they were not to be deliberately sacrificed in a delaying action then this was an appalling decision.

On the other side of the line, and having succeeded dramatically in

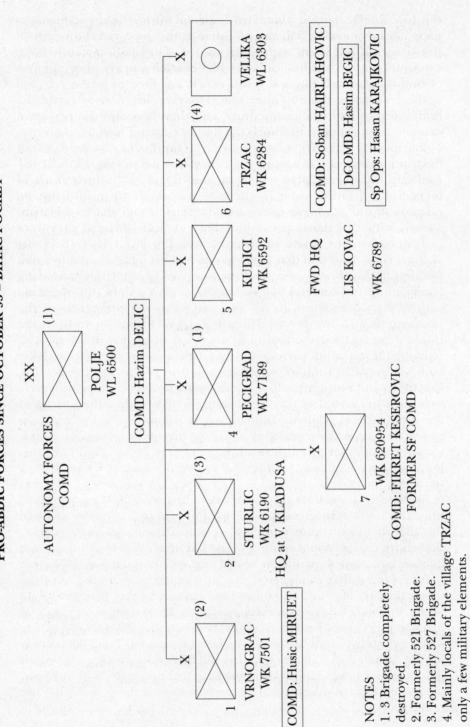

PRO-ABDIC FORCES SINCE OCTOBER 93 – BIHAC POCKET

XX

AUTONOMY FORCES COMD

POLJE
WL 6500
(1)

COMD: Hazim DELIC

1 — VRNOGRAC WK 7501 (2)

COMD: Husic MIRUET

2 — STURLIC WK 6190 (3)
HQ at V. KLADUSA

4 — PECIGRAD WK 7189 (1)

5 — KUDICI WK 6592

6 — TRZAC WK 6284 (4)

VELIKA WL 6303

COMD: Soban HAIRLAHOVIC

DCOMD: Hasim BEGIC

Sp Ops: Hasan KARAJKOVIC

FWD HQ

LIS KOVAC
WK 6789

7 — WK 620954
COMD: FIKRET KESEROVIC
FORMER SF COMD

NOTES
1. 3 Brigade completely destroyed.
2. Formerly 521 Brigade.
3. Formerly 527 Brigade.
4. Mainly locals of the village TRZAC only a few military elements.

the past weeks, neither Dudakovic nor any of his field commanders particularly wanted to halt the offensive at this time but the reality of the situation left them with little choice. They had certainly been successful but the attrition of battle had exacted a heavy price in terms of both human and physical resources. It was time to take a rest and nothing could be done to alter that. However, in order to retain the initiative they had to do something, and there was also the persistent demand from Sarajevo to 'finish the job' to contend with. It was in this scenario, still effectively under siege in the Pocket by Serbs of all descriptions,[60] and left completely to his own devices, that Dudakovic came up with a new plan which turned out to be nothing short of incredible. Another twist in the tale was about to unfold but no mention of this was made to the EU Monitors as they shared a glass of slivovic with Dudakovic two nights beforehand.[61] Instead they were introduced to the latest Commander of the 101st HVO Brigade, Colonel Grgic, and told that Vlado Santic had been transferred to a new position in the Mostar area. At thirty-two years of age Grgic was taking command of just under 1,000 troops, 97 of whom were still operating with Abdic's permission in APWB territory as the protectors of the Croat minority living there. Officially the HVO were 'neutral' in the internal conflict but the reality as usual was somewhat different. The only solid information parted with that night was the fact that the HVO had lost over 250 soldiers, killed in action in recent weeks, and this, together with Santic's prolonged absences in Zagreb, may well have explained the arrival of this new appointee. When the Monitors asked the three officers (Colonel Selmanovic, Dudakovic's Chief of Staff was also present) how they intended to pursue the campaign against Abdic, no information was given. Instead the conspirators burst out laughing, leaving the Europeans wondering what they had said that was so funny.[62]

The answer, or at least part of it, was delivered at 0530 hrs on 7 July, when the Monitor Team was awoken by 5th Corps military police and told that they were now confined to their accommodation until further notice. The entire civilian population were also put under curfew although they did not have armed guards on sentry duty outside their homes. Zagreb radio reported that elements of the 5th Corps had mutinied but from where the Monitors and the other international agency personnel were sitting, they were unable to confirm or deny it. Local radio broadcasts said that a terrorist group was operating in the area and at 1800 hrs mortar fire was heard north-west of the town. The only information Team Bihac could send to Zagreb that night was that they still had no idea what was going on but the efficient way in which the international personnel were confined suggested 'detailed planning'. This assessment turned out to be 100 per cent correct.[63]

NOTES

1. A typical example of this type of shelling is recorded in RC Zagreb's daily report of 16/2/94. On Saturday 12 February the Red Cross building in Bihac town was shelled by the Bosnian Serbs for no apparent reason, and one shell impacted right in the middle of the public kitchen, badly wounding a woman and destroying food parcels and other items which were stored there. Needless to say the building had no strategic value whatsoever.
2. RC Zagreb Daily Report: 17/2/94.
3. CC Plitvice Daily Report: 17/2/94.
4. Team Bihac Daily Report: 18/2/94.
5. RC Zagreb Daily Report: 19/2/94.
6. RC Belgrade Daily Report: 22/2/94.
7. Milan Celeketic was born in 1947 and was forty-seven when he assumed command of the Krajina Serb army, having previously commanded the 16th Bde of the JNA's 1st Corps in Banja Luka, and from 1992 the 18th Corps of the Krajina Serb army in Western Slavonia. Married with two daughters, this clear-thinking, non-drinking former JNA tank officer had been handed the task of bringing some order to the Krajina's military who, up to that point, had effectively operated as independent units. His task would not be easy but his appointment represented a clear policy statement by the politicians in Knin and in the longer term this was very bad news for Bihac.
8. Team Kostajnica Daily Report: 26/2/94.
9. RC Zagreb Daily Report: 28/2/94.
10. Team Bihac Daily Report: 5/3/94.
11. RC Zagreb Daily Report: 6/3/94.
12. RC Zagreb/Team Bihac Daily Reports: 7/3/94.
13. CC Plitvice Daily Report: 8/3/94.
14. RC Zagreb Daily Report: 11/3/94.
15. Team Bihac Daily Report: 14/3/94.
16. Team Bihac/RC Zagreb Daily Reports: 15/3/94.
17. RC Zagreb Daily Report: 19/3/94.
18. Team Bihac/RC Zagreb Daily Reports: 2/3/94.
19. BH Command was the name given to that element of UNPROFOR operating in Bosnia-Hercegovina. Still based in Kiseljak its new commander General Sir Michael Rose would shortly move the whole operation to Sarajevo.
20. RC Zagreb Daily Report: 24/3/94.
21. WTN Interview/RC Zagreb Daily Report: 25/3/94.
22. Mr de Mello met with Dudakovic and Abdic on 26/3/94 but achieved nothing.
23. RC Zagreb Daily Report: 26/3/94. Mr Veladzic, the Minister for Coordination of the Bihac Region, told ECMM that the government position was unambiguous. 'We don't want to discuss [anything] with Abdic. He has to surrender [first] and will then get an amnesty.'

24. Team Bihac Daily Report: 26/3/94. Assessment by Colonel Legrier and confirmed by ECMM.
25. RC Zagreb Daily Report: 1/4/94.
26. 5/4/94.
27. Team Bihac Daily Report: 9/4/94.
28. RC Zagreb Daily Report: 7/4/94.
29. RC Zagreb Daily Report: 12/4/94
30. CC Plitvice Daily Report: 13/4/94.
31. ECMM Special Report: 16/12/94.
32. When APWB broke away from the remainder of the Pocket the HVO initially adopted a more or less neutral position on the matter, there being Croat communities and HVO troops in both jurisdictions. However, as time went on, this position shifted and while still taking their instructions from Zagreb their alliance with the 5th Corps became more solid. When General Vlado Santic returned to the Pocket on 5 May he brought with him clear instructions to make this relationship even stronger still.
33. Team Bihac Daily Report: 17/4/94.
34. Interview with Colonel Crnkic, Commander 511 Brigade, 5th Corps: 22/4/94.
35. HINA News Agency: 18/4/94.
36. 21/4/94.
37. Team Bihac Daily Report: 28/4/94.
38. This picture was constructed over time by the Brigade Intelligence Officer, drawing on all information as it came to hand, including the interrogation of prisoners of war and a detailed examination of the personal effects of enemy troops killed in the fighting.
39. RC Zagreb Daily Reports: 10,11,12/5/94.
40. Team Bihac Daily Report: 13/5/94.
41. Team Bihac Daily Report: 20/5/94.
42. RC Zagreb Daily Report: 3/6/94.
43. RC Zagreb Daily Report: 4/6/94.
44. CC Plitvice Daily Report: 10/6/94.
45. RC Zagreb Daily Report: 11/6/94.
46. RC Zagreb Daily Report: 13/6/94.
47. ECLO North/RC Zagreb Daily Reports: 15/6/94.
48. In an interview with Former Sector North UNMO: 15/3/96.
49. The practice of identifying newly liberated villages on the radio quickly stopped when the Krajina Serbs began to tune in and, having identified the locations on the map, promptly shelled them.
50. Team Bihac Daily Report: 15/6/94.
51. Team Bihac Daily Report/Source, Frenchbatt: 17/6/94.
52. RC Zagreb Daily Report: 16/6/94.
53. Team Bihac Daily Report: 17/6/94.
54. This assessment was correct and the trade route between Velika Kladusa and

Zagreb was drying up, resulting in increased black-market activity with prices increasing by approximately 100 per cent. Team Bihac Daily Report: 21/6/94.

55. RC Zagreb/Team Bihac Daily Reports: 20/6/94.
56. RC Zagreb/Team Bihac Daily Reports: 21/6/94.
57. RC DR: 24/6/94.
58. RC Zagreb Daily Report: 1/7/94.
59. Team Bihac Daily Report: 1/7/94.
60. The Pocket was now surrounded by Serbs. To the north and west by the Banja, Kordun and Licka Corps of the ARSK, and to the south and east by the 2nd Krajina Corps of the Bosnian Serb army, who were now supported by other ARSK troops from the 12th Corps from Eastern Slavonia and the 18th Corps from Western Slavonia.
61. Slivovic is traditional home-made plum brandy and tastes like white spirit or turpentine. It is, to say the least, an acquired taste!
62. RC Zagreb Daily Report: 6/7/94.
63. Team Bihac Daily Report: 7/7/94.

CHAPTER EIGHT

Operation Tiger-Liberty

Before he could make any attempt to reverse his fortunes with the Serbs in the south and east Dudakovic knew that he had first to deal with Abdic and his rebel colleagues in Velika Kladusa – preferably driving them out of the Pocket altogether. To this end he began planning an operation, codenamed 'Tiger-Liberty', and he called in his most trusted subordinate, Lieutenant Colonel Hamdo Abdic, to carry it out.[1] The plan envisaged a number of 5th Corps officers convincing Fikret Abdic that they were leading a mutiny against Dudakovic and were asking for APWB support to ensure success. Then, at an opportune moment, they would either arrest Fikret Abdic or kill him, whichever proved more practicable, and thereafter the APWB would fall apart. So, on 7 July, Hamdo Abdic, Mohammed Babic and some other senior 5th Corps officers made their way through the front line, eventually making contact with Fikret Abdic and convincing him of their defection. He immediately agreed to support them.

Returning south the 'mutineers' then set up their headquarters near the village of Izacic, close to the border with the Krajina, and received food, fuel, cigarettes, 1,200 Kalashnikov semi-automatic rifles, over 200,000 rounds of ammunition, grenade launchers and some anti-tank missiles from APWB stockpiles.[2] Then, on 8 July, several explosions were heard in Bihac town, the members of the District Assembly were arrested, road blocks were set up all over the place, and Radio Bihac broadcast a series of bulletins which indicated that a coup was indeed in progress and that Dudakovic was reported to have handed himself over to the Bosnian Serbs. This was picked up in Velika Kladusa and Radio Velkatron, the APWB's own station, then spread this disinformation even further afield. By nightfall the coup was declared a complete success and a victory celebration was organized in Izacic for all concerned. This was the point when Fikret Abdic was meant to be arrested but for some unexplained reason he failed to turn up.

In any event, when it began to emerge that the whole thing was in fact a hoax, Colonel Branko, the Krajina Serb Liaison Officer, apparently tried to leave the area and was shot dead in the process. Razim Bazic, Fikret Abdic's senior security officer, and his driver were also killed, while the APWB Defence Minister, Ifran Saracevic, was arrested, although his driver, Addis Shabic, mysteriously vanished. Other than these incidents the whole operation had been bloodless and later that night, when

Dudakovic walked into the French UN headquarters in Bihac town dressed as a mutineer, with the tell-tale white ribbon in his epaulette, the reality of the situation began to unfold.[3] It was not until 10 July that the full story emerged and while some of the minor details remain disputable the RC Zagreb Daily Report, as written up that night by Irish EU Monitor Jim Bourke, gives an excellent account of what constituted the truth of the situation.

> 5 CORPS LO informed team BIHAC that the recent military activity in BIHAC had been a deception operation designed to induce the APWB to supply weapons and ammunition to BIHAC rebels. The LO had deliberately spread disinformation to agencies that elements of 502 Bde ('Tigers'), had switched allegiance and had seized the crossing at IZACIC (WK 6370). Part of the pact with APWB was that the 5 CORPS command building should be shelled during the night of 8 July. The team can confirm this took place. APWB attempted to supply the 'rebels' with over 800 rifles, 100,000 rounds of ammunition, food and cigarettes, delivered apparently by the RSK at IZACIC. The RSK security officer in control of the operation and one of ABDIC's military assistants were allegedly killed during the exchange. The LO stated that the operation was designed to continue for a further 1–2 days but it was felt by 5 CORPS that they could not maintain the deception for much longer. They had hoped to receive additional heavier weapons during this period. Team Comment: the facts presented by the LO broadly fit the events on the ground. SARAJEVO knew little of it, the entire operation being master-minded by 5 CORPS.[4]

Anxious to ascertain further information in an attempt to determine what might happen next, ECMM's Deputy Head of Mission, Brigadier General Bruno Cailloux, was dispatched into the Pocket and on 19 July he was invited to join Dudakovic for lunch. With his popularity soaring since news of his recent escapade had begun to circulate, Dudakovic looked upon this meeting as yet another opportunity to promote his own genius, and while he was more than willing to discuss Operation Tiger-Liberty in detail, nothing new emerged. Naturally enough he claimed to be the originator and author of the whole thing, and said he was completely satisfied with the outcome. He also said that some APWB troops were captured during the operation, had now seen the error of their ways, and had enlisted in the 5th Corps. When pressed about his future intentions all Dudakovic would confirm was that he was quite optimistic about further military progress on the internal confrontation line, and as Cailloux headed north to Velika Kladusa for his four o'clock meeting with Abdic, his only comment was that the 5th Corps

Commander had become 'self-satisfied to the point of arrogance'.[5] If he thought that was bad, the reception he was about to receive from the APWB leadership would turn out to be even worse.

The meeting with Abdic took place in his castle fortress that dominates everything else in Velika Kladusa, and was also attended by Abdic's 'chef de cabinet' Mr Kostic, and Defence Minister Saracevic, who had somehow managed to escape the clutches of the 5th Corps. Right from the outset Abdic insisted that APWB would not be seen as a problem for anyone in Bosnia if they chose to view it instead as a model for future peaceful coexistence, taking account of all ethnic aspirations and differences. As far as he was concerned, none of the current political leaders in Bosnia would be acceptable in the longer term and he felt it was time for new people, untainted by allegations of war crimes, to take charge. He saw himself fitting into this category and suggested that Jadranko Prlic, the Prime Minister of CRHB, might be another. For this to happen, he said, he needed access to the media and free elections in order to counter what he called 'Izetbegovic's propaganda', and while economic links with Zagreb were now closed he was in favour of the Contact Group plan because it articulated the need for all three ethnic groups to interact with one another. This was something he had been preaching for a very long time. So the meeting ended with little new information discovered and while the success of Tiger-Liberty had obviously been demoralizing and embarrassing for Abdic, General Cailloux was unable to conclude that APWB was on the verge of collapse. Rather it appeared that nothing much had changed, and life in Velika Kladusa and its environs was going on more or less as it had been for some time.[6] This, however, was not the case and this semblance of normality was about to evaporate.

Flushed with the success of Tiger-Liberty and having pushed Abdic back into an area which now consisted of less than one quarter of the whole Pocket, Dudakovic ordered his troops to begin the 'push' once again. On Thursday 28 July 5th Corps forces launched a new offensive along the ever-contracting internal confrontation line and began to make further progress against what had now become a badly organized, ill-disciplined and very confused APWB force. The only group putting up any serious resistance was the 500 members of the 4th Brigade, now holed up in the deserted town of Pecigrad, but with the 5th Corps virtually surrounding them, and bombarding the town at the rate of one projectile per minute, this courageous last stand was not expected to continue much longer. However, Dudakovic was anxious to press on and rather than waste any more time on Pecigrad he decided to by-pass it and head for Velika Kladusa with all speed. When he carried out this manoeuvre he discovered that the front line had moved further north than he thought and was now less than 7 miles from Abdic's headquarters.

Across the border in the Krajina neither the Banja or Kordun Corps were sure what was going to happen next and as a contingency measure raided the UN weapons storage sites in Sector North. UNMOs on the ground also reported increased Serb artillery support for Abdic but the difficulty here was, because the confrontation line was creeping northwards, they would shortly end up shelling the outskirts of Velika Kladusa itself.[7] The following day, as Abdic was sending his civil police to the front line in a last ditch attempt to keep the 5th Corps at bay, news filtered through that Pecigrad had fallen. As General Rose inspected the scene of this heroic defence, his press officer in Sarajevo, Major Rob Annink, announced that, 'the commander of the 4th Bde has been killed, his deputy captured, and the white flag raised over the town'. With the road to the north now open most of Dudakovic's military problems were over. His only remaining dilemma was how to complete the job and push Abdic out of the Pocket completely without killing thousands of innocent civilians who had fled to the north before the 5th Corps' advance and were now crammed into Velika Kladusa and its immediate environs. Before he had made up his mind how to handle this situation, on 5 August Abdic announced publicly that he was ready to enter negotiations with Sarajevo. This encouraged General Rose sufficiently to alter his schedule and fly to Velika Kladusa to talk to him. What Rose did not know was that Dudakovic was under strict instructions from Izetbegovic to finish Abdic off once and for all; to permanently resolve the military situation lest it develop again in the future and thereby distract the 5th Corps from carrying out their primary mission, which was holding the external line against the Bosnian Serbs. Nevertheless neither Abdic nor Dudakovic would ever be forgiven if they murdered thousands of innocent civilians and in an attempt to avert this an amnesty was offered by Sarajevo on the morning of 9 August.

On the basis of Amendment II, point 5, item 3 of the Constitution of the Republic of Bosnia and Herzegovina, the Presidency of the Republic of Bosnia and Herzegovina passes this

REGULATION HAVING THE FORCE OF LAW
AND REGARDING AMNESTY

Article 1. Amnesty is given to all members of paramilitary formations of the so-called Abdic Army and para-state organs of the so-called Autonomous province of Western Bosnia, as well as to other persons who, in working for the realization of their goals, have committed the following:

1. Crimes against the basis for social order and security of the Republic of Bosnia-Herzegovina – Heading XV, and crimes against the Armed Forces

of the Republic of Bosnia and Herzegovina, – Heading XX, as anticipated in the Penal Code of the Republic of Bosnia and Herzegovina ('Official Gazette RB-H', number 2/92, 8/92, 10/92 and 16/92) and in the Law on Application of the Penal Code of the Republic of Bosnia Herzegovina ('Official Gazette RB-H', number 6/92, 11/92, and 21/92).

2. Crimes of inciting to resistance from article 201 and the crime of spreading false information from article 202, anticipated in the Penal Code of the Republic of Bosnia-Herzegovina ('Official Gazette SRB-H', number 16/77, 32/84, 19/86, 40/87, 33/89, 2/90 and 24/91) and 'Official Gazette RB-H', number 16/92 and 21/92.)

Article 2. Amnesty applies to all persons from article I of this regulation, if they, by 16 August 1994, register at the nearest administrative body competent for matters of defence, or to a unit, headquarters or command of the Armed Forces of the Republic of Bosnia-Herzegovina.

Article 3. If a penal proceeding has not been instituted against persons from article I of this regulation, then no such proceeding will be instituted, and if a penal proceeding is in process, it will be discontinued. If a person from article I of this regulation has been enforceably sentenced to a term of imprisonment, he will be freed from serving that sentence, and if he has begun to serve the sentence, he will not serve the rest of the sentence.

Article 4. The Minister of Justice is authorized to make, in cooperation with the Minister of Defense, instructions for implementing this regulation.

Article 5. This article takes effect on the day it appears in 'Official Gazette RB-H', number 1688/94, 9 August 1994, Sarajevo.

Signed
President of the Presidency
of Bosnia-Hercegovina.

Alija Izetbegovic

While the terms of this were not particularly unreasonable Abdic still refused to capitulate and pledged to remain with his people, offering to open discussions with Izetbegovic through the good offices of General Rose – but the Bosnian President would not agree to this.[8] Abdic then asked Krezimir Zubak to become involved but nothing materialized there either and his situation became more untenable by the hour.[9] His only consolation was that the 6th APWB Brigade had successfully disengaged from the battle west of Pecigrad and, having crossed into the Krajina where they knew the 5th Corps would not pursue them, had arrived in Velika Kladusa more or less intact.[10] With them, however, came an additional 7,000 civilians and however happy Abdic might have been to see them, an already dreadful humanitarian situation became appreciably worse. In response to this new influx and the unrelenting shelling some 50,000 displaced people grabbed what little they could carry and moved across the international border into the Krajina, thus becoming refugees.

In the midst of this chaos and disorder ECMM's Head of Mission, Ambassador Paul Joachim von Stulpnagel, went to Velika Kladusa on the morning of 12 August and met with Abdic who appeared to be oblivious to the turmoil going on around him.[11] When the meeting concluded Abdic then went through the bizarre performance of holding a press conference by phone with the world's press, who had assembled in the Intercontinental Hotel in Zagreb. With his assembly speaker, Bozidar Sicel, physically present in Zagreb, Abdic announced, to the amazement of all present, that an interim solution to the problems in Bihac had been found and he was personally prepared to fund a Mostar-type settlement, whereby the entire Pocket would be demilitarized and become a protectorate of the European Union, with a French national appointed as the European Administrator.[12]

This development came as a complete surprise and raises the question of where this notion actually came from in the first place, or who suggested it. Whatever hope such a 'solution' might have provided some months previously, when both sides could have bargained from comparatively equal positions, it now stood absolutely no chance of acceptance given that the 5th Corps, and by inference the Sarajevo government, were well and truly ready for a final battle. When pressed by the media to state just how much territory his forces still retained Abdic declined to answer, and refused also to comment on the latest UNPROFOR assessment which indicated that at best he only controlled about 50 square km in the immediate vicinity of Velika Kladusa. As the conference rambled on he again said that he was willing to negotiate with Sarajevo and that he always acknowledged the integrity of Bosnia-Herzegovina's internationally recognized borders. But in the same breath he continued his verbal assault on Izetbegovic, condemning the President's apparent new willingness to talk to Karadzic about partitioning the country while he stoutly refused to talk to APWB about peace.

A meeting between delegations from APWB and the 5th Corps did take place on 15 August but this stalled because the APWB side were insisting on a formal cease-fire prior to political negotiations, and the Bihac authorities, including Dudakovic, wanted it the other way around. When they got together again on the 17th some progress was made until the APWB representatives began looking for a 'constitutional expert' to draw up the political settlement. Unable to proceed any further another meeting was scheduled for the 20th but this would never take place. As Messrs Delic, Hirkic, Kajtazovic and Kostic made their way back into Velika Kladusa fighting erupted all around them. A Gazelle helicopter was seen flying out some of Abdic's personal staff and by 1730 hrs over 500 townspeople had decided it was time that they too departed and were now dispersed along the main road out of town, leading northwards into the Krajina. Another 700 miserable and confused souls had gathered 7 miles further south near the village of Mala Kladusa and, as they swarmed about in the middle of the road, they suddenly realized that the leading elements of the 5th Corps were almost upon them. Very quickly they organized themselves and pointing their laden-down cars, tractors, horses, carts, donkeys, wheel-barrows and bicycles in the general direction of the Krajina, they grabbed what few remaining possessions they could carry and began an odyssey into living hell. By now the APWB authorities had also started to panic and the situation spiralled out of control when the word went out that all civilians were now advised to leave Velika Kladusa by midnight. The APWB military – or what was left of them – would theoretically remain for a further twenty-four hours to make sure that everyone got away.[13]

Meanwhile, across the border in the Krajina, the civil and military authorities were faced with an impending humanitarian disaster as thousands of refugees began pouring into a jurisdiction that could barely sustain itself. Initially the plan was to facilitate the safe passage of all these people through the Krajina and then have them disperse into Croatia proper but it quickly emerged that this was not going to happen.

NOTES

1. No relation to Fikret. The name Abdic is as common in Bihac Pocket as Murphy is in Ireland.
2. Roderick de Normann, 'The Miracle of 5 Corps', *Jane's Intelligence Review*, 1996.
3. 'Bihac Pocket – A Tactical Appreciation', Bill Foxton, ECMM Papers: 17/2/95.
4. RC Zagreb Daily Report: 10/7/94.
5. Special Report, D/HoM Ops: 22/7/94, part 1.
6. Special Report, D/HoM Ops: 22/7/94, part 2.
7. Reuters Zagreb: 3/8/94.
8. Reuters Zagreb: 10/8/94.
9. HINA News Agency: 10/8/94.
10. Reuters Zagreb: 10/8/94.
11. Head of Mission's Special Report/ECMM Papers: 13/8/94.
12. Zarko Modric: 12/8/94.
13. RC Zagreb Daily Reports: 15,17,/8/94.

CHAPTER NINE

Turanj Crossing and Batnoga Camp

When the first fifty-nine APWB refugees arrived at the Croatian police checkpoint at Turanj, near Karlovac, they were allowed to pass through as their documents were considered to be in order. However, when the scale of the migration became clear, the Croatian government decided that it could not take responsibility for the numbers involved and the crossing point was closed. Later on, when another 700 arrived, they were allowed through the Serb checkpoint and into the UN-controlled 2 km separation zone between the two forces, but when they attempted to pass into Croatia they were turned back by Croatian police. As if that was not bad enough when they then attempted to return to the Krajina the Serb police refused to let them back because another 2,000 had arrived at the checkpoint in the meantime and the place had become completely blocked.

In an attempt to bring some order to the scene an ECMM team from Karlovac sought out the local Croatian chief of police, who was now personally manning the checkpoint, and pleaded with him to give some assurance to the unfortunate people who were now trapped in no man's land. All this futile exercise elicited was a display of arrogance by the Croat who announced that as far as the Croatian government was concerned, an agreement had been signed with UNPROFOR ten days previously in which the UN had assumed responsibility for refugees in the Krajina, and as these people were still technically in the Krajina the UN could look after them. As darkness fell, and unable to proceed or return from whence they came, all that these victims of the conflict could do was bed down were they were and hope that things would get better in the morning. But the situation just got worse.[1]

At 0530 hrs on the morning of 21 August the final 5th Corps attack on Velika Kladusa began and evolved quite quickly into a series of street battles, which continued throughout the day. By early evening resistance had evaporated and at 2030 hrs Dudakovic entered Abdic's castle fortress while his troops poured on to the deserted streets, drinking and celebrating a famous victory. They also managed to plunder and loot a number of premises before a detachment of military police arrived to restore some order. Whether this was a deliberate tactic by Dudakovic remains unclear but either way to the victors went what few spoils of war were worth taking from Velika Kladusa that autumn evening. In the meantime all of the unfortunate people who had fled the Pocket were assembling in a variety of makeshift refugee camps across the Krajina. In addition to the 2,500 still trapped at Turanj more were gathered near Topusko, another group had arrived at Katinovac, but by far the largest concentration was now to be found in a miserable God-forsaken place called Batnoga, where upwards of 20,000 people were crammed into a filthy disused chicken farm. Of these, 80 per cent were women and children, and as the enormity of the situation began to dawn on the international agencies, UNHCR negotiated successfully with the Serbs to allow them to supply the camp with humanitarian aid. The first consignments there consisted of basic requirements such as bread and water, and tents to accommodate those who could not fit into the farm's twenty-four sheds.[2]

At a crisis meeting in Zagreb the following day Mate Granic, Croatia's Foreign Minister, and Ivan Jarnjak, the Interior Minister, having first discussed the matter with Bosnian Prime Minister Haris Silajdzic, then went to Yasushi Akashi and effectively washed their hands off the whole problem. Conveniently forgetting that in the not too distant past their president, Franjo Tudjman, had been one of Fikret Abdic's greatest supporters, and had gone to great lengths to legitimize him as an international figure, the citizens of APWB were now to become the latest sacrifice to political expediency. The rules had changed. The Americans were calling the shots now and Izetbegovic was back in favour. The two ministers spelt it out to Akashi that these refugees were in what was supposed to be a UN protected area, so the UN could go and look after them or, more preferably, encourage them to go back to where they came from in the first place.[3] In typical fashion the Krajina was occupied territory when the Croatian government was talking politics but someone else's responsibility altogether when there was a real problem to be dealt with. As Akashi left the meeting he was under no illusions as to who would have to take up this problem and run with it. Once again it would be UNPROFOR, UNHCR, ICRC, ECTF and ECMM, with European Union taxpayer's money funding whatever relief programme would eventually be put in place.

In the midst of all this confusion twelve members of the 5th Corps, who had become disoriented in the fighting, also turned up at Turanj complete with their personal weapons and demanded to cross into Croatia. They were refused permission and told to go back and join the other refugees. Thankfully some UNCIVPOL personnel who were present at the time apprehended them and probably saved their lives, but the fact that they had been able to make the journey in the first place, armed and in uniform, is a fair statement of just how confused the whole situation had become. As each day passed more and more people continued to stream into the refugee camps with Fazilla Abdic, Fikret Abdic's wife, taking on the role of a refugee leader at Turanj while her husband and his armed praetorian guard apparently enjoyed unrestricted freedom of movement as they travelled around the Krajina to one meeting after another.[4] Dudakovic for his part made an appeal to the refugees to return to their homes which he claimed were intact and untouched, but nobody was prepared to believe him.[5]

They were right not to. Roger Bryant, the EU Monitor who was team leader in the Pocket at the time, made a very telling comment in his report on the aftermath of the Bosnian army's return to Velika Kladusa. '5 Corps followed up with looting, car vandalism and theft, stealing fuel from abandoned cars, and stealing from abandoned refugees' belongings. The town this morning [22 August] looked as if a disappointed English football crowd had given the centre some serious attention.'[6] This report is consistent with what the 5th Corps got up to in other places as they made their way northwards and the refugees were well aware of the real situation.[7]

Over the next few days, as the 5th Corps began sending most of their troops and equipment back to the south, the streets of Velika Kladusa remained deserted. UNPROFOR figures indicated that there were at least 23,000 refugees scattered throughout the Krajina and probably many more holed up in remote places that had not been discovered.[8] An ECMM team from Glina caught up with Abdic as he addressed the refugees who had gathered at Stara Selo near Topusko. His basic message was that they should continue to hold out for independence – compromise with the 5th Corps was not an option.[9] Later that evening 300 refugees on the Krajina side of the Polish UN checkpoint in the middle of Turanj surged forward and approached the Croatian police, demanding to be let in. Reinforcements were summoned from Karlovac, the Croats stuck to their guns, sandbags and armoured vehicles, and the refugees remained where they were. By now a variety of celebrities, including the American Ambassador Peter Galbraith, were touring the area and actively encouraging the refugees to return to Velika Kladusa where a new municipal authority, led by Sefik Stulanovic, was now in place. Deriving no confidence from this development, largely because Stulanovic had spent the previous eight months in jail in Velika Kladusa for opposing APWB rule, and with Abdic continuing his 'no surrender' routine, the numbers at Turanj continued to swell.

By the evening of 25 August the refugees at Turanj had risen to over 12,000,[10] thanks primarily to the operation of a six-bus shuttle service which began ferrying people from Topusko. The majority of these unfortunate people were now crammed into the 1 km stretch between the Polish soldiers in the middle of the crossing and the Croatians on the Karlovac side. With APCs and lightly armed police at the checkpoint, more heavily armed police immediately behind them, and special police a little further to the rear, the Croats were ready to act in the unlikely event that these hungry, filthy, frightened and confused people, who were now stranded in the middle of nowhere, would attempt to invade the Croatian state! Even more police were on call back in Karlovac police station and thousands of soldiers not very far away.[11] Just what exactly they thought the threat was remains anybody's guess.[12] A detailed report compiled at the time by a 'Feed the Children' team on the ground puts everything into perspective.

> Turanj is a town left destroyed by war. It is now home to between 16,000 and 20,000 Bosnian refugees. A few live in tents and buses that they brought with them from their home towns but most are living in the remnants of a trashed town. In one small house there were 20 occupants, in another larger house 100 sheltered, crammed 9 and 10 to a room. Almost all of the houses smell of the burning left by the 'ethnic cleansing'. There is no electricity, the water is brought in by UNPROFOR tanker. Toilets are improvised and an appalling health risk. Rubbish is left to rot, or to the local rat population. The only fuel they have is wood. Hardly any of the houses have windows, many have no doors or roofs. Plastic sheeting is used to keep out the worst of the rain but it will not keep out the cold. The most dangerous aspect of Turanj is live explosives. Mines, unexploded mortars and artillery shells are everywhere. A 12 year old boy was brought to the makeshift casualty tent with blood pouring from leg and chest wounds. He was bandaged and taken by ambulance to hospital in Karlovac, 5 km away. A few minutes later a second ambulance brought another boy. There was nothing anyone could do for him – his left leg and the left side of his head had been torn off by the blast from a mine he had stepped on. Ahmed was 16 years old. He sought sanctuary in, and died at, Turanj.[13]

In Batnoga the situation had already taken on an air of permanence with the emergence of a refugee leader in the person of Sead Kajtazovic, one of Abdic's right-hand men, and the holding of formal meetings between the refugees and the plethora of UN officials who had by now descended upon the place. At a meeting on 26 August Kajtazovic announced that there were now between 32,000 and 35,000 people in the camp and remained adamant that they could not return to their homes because UNPROFOR would not be able to protect them, especially at night. He then asked the EU monitors present to go back to Velika Kladusa and

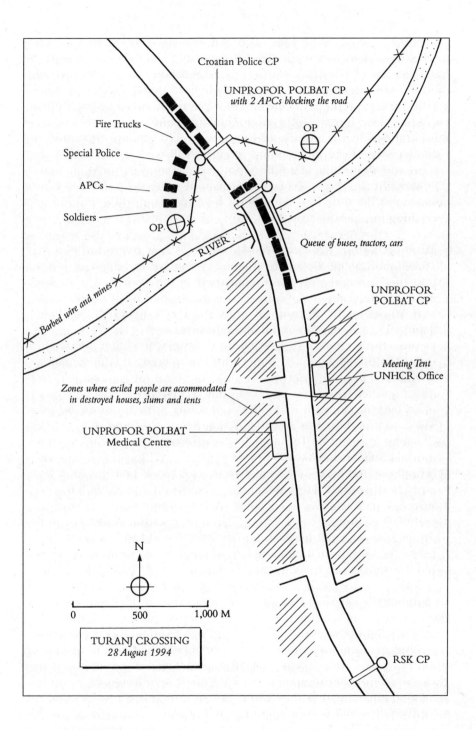

Croatian Police CP

UNPROFOR POLBAT CP
with 2 APCs blocking the road

Fire Trucks

Special Police

APCs

Soldiers

OP

OP

RIVER

Barbed wire and mines

Queue of buses, tractors, cars

**UNPROFOR
POLBAT CP**

Meeting Tent
UNHCR Office

*Zones where exiled people are accommodated
in destroyed houses, slums and tents*

UNPROFOR POLBAT
Medical Centre

N

0   500   1,000 M

TURANJ CROSSING
28 August 1994

RSK CP

find out what was going on but even as they headed off, he began asking for transportation to take more people to Turanj. Undeterred the Monitors made their way back into the Pocket and met with the commander of the French UN Battalion, the new Mayor of Velika Kladusa, and representatives from both UN Civil Affairs and UNCIVPOL. The new regime again guaranteed the safety of any returnees and invited the monitoring agencies to put in place whatever measures they thought necessary to monitor the situation properly.[14]

Every suggestion that was put to them they readily accepted, including the visit of some refugee leaders to inspect the town and the making of a video by UN TV. It can of course be argued that all these concessions were agreed to because they knew full well that nobody was coming back anyway. In the best traditions of Balkan politics, where the 'truth' is generally a 'lie', it is highly probable that the new authorities in Velika Kladusa were well aware that, as they spoke, yet another 356 tractors and 112 horses and carts, carrying upwards of 2,500 more refugees, were making their way across the Krajina towards Turanj.[15]

With the situation deteriorating by the day and the Krajina Serbs struggling to keep pace with the number of international personnel who were now at large in their territory, ECMM's Head of Mission, Ambassador von Stulpnagel, went back to Topusko for another meeting with Abdic. There was no press conference on this occasion, largely because no compromise was possible. At Turanj and Batnoga EU Monitors had managed to talk freely with some of the refugees, many of whom were quite willing to return to their homes and take their chances with the 5th Corps, but they maintained they really had no choice. They had to obey Abdic and his appointed leaders in both camps.[16] The sight of Abdic walking around Batnoga in the company of US Ambassador Peter Galbraith and his entourage certainly gave the impression that the Autonomous Province of Western Bosnia, 'in exile', had now attracted American support, although nothing could have been further from the truth. However, as far as the refugees were concerned, perception was reality, and this provided further 'evidence' that Abdic was still an important figure and working away on their behalf. The main problem with this approach was that the longer they stayed as they were the more difficult it was going to be to return voluntarily, and Abdic was well aware of this.

Galbraith moved on to Velika Kladusa for a meeting with Dudakovic, representatives from UNPROFOR and all the other agencies now operating there. After one and a half hours of discussion it emerged that the new authorities had agreed to establish refugee resettlement centres throughout the Pocket and UNPROFOR, even though it had no authority for this kind of activity and could barely protect itself, would shelter the returning refugees for a period of six months. Then the people could reintegrate into the community or leave and live in the Krajina if they wished. None of the APWB military would be forced to serve in the 5th Corps, but if they wanted to join voluntarily then that would be acceptable. UNCIVPOL, ECMM and the other international organizations would oversee the whole thing.[17] Sadly this solution, such as it was, was not attractive enough to encourage anyone to break ranks with Abdic.[18] The refugees stayed where they were and the humanitarian situation got progressively worse, notwithstanding the arrival of an UNICEF mobile health clinic and the provision of two heavy duty generators from the Polish UN battalion. With the refugees now grasping at every straw that was thrown to them the EU Monitors attending the daily meeting in Batnoga on 29 August thought they detected a change in Kajtazovic's attitude, when he indicated that he might be prepared to tell the people to go home, if UNPROFOR could really guarantee their safety.

Wasting no time the EU Monitors immediately set out for Velika Kladusa and after some discussion with the Mayor, he agreed to provide them with a letter for the refugees that would outline in detail the type and level of protection they could expect from the new administration.[19] Ironically, when the team attempted to get back into the Pocket the following day to collect the letter, the Serb police refused to let them through on the grounds that their papers were not in order. Fortunately the Bihac team were in the area, managed to pick up the letter, and took it to Batnoga where both Kajtazovic and Abdic were having a meeting at the time. Having read the document Kajtazovic then announced to the disappointed and frustrated Monitors that as far as he was concerned the document was not legal as it had been issued by an 'illegal authority'. He went on to condemn the 5th Corps as 'conquerors and dictators' and said that while the refugees certainly wanted to go back, they would only do so if governed by Abdic and if the place had some kind of 'protectorate status'. Two days of shuttle diplomacy turned out to have been a complete and utter waste of time. The reality of course was that no matter how much talking was done, or what kind of demands Kajtazovic made, the refugees would be allowed back only on terms which were acceptable to the Sarajevo government. Abdic knew it, Izetbegovic knew it, Galbraith knew it, and now everyone else knew it too. On the other hand it was also clear that Abdic needed the refugees far more than they needed him but for as long as the camp leaders remained loyal to him he retained control, and the world would have to continue dealing with him whether they liked it or not.

From the perspective of the Krajina Serbs, however, this situation was really little more than a distraction, and if nothing else it ensured that for as long as the crisis continued they could look forward to taking their percentage of all humanitarian aid that crossed their borders en route for the refugees. The Croats, of course, had a different approach that was spelled out by the Zupan of Karlovac to ECMM's Chief Humanitarian Officer Jan Uwe Thoms in the course of a volatile meeting on 30 August. Unbelievably the Croats were more concerned about the 'damage' the refugees were allegedly doing to deserted Croat houses in the separation zone, and the matter of who was going to pay for this, than helping to alleviate the situation. By liberally interpreting the Cease-fire Agreement of the 29th March the Zupan had determined that the UN should foot the bill for the alleged damage. He continued in this vein by expressing concern that the refugees were polluting Karlovac's water supply because they were using water from the nearby Korona river, and this would pose problems for his people in the near future. Clearly the Croats would have much preferred the refugees to remain living in the open, in filth and squalor, and refrain from washing, cooking, drinking or eating in order that the citizens of Karlovac could continue to enjoy the lifestyle to which they had become accustomed.

It was now clear also that the longer the situation remained unresolved the greater the risk that both refugee camps would become permanent fixtures. In Velika Kladusa

life in the area has by and large returned to normal, and people in the streets do not seem to be suppressed by the new authorities. There is, however, a certain tension since it looks as though everything which might be of use to the armed forces has been stolen by them, especially cars. Farmers and their families who remained are working the fields. Several houses were seen that had been destroyed in the fighting, and one house which had been deliberately blown up. There is evidence of civilians looting deserted houses and this is still happening. The only way of stopping this looting is for UNCIVPOL, and UNPROFOR, together with the civilian police, to patrol more often and in greater numbers. But the longer the refugees stay away from their homes, the more houses will be looted.[20]

Colonel Dequen, the Commanding Officer of the French UN troops in the Pocket, also rejected the concept of 'resettlement centres', on the basis that he was neither mandated nor in a position to guarantee anyone's protection. As far as he was concerned the matter of resettlement was the responsibility of the Sarajevo government and he was absolutely right. Unfortunately this development also played into Abdic's hands and he now had a statement from a senior UN officer to support what he himself had been preaching for two weeks.

In the camps themselves the law of the jungle began to set in; weapons were fired to settle disputes at Turanj and the camp leadership in Batnoga became completely confrontational, with the international agencies continually berating them for supposedly doing nothing. It also emerged that the Serb militia positioned around Batnoga were also arresting people they thought were trying to escape and herding them off to prison in Vojnic and elsewhere. For those who managed to evade capture there was then the matter of mines to contend with, and the camp was alive with stories of several unsuccessful escape attempts.[21] And then, just when people had begun to forget the military side of life, two Orkan rockets ploughed into Velika Kladusa at 1050 hrs on 9 September. UNMOs confirmed that five rockets had been fired from east of Otoka in Bosnian Serb-held territory and this tied in with other attacks on Buzim and Cazin over the previous few days. The only matter at issue was which type of Serb – Krajina or Bosnian – had actually fired them, and at the end of the day it hardly mattered. The message for Dudakovic was very simple; he may have won a battle but the war was far from over, and as he handed in another official protest to the ECMM team in Bihac town he was acutely aware that there was more work to be done before the Pocket could be considered secure.[22]

NOTES

1. RC Zagreb Daily Report: 20/8/94.
2. RC Zagreb Daily Report: 21/8/94.
3. RC Zagreb Daily Report: 22/8/94.
4. Abdic's control over his people can in the first instance be attributed to the fact that he was their elected representative but this accounts for only half the story. It was widely believed at the time that he also controlled an Austrian bank account into which former residents of the Pocket then working throughout Europe were encouraged to deposit whatever they could afford, to be held in credit for members of their families still living in the Pocket. Once the transaction was complete Abdic would then arrange to have vouchers issued to the relevant beneficiaries who could then exchange them for food at distribution points manned by APWB officials. Such an operation could be seen as either a marvellous work of charity, or alternatively as one huge rip-off, but people needed food to survive physically and Abdic needed the people to survive politically. When they all moved into exile in the Krajina their status might have changed from resident, or displaced person, to refugee but their relationship with Abdic remained the same. It was, without doubt, a very vicious circle.
5. Vjesnik: 23/8/94.
6. Special Report to ECMM HQ: 22/8/94. I knew Roger Bryant well, and coming from this mild-mannered, quietly spoken, former British Naval Officer, a comment such as this can safely be taken to mean that the place had in fact been completely vandalized.
7. Further evidence of what really happened is provided by Sefija Delanovic who became just another statistic of war, having been driven from her home

by the advancing 'liberators' in the 5th Corps. 'They entered our village, burned our house, and took our sheep and horses away,' she said. Richard Meares/Reuters: 4/8/94.

8. Team Bihac Daily Report: 23/8/94.
9. Team Glina Daily Report: 24/8/94.
10. Team Karlovac Daily Report: 25/8/94.
11. RC Zagreb Daily Report: 25/8/94.
12. It later emerged that the Croats had convinced themselves that this was an opportunity for the Serbs to infiltrate Croatia and take some more of their territory. Instead of doing something to alleviate the humanitarian crisis, which was staring them straight in the face, their energies were deployed instead in erecting sandbag bunkers from which they would repel the Serb hoards when they 'attacked'. Whoever made this assessment certainly got it wrong.
13. Feed The Children Report: 26/10/94.
14. Team Plaski Daily Report: 27/8/94.
15. CC Topusko Daily Report: 26/8/94.
16. An ECMM team in Batnoga on 27 August estimated that up to 90 per cent of those present would go back to Velika Kladusa if they had a free choice. Team Plaski Daily Report: 27/8/94.
17. Galbraith also tried to convince Abdic that under the Washington Agreement the Bihac region would enjoy far greater autonomy than it had before and for that reason he should accept the amnesty and return. While this was true it did not address the main point, which was that Sarajevo would never tolerate Abdic again, nor he them.
18. Both ECMM and UNPROFOR also provided further confirmation that most of the houses in Velika Kladusa had indeed been looted and in some cases Muslim refugees from other parts of Bosnia had also begun moving into the recently abandoned properties. Team Plaski Daily Report: 28/8/94.
19. Team Plaski Daily Report: 29/8/94.
20. RC Zagreb Daily Report: 2/9/94.
21. Team Velika Kladusa Daily Report: 7/9/94.
22. Team Bihac Daily Report: 9/9/94.

CHAPTER TEN

The 5th Corps' Southern
Offensive: Operation Grmec

With September drawing to a close and the weather beginning to deteriorate right across the Balkans, the predicament of the refugees in the Krajina began to take on a permanence that no one except Abdic and his associates wanted to maintain. These people had by now become pawns in a dirty political game, which revolved around keeping them where they were for as long as possible, in ever-deteriorating circumstances. Then, when the tragedy became overwhelming, Abdic would reappear to demand international intervention which in turn might pressurize Izetbegovic to compromise sufficiently and thereby allow the re-emergence of APWB, in one guise or another. This was the strategy but in the meantime life continued for the refugees almost in defiance of their worsening circumstances.

At Turanj a public phone was installed and a local butcher arrived to sell meat and fish to those who could pay for it.[1] In Batnoga, however, babies were born, and adults and older children died from the usual variety of causes[2] as UNPROFOR engineers began to build showers and toilet facilities, and a US medical team was doing its best to provide basic services for those worst affected.[3] From time to time, when their leaders felt the refugees might be getting too happy with their lot, a row would conveniently break out over whether or not UNPROFOR had the requisite permission to deliver food aid to the camp in the first place. The Serb militia guarding the perimeter would begin this argument,[4] while the next day the refugee leadership themselves would find a reason to turn the food away, and from time to time they even went to the trouble of organizing hunger strikes among selected refugees, in order to protest their belief that the International Community was not doing enough to help them.[5] And so it went on. The refugees had become an international problem,[6] and Abdic and his close associates continued to exploit the situation to further their own political objectives.[7]

In Velika Kladusa those who remained and those who had moved into the town from elsewhere began picking up the pieces of their shattered existence. Right around the perimeter of the Pocket the 5th Corps and the Serbs continued to spar with one another in limited low intensity

101

offensives which saw the confrontation line shift a few metres one day, and then back again the next. The salient points of Jim Bourke's daily report from ECMM's regional centre in Zagreb on the night of 19 September read as follows:

Radio 'Petrova Gora' carried a report at 1700 hrs this evening on the two meetings that Mr ABDIC attended over the last two days, namely the Crisis Staff Meeting [with the Krajina authorities] and the meeting with ECMM's Head of Mission this morning. It stated that the tone did not give any cause for optimism and no solutions emerged from either meeting. 'Nobody will listen to us,' says Abdic.

UNMOs in Sector North have informed ECMM teams that one UNMO has been killed and one injured at Kunic as a result of a mine explosion. Confirmed by Team Plaski the officer who died was Danish, and the injured one is Polish.

Team Sisak have received an unconfirmed rumour that General Mladic, the Commander of the Bosnian Serb Army, was arrested, injured and probably killed last week by the 5 Corps near D. Zinovac.[8]

UNCIVPOL Vojnic report that there are currently seventy-seven Muslims imprisoned in Vojnic by the Krajina Serb authorities. They are being interned for illegal border crossing and unsatisfactory identity checks. After investigation they are expected to be moved to Batnoga or Turanj.

Team V. Kladusa reports that the market in V. Kladusa is again in operation. Most of the foodstuffs come through the black market and at very much inflated prices.

Team Plaski attended the daily camp meeting at Batnoga Refugee Camp, the main item discussed was the 'demonstration' four days ago in which 1,000 young people participated. Their action culminated in them breaking into the stores of the Aid Agencies and taking away some mattresses. They were apparently complaining about lack of food and water. RC Comment: it is probable that this action was orchestrated by the camp committee or some of the older people in the camp.

As winter approached one of the main problems for the international agencies operating in Batnoga was to establish just how many refugees were actually living there. Several attempts were made to physically count them but this proved impossible and certainly the suspicion was that the camp leadership was determined to keep the matter in dispute as a mechanism to claim humanitarian aid for the greatest number possible. Accordingly the numbers varied from day to day and, depending on who you spoke to, rose on occasion to over 25,000. Michael Cleary, a Senior

Officer in the Irish Army and then ECTF's Infrastructure and Food Co-ordinator in Former Yugoslavia,[9] visited the camp on 19 October and his account of what he found was probably one of the more vivid and accurate.

There are now 16,000 persons living in the 24 chicken farm huts. Attempts are being made by the refugees themselves to create partitions between families in the huts, by using any form of sheeting such as cardboard, plastic or timber that is available, even the discarded corn stacks from the fields are being used. There are only a few stoves in each of the buildings which are being used for both cooking and heating. Much of the heating is carried on outside the buildings on makeshift ovens. This will cease when the weather becomes wet. Stovepipes within the buildings are in many cases not long enough to exit through the roof ventilator and are causing considerable smoke problems within the buildings. The walls of the building will give very little insulation when the cold weather arrives. The water pump in the camp is broken. The existing latrines are full and new ones need to be dug. a field has been identified close to the camp and the refugees themselves will dig the holes with the help of an excavator from UNPROFOR. Some kind of shower unit is badly needed and if a military type unit was provided, a Mr Amir, who previously was the water supply engineer in Velika Kladusa, could fix it up. The refugees at present are sleeping on mattresses on the ground of each of the chicken huts. If bunk beds of the type used by the military worldwide were supplied I consider that a major improvement could be made to the space problem. I recommend that this course of action be pursued at the Member States Meeting on Thursday.[10]

Meetings with the refugee leaders were also becoming more hostile now as the effects of winter began to set in. Sead Kajtazovic, operating through an interpreter, began listing one demand after another, while nothing UNHCR or any other agency was doing appeared to satisfy him. As the smell produced by dampness, sweat, dirt, smouldering wood, scattered refuse and latrines full to the brim with tons of untreated sewage became pervasive, an already critical situation was getting worse by the minute. The latest arrivals were unable to find any space in the already chronically overcrowded huts so they began squatting wherever they could find some space, and using plastic sheeting, cardboard boxes, wood or whatever else was to hand, they made makeshift tents and settled down for the days and nights ahead. The sight of very small children and the elderly, condemned to suffer in conditions unfit for animals, was absolutely heartbreaking but there was nothing much in real terms any foreigners could do to help them. The man who certainly could have done something to resolve the matter was nowhere to be found, and rumoured instead to be commuting daily between the camps and his apartment in Zagreb. Had Fikret Abdic been condemned to live in Batnoga, and awake hungry and cold every morning to be overwhelmed by the stench of the place, he might well have had a different outlook on life. But he was not and did not, and his struggle went on at his people's expense.[11]

An eye-witness account of a journey through the area at that time now provides an interesting insight.

It was cold and damp that Sunday morning as we started out from Plaski for our weekly meeting with the other Monitors operating in our area. Today we were heading for Velika Kladusa, in the extreme north-west corner of Bosnia, and as I sat in the back of the Landrover I was assailed by plumes of smoke coming from the two chainsmokers in the front, and a noxious smell of diesel coming from the five jerry cans bouncing around in the back. It was all bleak and grey outside, and the shells of burnt-out houses emerged all too frequently from the cold fog, which seemed to permanently envelope everything. I shall always remember the cold and the fog in the Krajina. It was almost as if it was nature's way of imposing peace and tranquillity on the pain and torment which the landscape had witnessed in the very recent past.

As the road wound its way from Slunj and into the valley beyond, isolation gave way to desolation as we approached a teeming humanity crammed into a disused chicken farm in a place called Batnoga, where 25,000 people were now living like animals, and in many cases faring no better than the previous inhabitants. These people were some of the real victims of Yugoslavia's war of dissolution, having been routed in terror from their homes and possessions with no future and no hope, and little option but to follow the orders of their leaders who had led them into this miserable situation in the first place.

And as we drove along the dirty road between the wooden chicken sheds and the filthy plastic polythene campsite I could feel the stench of the place seep into the comparatively sanitized atmosphere of our car. I had left my window fractionally open to allow the smoke and diesel fumes escape, but now another smell assaulted me, clung to my clothes, and seeped up my nose. I only barely managed not to get sick.

And as the road climbed towards the village of Cetingrad we found three Serb tanks parked by the side of the road in full view of the camp. At first glance these looked no different to any other day, but as we drove by and exchanged the usual 'Dobar Dan' with the tired, bored soldiers I almost missed the subtle change that had taken place. The gun barrels were no longer pointed towards Batnoga. They were pointed now back into Bihac Pocket. What could this mean? The date was 23 October 1994 and within a few days we would all be well aware of what was afoot.[12]

While the refugee problem caused severe problems for the Serb authorities and the International Community alike, the absence of dissension within Bihac Pocket allowed the 5th Corps to regroup and the overall situation quickly became comparatively stable. This prevailed until the end of October when reports began to indicate that a new 5th Corps offensive might be under way from the south of the Pocket into Bosnian Serb territory. The motivation for this initiative was initially unclear. One explanation suggested that it was an attempt to distract the Bosnian Serbs from other Muslim and Croat operations in Central Bosnia. Another indicated that it was purely an attempt to extend the size of the Pocket to the boundaries defined in the Contact Group Peace Plan of July 1994 on the basis that it would ultimately be easier to claim this area at the negotiating table if the Muslim Armija actually controlled it to begin with.

Whatever his motivation, on 26/7 October Dudakovic launched his forces on a two-pronged attack deep into Serb positions to the south and south-east of the Pocket, which quickly took them across the Una river, forward to the villages of Ripac, Gorjavac and Racic, and into the outskirts of Bosanska Krupa from where they had been evicted over two years previously. In the days that followed the 5th Corps continued to develop the situation and advanced as far south as Kulen Vakuf and Vrtoce, sweeping all Serb opposition before them. By the 29th, however, Dudakovic's bold initiative had run out of steam and ground to a halt. Thanks to CNN and Sky News, this campaign was portrayed internationally as a legitimate military operation in pursuit of 'rebel Serb forces',[13] and for a short period it did appear as if the Bosnian Serb army was about to crumble before them. Other Serb setbacks in central Bosnia, mainly in the Kupres Salient and the Brugle Finger, seemed to indicate that perhaps the BSA were about to be brought to their knees throughout the country after all, and triumphal sounds began to emanate from Sarajevo. This would not last long.

As the offensive ground to a halt Dudakovic found his limited resources now stretched over a distance of 80 km – from Velika Kladusa in the north to Kulen Vakuf in the south – and he now became extremely vulnerable to counter-attack as all the logistical problems associated with such a rapid advance began to bite hard. He had moved too far much too fast, even though assessments at the time did not indicate that the Bosnian Serbs were capable of mounting a swift counter-offensive, nor that the Krajina Serbs might be prepared to become significantly involved.

But why had Dudakovic put himself in such difficulty in the first place? The answer is that probably for the first time in almost a year and a half he no longer had to divide his forces in two and fight simultaneously on two fronts which were over 50 km apart. Now he had several brigades on call and the opportunity was there to resolve a long-outstanding problem with the Bosnian Serbs. Conventional wisdom suggests that initially he never intended to do anything more that push the Serb artillery out of range of Bihac town, and perhaps reclaim Bosanska Krupa as well, but as the situation developed he simply got carried away with his achievements.

The first phase of the operation began at midday on 24 October and by 2300 hrs the headquarters of 2 Krajina Corps (BSA) had issued orders for the forward elements to begin withdrawing. Striking out from the Pocket in two columns with the 501, 502 and 517 Brigades pushing south-west, and the 503, 511 and 1st Liberation Brigades heading north-east for Bosanska Krupa, Operation Grmec 1994 had begun. With the Serbs reeling before him Dudakovic stopped his forces after three days and conducted a classic 'relief in place'. It was then he decided to push further south towards Kulen Vakuf. In the east progress was much slower and although Bosanska Krupa was reclaimed, the area immediately surrounding it was not. With his corps now strung out over a distance of 80 km, from Velika Kladusa in the north to Kulen Vakuf in the south and eastwards to Bosanska Krupa, it quickly became apparent that there was no possibility whatever of supporting this advance with either men or materials.[14] Elements of the 101 Brigade HVO, who were also involved, were ordered to abandon Kulen Vakuf less than forty-eight hours after having taken it, and a very disorderly withdrawal developed into something of a rout as the Serbs, recognizing that Dudakovic was in trouble, began to throw as much artillery at him as they could muster.

In open countryside the 5th Corps were systematically beaten back into the Pocket.[15] When they returned they soon discovered that all was not well in Velika Kladusa either as Abdic, once again supported by the Krajina Serbs, was on the verge of a comeback. Within the space of three weeks Dudakovic had turned a comparatively secure position into one tottering on the brink of total defeat. The 'safe area of Bihac' was about to become another Gorazde as the world focused on 'beleaguered' Muslims surrounded by 'rebel Serbs' of one sort or another. This version of events was far from correct and it conveniently ignored that the Muslims had brought most of this upon themselves. Once provoked the Serb response was always going to be punitive and disproportionate, and this did not come as a surprise to Dudakovic. Baying for blood, General Manojlo Milovanovic, the Bosnian Serb army's Chief of Staff, who had taken control of all Serb elements attacking Bihac, was quoted as saying, 'Since the soldiers of the 5th Corps did not accept my asking them to surrender, I am compelled to continue defeating the Moslem army, no matter in which area or settlement its members are . . . Jihad warriors must be prevented from taking part in combat actions'.[16]

On 4 November the Bosnian Serb counter-attack had begun and by the 6th Kulen Vakuf had been retaken. On the 8th Ripac returned to Serb hands as did the bridge at Bosanska Krupa and during the next week (7–13 November) the Bosnian Serbs regained over 90 per cent of the territory lost in the previous three weeks, thereby returning them to a line just south of the Pocket. In the north a force of 5,000 soldiers loyal to Fikret Abdic, and again supported by the Krajina Serbs, launched an attack on Velika Kladusa on 16 November.[17] The bulk of these troops had been withdrawn from the refugee camps during the preceding days, and were organized and equipped by the Serbs. Struggling now to defend a very hot front line in the south, Abdic drew Dudakovic back to the north to fight on a second line, while the Krajina Serbs were clearly in the business of establishing a third in the west. By 17 November the 5th Corps was committed on three fronts and indications were that their position was becoming untenable. On the 18th two Serb Orao aircraft took off from Udbina airbase in the Krajina and dropped napalm and cluster bombs on Bihac town.[18] The following day a further air attack from the same base resulted in one of the aircraft smashing into an apartment block in Cazin causing wholesale death, injury and destruction. Significantly enough the pilot, who was born in Serbia, was flying a Bosnian Serb aircraft from an airfield in the Republic of Srpska Krajina!

With almost 1,300 UN Bangladeshi troops now operating throughout the Pocket, having recently replaced the French, and the so-called 'safe area' having become probably one of the most unsafe places in the world, the UNPROFOR leadership knew full well that once again they were on public trial. In a special report to Kofi Annan in New York on 15 November, Akashi referred everything back to a draft report on safe areas, which he had submitted to New York on 29 April but upon which no decision had yet been taken.[19] In that document UNPROFOR had recommended the creation of a very limited safe area around Bihac town, purely on the basis that this was all they could reasonably be expected to defend with the limited resources they had available. Seven months later the manpower levels were approximately the same, although the Bangladeshis had the added difficulties of having been deployed in the Pocket with half their equipment and only one rifle between every four of them. This appalling mess was the product of a system where countries were encouraged to supply troops to UNPROFOR on the understanding that their equipment would then be sponsored by a more wealthy nation. In this instance not all of the equipment had been provided by the date of deployment and while in normal circumstances the logistics would have eventually caught up with them and all would have been well, on this occasion the conflict erupted all around them, and the ever-smiling, good-natured Bangladeshis were caught in the middle of a nightmare. Some commentators took a perverse delight in criticizing their officers for allowing this situation to develop in the first place, the implication being that these were a bunch of unprofessional people who should never have been allowed into UNPROFOR in the first place. This was totally unfair and unwarranted, and indeed the Bangladeshis were every bit as good, if not in fact a good deal better than most of the troops that made up the 24,087 'blue helmets' in Bosnia at that time.[20]

In this context then it was not surprising to find that Akashi had written 'The fundamental issue in dealing credibly with the Bihac situation is that UNPROFOR's responsibilities must to the extent possible be brought into line with our capabilities'. Weighing up all the possibilities as best he could he suggested that, 'We will have to deal with this situation as and when it develops', although a military exclusion zone around Bihac town was completely ruled out on the grounds of insufficient manpower. So the 'let's make it up as we go along' school of thought was very much in evidence until events on the ground effectively forced the Security Council to make a decision. On 19 November UNSC Resolution 958 authorized close air support and airstrikes in the Krajina if such action was deemed necessary by Akashi. In tandem with this it was discovered that, as of now, the 'safe area of Bihac' was indeed confined to Bihac town and its immediate surroundings, with demilitarization and separation of forces central to any implementation process.

If this were properly implemented the 5th Corps would not be entitled to keep any weapon of greater calibre than an 81-mm mortar within that area; no military headquarters could be sited there; no munitions could be produced or stored there; and no combat troops would be allowed take refuge within this delineation. To safeguard the status of Bihac and the other five safe areas in Bosnia an additional 34,000 UN troops would be needed to do the job properly, and with the UN barely able to balance its budget as it was it became quite clear that the chances of any of this happening were nil. Instead what occurred was another punitive disproportionate response, this time by NATO when the Krajina Serb air base at Udbina was bombed repeatedly. This was not linked in any serious way to proposals for a peaceful settlement and Akashi and his advisors were once again left to jump from one crisis to another.

Having embarked upon a strategy of calling in NATO to respond to Serb aggression around Bihac the question then arose of how far Akashi and General Rose were actually prepared to go on this issue. In the immediate aftermath of the attack on Udbina much was made of the size of the NATO strike force and the fact that it was the first such operation in NATO's history. What was not alluded to at all was that the Serbs knew full well this attack was coming and had diverted most of their aircraft to other areas as a precaution.[21] Of equal or perhaps more significance was

*General Atif Dudakovic, Commander of the 5th
Corps of the Bosnian Muslim Army.* (Roderick
de Normann)

*Fikret Abdic, leader of the breakaway
'Autonomous Province of Western Bosnia'.*
(Roderick de Normann)

Danish UN peacekeepers investigating events around Bosanska Krupa in April 1992. (H. O'Donovan)

General Vlado Santic in December 1994. (Anon.)

A shoulder flash from the forces of Fikret Abdic – the APWB. (Author's Collection)

The staff of the 'information cell' at ECMM HQ, 31 December 1994. From left to right: Klaus Cramer (GE), Jean Michel Happe (FR), Holger Aulike (GE), Phillipe Joley (FR), Joss Gannes (BE), Hubert Krauss (GE) and Brendan O'Shea (IRL). (Author's Collection)

Bill Foxton, ECMM's Team Leader during winter 1994 and spring 1995. His armoured Mercedes Landrover served him well on more than one occasion. (Roderick de Normann)

The only link with the outside world for most people in 1994 – ECMM's satellite telephone.
(Author's Collection)

ECMM on patrol in the town of Lipik in Sector West during February 1995. (D. Galvin)

'The German Connection.' German and Croatian flags unashamedly fly side by side on the main street in Citluk, Bosnia-Hercegovina, February 1995. (Author's Collection)

Members of the 5th Corps display a Krajina Serb M-48 tank captured during Operation Storm in August 1995. A Bangladeshi UN peacekeeper also expresses an interest in Dudakovic's latest prize. (Bill Foxton)

Ambassador Albert Turot (FR), ECMM Head of Mission from January to July 1995, presenting an ECMM medal to General Dudakovic. (Roderick de Normann)

A refugee in Turanj sums up the utter desperation of the situation, October 1994. (Philippe Graton © Mediaworks)

The unsanitary conditions endured by the refugees, October 1994. (Philippe Graton © Mediaworks)

The scene near Bosanska Petrovac after a successful 5th Corps ambush on a Bosnian Serb convoy in September 1995. (Bill Foxton)

5th Corps troops overlooking the burning town of Pritoka near Bihac following its 'liberation' in August 1995. (Bill Foxton)

A monument to ethnic cleansing in the Krajina. (Julien Neil)

The only purpose of this level of destruction was to ensure the civilian population never came back, and it worked. (Julien Neil)

the fact that the alternative runway at Udbina, the Korenica–Udbina road, which had long ago been adapted for use as a second runway and ran dead straight for over 3.5 km, was neither targeted or damaged by any of the eighty bombs which were used in the raid. This effectively meant that as soon as NATO had completed its mission the airfield became operational again as none of the flight control equipment had been targeted either, and by evening a Serb helicopter had resumed firing rockets against 5th Corps targets just north of Bihac town.[22] So what kind of message was this supposed to send to the Serbs?

General Mladic responded immediately by letter to the UN Force Commander General De Lapresle in which he bluntly said, 'It is sad that you are partial. . . . You are, General, responsible for the escalation of the war here and your offer that you and General Rose continue to mediate in establishing a cease-fire is senseless.' Accusing UNPROFOR of being no better than 'those who from 1941 to 1945 have spread death in these areas', Mladic refused to guarantee the safety of any UN soldier in Bosnia and concluded defiantly, 'be assured that you cannot bring peace using NATO bombers'.[23] Karadzic's letter to Akashi was even worse.

РЕПУБЛИКА СРПСКА	REPUBLIC OF SRPSKA
ПРЕДСЕДНИК РЕПУБЛИКЕ	PRESIDENT OF THE REPUBLIC
САРАЈЕВО	SARAJEVO

H.E. Yasushi Akashi SRSG

22 November 1994

Excellency,

I have just received a verbal threat from the UN B-H HQ that we shall be bombed at Debeljaca hill near Bihac unless we withdraw before dawn.

It is claimed that we are about 4 km inside the safe area of Bihac. As you know well, Excellency, an area is a safe area when the sides to the conflict agree about it and about delimitation of such an area. After that, in such an area there can only be civilian population and no combatants.

We have never delimited the 'safe area' in Bihac Pocket, nor was it demilitarized. As a matter of fact the Bihac Pocket is a stronghold of the B-H Army. A few weeks ago the Moslem side launched attacks from the Bihac area, captured great portions of the Serb territory and killed many Serb soldiers and civilians. The UN and NATO did not react. Now we are receiving the threat which is absolutely unacceptable. After our experience with Igman Mt and the other localities we will never withdraw from any territory before we sign a peace treaty with our enemies.

I regret, Excellency, that I have to inform you that we will not tolerate or accept any kind of attack by NATO in the Bihac area or elsewhere which can happen only if you and other UN officials approve it. If it happens anyway it would mean that further relationships between yourselves and our side will be rendered impossible because we shall have to treat you as our enemies. It would be regrettable if we came to a situation whereby all UNPROFOR forces as well as all NATO personnel would have to be treated as our enemies.

The establishment of peace in the Bihac pocket is possible only when the Serb and Moslem sides agree to the extent and character of the so called 'safe area' on the basis of international conventions.

Until such time we retain the right to hunt down every armed Moslem in the area.

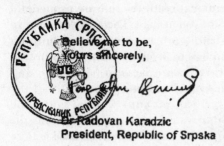

Believe me to be,
Yours sincerely,

Dr Radovan Karadzic
President, Republic of Srpska

Clearly the NATO airstrike was not having the desired effect on the Bosnian Serb leadership, and while objectively one might have been inclined to accept that Karadzic had indeed made one or two valid points, his appalling arrogance ensured that little notice would be taken of them. However Akashi's response was anything but resolute.

UNITED NATIONS PROTECTION FORCE

Special Representative of the Secretary-General for the Former Yugoslavia

23 November 1994

Dear Dr Karadzic,

I have read with great interest and concern your letter of 22 November 1994 on events around the town of Bihac.

In the absence of agreement among all concerned, UNPROFOR had delineated a safe area around Bihac in order to provide refuge for civilians who are already entering the town in large numbers. The boundaries of this area have been passed to your military headquarters by our Bosnia-Herzegovina Command. A copy is attached.

Military activities around the town of Bihac are now at the most critical point. It is of the utmost urgency and importance that your forces neither enter nor fire into the delineated area.

I also repeat the call in my letter of 21 November 1994 for an immediate cease-fire in Bihac and request your urgent response. I am at your disposal to discuss its implications and application at any time by telephone, correspondence, or in person.

In our reports we have made the Security Council fully aware of the several difficulties pertaining to implementation of the safe area concept. I have had opportunities to explain this to you at Pale. The Security Council has directed us to explain resolution 959 to provide recommendations on the modalities of implementation, as well as to propose further measures to stabilize the situation in Bihac and to demilitarize Sarajevo.

You and your people stand at a historical turning point. With all the seriousness I can convey, Excellency, I call on your wisdom and good judgement in exercising the maximum restraint. It is essential that the situation not be permitted to become further inflamed, which will lead to consequences that serve only those who seek a military rather than a diplomatic solution to the conflict.

Yasushi Akashi

Yasushi Akashi

Akashi's gesture of including a map that delineated the 'safe area' could almost be interpreted as accepting that Karadzic did not understand where the safe area was supposed to be in the first place. Equally, asking him to exercise 'maximum restraint' was a far cry from laying down the law, and if the Serbs saw this as indecision on the part of the UN they were absolutely correct. With no act of contrition forthcoming from Pale the overall situation took a turn for the worse on 23 November when at 0900 hrs two British Harriers on a reconnaissance patrol in the Bihac area were locked on to by an SA-2 'Fan Song' radar system and, in compliance with their orders from Admiral Leighton-Smith, the pilots acting in self-defence, engaged the system with Harm missiles and destroyed it. In response to this NATO then launched additional sorties which attacked two SAM missile sites near Otoka and Dvor with similar effect.[24] At a news briefing in Naples that evening Captain Jim Mitchell showed a video of the second strike as filmed by one of the attacking US F-15 Strike Eagle jets, which showed 225 kg laser-guided bombs scoring direct hits on a mobile missile launcher in a field near a farmhouse somewhere near Otoka.[25] News of this was not well received in Pale and all Serb checkpoints were immediately closed to both UN and civilian traffic. Flights in and out of Sarajevo were then suspended following Serb threats to shoot down incoming aircraft and numerous sniping incidents took place, including an attack on a tram just outside the Holiday Inn.

West of Sarajevo, near the town of Ilijas, fifty-five Canadian UN troops were taken hostage by the Bosnian Serbs and having been disarmed of everything except their side arms they were then taken away to six different locations. Further north in Brcko the UNMO team was evicted from the area and sent off along the road to the Serbian border where they were robbed of their armoured Landrover and personal belongings.[26] In Banja Luka the UNMOs in the town were taken under escort to the airports at Zauani and Mahovljani and forced to sit on the runways as a deterrent to further NATO attacks.[27] In Bihac the level of Bosnian Serb shelling increased dramatically, leading the UN to report that 'the Krajina and Bosnian Serb forces have, for all intents and purposes, effectively cut off Bihac town'.[28] The next day the overall situation deteriorated even further when 350 UN troops in central Bosnia – French, British, Ukrainian and Russian – were surrounded by Bosnian Serb forces as they manned weapons collection/storage sites and were denied permission to leave.

Panic then set in. General Gobilliard, the UN Commander of Sector Sarajevo, denied that his troops were being held as hostages, preferring instead to see the situation as one where they were just being restricted in their freedom of movement! General Rose then went public with a plan to arrange a cease-fire so that Bihac could be demilitarized like Srebrenica, Zepa and Gorazde. Haris Silajdzic, speaking after his meeting with Rose, unbelievably went along with this, while Karadzic dismissed the pair of them and continued to insist that, 'Bihac will only become a protected zone when the Serbs have disarmed the 5th Corps, making it then possible for the Moslem civilian population to lead normal lives'.[29] He failed to clarify what he thought 'normal life' should be.

Meanwhile, back in Bihac, Dudakovic was hanging on by his fingernails as Abdic continued to make gains in the north and the Serbs moved to within 1,000 m of Bihac town itself in the south. In a surprise move that evening Dudakovic sought out ECMM's Francis Bonal, a French Monitor who had been operating in the town on his own now for over a month, and between the two of them they agreed that a cease-fire was required at this time. Using the satellite phone in Bonal's Landrover they then attempted to contact Karadzic in Pale, Dudakovic apparently knowing the number by heart, but despite their best efforts they failed to raise him.[30] The unproved suspicion here was that Karadzic was well aware who was looking to speak with him but availed of the confusion to allow General Milovanovic time to continue pressing home his military advantage.

19. OCT. 1994.

Base Data Concerning Situation on Bihac Pocket – V Corps BH
Strength: 15,000–20,000 Soldiers

COMMANDING OFFICER – BRIGADIER GENERAL DUDAKOVIC, ATIF.

1. **501 BDE** – CO: BRIGADIER SARGANOVIC, SENAD,
                    AOR: WK 7264–WK 7671 (OSTROZAC AREA)

2. **502 BDE** – CO: COLONEL ABDIC, HAMDO,
                    AOR: WK 7264–WK 7359 (BIHAC AREA) AND
                    WK 6164–WK 6280 (IZACIC AREA)

3. **503 BDE** – CO: BRIGADIER DELALIC, MUHAMED,
                    AOR: WK 8471–WK 7671 (MIOSTRAH AREA)

4. **505 BDE** – CO: BRIGADIER NANIC, ISMET,
                    AOR: WL 7307–WK 9380 (VRNQGRAC, BUZIM AREA)

5. **506 BDE** – CO: MAJOR MIRJKOVIC, MIAS,
                    AOR: WL 6203–WL 7307 (V. KLADUSA AREA)

6. **511 BDE** – CO: MAJOR SEDIC MIRSAD,
                    AOR: WK 9380–WK 8471 (BOS. KRUPA AREA)

7. **517 BDE** – CO: MAJOR NADAREVIC IBRAHAM,
                    AOR: WK 6280–WK 6296 (STURLIC AREA)

8. **BBL** – CO: 1ST LIBERATION BRIGADE
                  MAJOR AVDIC, AMIR
                  AOR: WK 6296–WL 6203 (POLJE AREA)

10. **101 HVO BBL** – CO:LIEUTENANT COLONEL GRGIC,
                    BDE AOR: WK 7359–WK 6164 (SOKOLAC AREA)

V CORPS BH WEAPONS:

2? × Tanks T54/55, 1 × APC BOV/M
1 × M53/59 PRAGA 30 mm/2; 3 × ZIS -3 76 mm;
Several Mortars 82 and 120 mm; ? × AA/A-Tank Guns.
Other Forces in the Pocket: Civilian/Military Police Units

NOTES

1. Team Karlovac Daily Report: 9/9/94.
2. Team Velika Kladusa/UNHCR Reports: 12/9/94.
3. RC Zagreb Daily Report: 13/9/94.
4. RC Zagreb Daily Report: 13/9/94.
5. Team Bihac Daily Report: 15/9/94.
6. On 16/9/94 Slovenia agreed to allow eighty-five of the refugees at Turanj, who apparently had correct documentation, to pass through the country en route to locations elsewhere in Europe. The Serbs had other ideas, however, and refused. These people would eventually escape their ordeal but not before bureaucracy and officialdom on all sides had registered their authority and been paid off. Unconfirmed reports indicated that 7,000 Deutschmarks per head was the sum required to effect safe passage to Croatia.
7. To this end a new radio station came on the air, Radio Krajina Cazin, and broadcasting from Korenica provided the inhabitants of Batnoga with a daily diet of anti-5th Corps propaganda and purported to give up-to-date information on the maltreatment of those who remained behind in the Pocket, as well detailing the burning and looting of their homes.
8 Several rumours abounded at this time that Ratko Mladic had been wounded and/or killed by the 5th Corps. However, neither UNMOS in the area, nor the senior operations officer at Sector North HQ in Topusko, nor the G2 personnel at UNPROFOR in Zagreb, could confirm that Mladic was even in that part of Bosnia at that time. A better assessment would have recognized this as clear 5th Corps propaganda.
9. ECTF was/is the European Community Task Force whose function was to coordinate the allocation and distribution of humanitarian aid in the region, given that the EU was paying for over 80 per cent of it.
10. Report to Head of ECTF, visit to Batnoga, 19/10/94, Michael Cleary.
11. ECMM Team Plaski Daily Report: 19/10/94.
12. Extract from the author's personal records, 1994/5.
13. Nobody bothered to remark that it could also be seen as 'an attack out of a UN safe area', which was supposed to be demilitarized in the first place!
14. Serb strategy has always revolved around the principle that if you cannot defend yourself properly today, you withdraw, keep your force intact, and then when the enemy is overstretched you strike back at a time and place which is most favourable to you, with a force quipped to do so. This is precisely what they did to Dudakovic and for a former JNA officer he certainly should have seen it coming.
15. Roderick de Normann, 'The Miracle of V Corps', *JIR*, 1996.
16. VIP News, Belgrade: 21/11/94.
17. Vecernji list: 17/11/94. On the evening of Wednesday 16/11/94 a message from Fikret Abdic was broadcast on Radio Velkatron aimed at the refugees in

the camps. He said he would guarantee their safety in Velika Kladusa as his troops numbered 10,000 (a gross exaggeration). He also called on the 5th Corps to surrender.

18. The napalm did not detonate.
19. UNPROFOR Report Z: 1714, 15/11/94.
20. UNPROFOR Fact Sheet: 31/11/94.
21. EU Monitors in Korenica were informed by the President of the municipality that three people had been killed in the Udbina raid with a further three taken to hospital in Knin. Whether this was true or not remains unclear as no mention of casualties is made in either the UN or ECMM reports for either 21 or 22 November.
22. UNPROFOR Chronology: 21/11/94.
23. Letter from Mladic to De Lapresle: 09/20–1051–22/11/94.
24. Daily Sitrep HQ BH Forward Command Sarajevo: 23/11/94.
25. Reuters, Naples, Italy: 24/11/94.
26. ECMM Daily Briefing: 25/11/94.
27. Ibid., para. 11.
28. Ibid., para. 5G.
29. Reuters Sarajevo: 24/11/94.
30. Team Bihac Capsat Message to HQ ECMM 2330 hrs: 24/11/94. At the end of his message Francis Bonal said he hoped to return to Zagreb the following day. Little did he know that it would be early January before he was able to make that journey having been trapped in the Pocket for seventy-six days as the battle raged around him. I caught up with him much later on in Medugorje and over dinner one night remarked that being an artillery officer he at least had the advantage of knowing what the Serbs were firing at him during his time in the Pocket. 'Yes, of course,' he replied, 'but that was not much consolation.' Bonal did very well on his own. Not everyone would have been able to handle the pressure.

CHAPTER ELEVEN

Boutros-Ghali goes to Sarajevo

As Dudakovic's continued to fight on three fronts in Bihac, Serb and Muslim officials met at Sarajevo airport on 25 November in yet another attempt to hammer out cease-fire terms.[1] UN sources were now reporting that no more than 300 members of the 5th Corps remained actively defending Bihac town, although the population had swollen to over 70,000 as a result of the huge influx of displaced people from villages to the south and west. The hospital was packed with casualties, the markets and shops were completely bare, and people sheltering in their homes were reported to be openly weeping with fear. Monique Tuffelli from UNHCR believed that while the ordinary people were very angry earlier in the week at the UN's perceived failure to protect them, they were now too overpowered by events to begin blaming anyone.

Later, as the airport talks concluded, Haris Silajdzic announced that he had been willing to agree a nationwide cease-fire but Nikolia Koljevic, while accepting the need for one, wanted further discussions before any final agreement could be reached.[2] Broadcasting on Bosnian Serb Radio News at 1900 hrs that night Koljevic outlined more of his plans and, repeating the Serb's willingness to stop the fighting if a peace agreement could be reached, he then insisted that Britain, France and Russia would have to guarantee the deal for the Serbs, as Germany and the US were likely to do so for the Muslims. Whether this was a serious proposal or just another delaying tactic is not exactly clear, but the international mediators were probably dismayed to discover that the very next item on the same news bulletin featured General Milovanovic threatening the 5th Corps with extinction if they failed to surrender within twenty-four hours.[3]

As far as the Bosnian Serbs were concerned it was clear that the right hand had not the remotest understanding of what the left was trying to do, and certainly of no concern to either limb of the leadership was a demonstration taking place that very evening, thousands of miles away in a place called Dhaka, where hundreds of Bangladeshis were marching by torchlight to highlight the plight of their troops in a place called Bihac Pocket. 'We strongly protest at the UN decision to put them on high risk duty without proper logistics. Today they are just like sitting ducks,' said a man whose nephew was serving with UNPROFOR.[4] This assessment was absolutely correct but neither Mladic or Milovanovic were likely to dwell on the matter of these foreign 'sitting ducks' whom they saw as essentially no different to the native variety if they happened to stand in their way. This very subject was also high on the agenda when the Croatian war council met in Zagreb that night to discuss how the Croats were going to increase support to the Sarajevo government in compliance with their 1992 agreements, and especially since tension levels throughout the Balkans were now steadily on the rise. A significant contribution to this debate was made by Denis Kuljis whose article in *Globus* on 25 November proved particularly effective. Entitled '20,000 Serb Soldiers from Croatia and Bosnia are Entering Bihac', and conveying graphic images of helpless Muslims and Croats about to be butchered by the Serbs, this was without doubt one of the best pieces of modern propaganda ever written. While this, of course, could have been easily dismissed by objective assessment, as far as Tudjman's war council was concerned these 'revelations' could not have come at a better time.

As fighting continued around Bihac General Rose warned the Serbs that further close air support was in the offing if they did not stop. Milovanovic promptly ignored him. NATO planes were then ordered into action but as the initial sortie was trying to locate a suitable target Rose had a change of heart and decided that the whole exercise was a waste of time. The mission was cancelled and even though the Serbs fired two badly directed SA-2 missiles at the departing aircraft, no follow up action was initiated.[5] Clearly the spectre of the 'Mogadishu Line' had appeared once more and Rose was not prepared to send his troops across it. This decision was greeted with derision by the government in Sarajevo but members of other agencies like, for example, those staff officers at ECMM HQ who had previously served with the UN in other missions, were convinced that he had acted correctly. In real terms there was nothing he or any other foreigner could now do to stop the carnage if the parties to the conflict were not themselves prepared to talk to one another. Had Rose gone ahead with the airstrike it was virtually guaranteed that by 0900 hrs the following morning even more UNPROFOR troops would have found themselves surrounded and held hostages pending the inevitable UN climbdown, which would have had to follow on in due course.

Accordingly UNPROFOR troops sat back and watched as the battles went on all over Bosnia. In Velika Kladusa, Bihac and Sarajevo the Serbs were certainly calling the shots, while in Stolice and Sapna in the north-east of the country the Muslims had begun and won a series of battles, which quite surprisingly had attracted no media attention whatsoever.[6] Attacks on a telecommunications mast sitting astride a marginally strategic hill were apparently not the stuff good copy was made of. In any event the significance of the overall situation was not lost on the members of the UN Security Council, who empowered the Secretary General on 28 November to go to Bosnia in the hope that his personal intervention might succeed where his emissaries had failed. It did not, and in fact served only to generate a new row that none of the mediators on the ground really needed at that time.

Flying into Sarajevo on the morning of 30 November and having written to Karadzic in advance, asking for a meeting,[7] Boutros Boutros-Ghali first went to meet Izetbegovic at the presidency building and immediately thereafter gave a press conference. He then returned to the airport for a meeting with the Serbs, having sent an earlier message to Karadzic informing him of the venue. The Serbs were outraged that the Secretary General would snub them by refusing to go to Pale. Karadzic then suggested that the meeting take place in the Serb part of Sarajevo, where all Boutros-Ghali had to do was cross a bridge, but unbelievably this was also rejected. Karadzic then decided that under no circumstances was he going to the airport and while a unique opportunity was indeed lost, it was hard not to concede that on this occasion the Serbs did have a valid point. At face value it certainly appeared as if the UN Secretary General was intent on spending as little time in Sarajevo as he could get away with, when by any objective standard he should have been prepared to stay there for as long as it took to bring all of the parties to their senses. He had nothing to gain from treating any of them differently and this begs the question of what was so terribly wrong with making the relatively short journey to Pale, or an even shorter walk across the river, in order to talk with the Serbs on their own territory. Clearly he had no wish to legitimize Karadzic and his ministers, and perhaps that was understandable, but if he was not prepared to compromise he had little business coming to Sarajevo in the first place. This was more than a lost opportunity, it was a tragedy, and it signalled to the Serbs that from now on they could not expect to be dealt with impartially. In his letter to Akashi on 1 December Karadzic put the matter rather well, and given the circumstances was quite well mannered about it.

I too regret the fact that the planned meeting between the Secretary General and myself did not take place yesterday. The Secretary General sadly could not bring himself to cross a bridge in Sarajevo and hold the meeting on our territory. This shows that he recognizes only Mr Izetbegovic as the legitimate leader of Bosnian Serbs. We take a dim view of this. Mr Izetbegovic is the leader of a rump illegitimate Presidency and he is, moreover, the leader of only a part of the Muslims. Although we have great respect for the UN as an institution, and for the person of the Secretary General, you must understand that no significant progress in our relations is possible if we are not treated on a basis of equality. I trust that you will see our point of view and I look forward to meeting you tomorrow.

NOTES

1. Chaired by General Rose, Generals Ratko Mladic and Rasim Delic also attended.
2. Reuters Sarajevo: 25/11/94.
3. News Report ECLO Sarajevo: 25/11/94.
4. Reuters Dhaka: 25/11/94.
5. ECLO Sarajevo Daily Report: 26/11/94.
6. ECMM Weekly Information Analysis Summary, no. 105.
7. In his letter to Karadzic on 28 November the Secretary General appeared to be genuinely pursuing a resolution of the problem when he said, 'I believe it is imperative at this moment to take all steps to stop the hostilities and alleviate the suffering of the civilian population. In order to further these aims I intend to visit Sarajevo on Wednesday 30 November 1994, and would like to meet with you at the airport.'

CHAPTER TWELVE

Croatia's Economic Agreement and the Z-4 Plan

With international attention now firmly focused on Bosnia a number of other very important events also took place. On 2 December, after several postponements, the ICFY-sponsored Zagreb/Knin Economic Agreement was signed in Zagreb. This agreement dealt with water supply and electrical distribution, the reopening of the Zagreb–Belgrade Highway through Sector West, and the opening of the oil and gas pipelines through Sector North. Of crucial importance was the acceptance that this was the basis for further negotiations, in relation to the return of refugees and displaced persons, the payment of Croatian state pensions, and the further opening of roads and railways. Signed by Sarinic for Croatia and Mikelic on behalf of the Knin authorities, this was a huge step into the unknown for the Krajina Serbs. While at one level it made perfect sense to cooperate with the Croats on these matters, on another it made none at all. Less enthusiastic was Milan Babic, who was firmly convinced that this was the first step in a process which would eventually erode the status of the Krajina altogether. When Sarinic then began insisting that if the agreement was not implemented in full by 20 January 1995 Croatia would refuse to extend UNPROFOR's mandate, Babic's worst fears were confirmed.

Mikelic on the other hand was far more upbeat and stated on Belgrade Radio that while he had not achieved all that he wanted on economic matters, he had 'managed to make the Agreement without Preambles, Security Council Resolutions, or Political Qualifications. Croatia has international recognition within its borders on paper . . . everything else is in our hands'. All of this went down well in Belgrade, where Mikelic was being used cleverly by Milosevic to pave the way for better relations between Belgrade and Zagreb, but it was immediately clear to all commentators that no matter what the Krajina Serbs conceded to Croatia, in the longer term it would never be enough.

With the ink barely dry on the Economic Agreement out stepped the 'Zagreb 4', which curiously enough consisted of five people: Leonid Kerestedzhjiyants (Russia), Peter Galbraith (US), Geert Ahrens (ICFY), Alfredo Cordella (ICFY) and Jean Jacques Gaillarde (EU). They produced their plan for a new political solution that was allegedly aimed at the peaceful reintegration of the UNPAs (i.e., the Krajina) into Croatia proper. While it looked as if some progress was being made here the overall situation in the Krajina actually remained as bad as ever. All troops were fully mobilized and rumours abounded in Knin that the Croatian army was operating inside Bosnia's international borders in order to creep into the Krajina by the back door. When this was put to General Gotavina, the HV Commander in Split, he responded by claiming that the Krajina Serbs were also operating in Bosnia (presumably he was referring to the area around Bihac), and that this more or less justified what his own troops were up to. By any reasonable standard it did not and UNPROFOR sources later confirmed that elements from at least three Croatian brigades (126th, 4th and 9th) were actually deployed in Bosnia in an area just north of Livno at that very time.[1] And so it emerged that the Croatians, in tandem with their Bosnian Muslim associates, were quite prepared to talk about peace and even sign agreements on economic matters, while simultaneously preparing for a new round of fighting. That they got away with this charade had more to do with the fact that the members of the International Community were totally divided on several key issues, not least among which was the central matter of whether UNPROFOR should stay put or go home. At the CSCE meeting in Budapest French Foreign Minister Alain Juppe made it clear that 'If there is no diplomatic progress over the next few weeks, we need to be ready and prepared to start a possible withdrawal operation', while on 7 December the British Foreign Minister, Douglas Hurd, announced that 'the British government wants the UN force to be able to continue its mission and the British contingent to continue to play a major part'. Meanwhile, and almost as if to prove that no one really knew what was going on, senior officers in UNPROFOR and NATO agreed to scale down Operation Deny Flight and limit it purely to reconnaissance flights. In the absence of any clear policy or strategy the military had decided to make the best of the situation, secure in the knowledge that the operation had failed anyway, and that in political circles no government was actually prepared to pay the price for enforcing this or any other similar measures. Confusion, disorder and disagreement had become the international order of the day, and the politicians of Former Yugoslavia, Muslim, Serb and Croat alike were thriving on it.

To compound matters further the UN General Assembly (UNGA) then went ahead with a vote on 9 December which for the first time labelled the Krajina as 'occupied territory' within Croatia's internationally recognized borders, and declared that any attempts to integrate these areas into a Federal Yugoslavia (i.e., Serbia) were illegal.[2] Taking this vote at this time was a serious mistake because it allowed Croatia to seize the high moral ground, and the UNGA appeared to have joined a growing list of agencies who for one reason or another were no longer prepared to act impartially in their dealings with the Knin authorities. Of course the Krajina was occupied territory. It was 'occupied' by people whose ancestors had lived there for hundreds of years, and even the most basic examination of the 1991 Census, or any one of a plethora of maps illustrating ethnic distribution in the Balkans, would have left this matter in no doubt whatsoever.

But nobody was interested, and no one was prepared to make any attempt to understand where these Serbs were coming from, or what was likely to happen to them once they were frogmarched back into a post-Communist Croatian state with an armed policeman on every street corner. All Serbs had been painted black by the media in the first instance and now apparently were also typecast by the International Community. No matter what any of them did, either politically or militarily from here on, that picture was never going to improve. That is not to suggest they did not deserve to be condemned for the atrocities they committed – of course they did – but for the International Community to begin taking sides at this point in the conflict was a crucial mistake. The time for taking sides had been in 1991 but none of the main players had been willing to commit their troops and proceed down that particular road at that point.

The history of the Balkans has never been simply black and white. More often than not there have only been shades of grey and by now the entire conflict had become very grey indeed. The EU summit in Germany on 10 December chose not to see this 'greyness' at all and condemned instead both the Bosnian and Krajina Serbs for their violation of Croatia's borders, and their ongoing campaign in Bihac. The Knin leadership were also told in no uncertain terms that if they knew what was good for them they had better sign up to the Z-4 Plan on political reintegration when it was announced formally a few weeks later.[3] That no self-respecting Krajina Serb could ever accept what was on offer seemed to bother none of the luminaries attending the summit. The overall political situation had now become very murky and was summed up rather well by Radovan Karadzic when he called the whole thing 'one great big mess'. For once neither his admirers or detractors could disagree with that assessment.

NOTES

1. ECMM Weekly Information Analysis Summary, no. 107.
2. Result: yes, 142; no, 0; abstentions, 18. The only European countries to abstain were Russia and Belarus.
3. ECMM Weekly Information Analysis Summary, no. 108: 16/12/94.

CHAPTER THIRTEEN

Casualties for Bangladesh

Back on Bosnia's many battlefields military commanders of all creeds sought to exploit the ongoing political indecision. Just inside the Bosnian border in a place called the Livanjsko Polje, professional units of the Croatian army continued their push against the Bosnian Serbs as Foreign Minister Granic and UN Ambassador Mario Nobilo struggled to agree on a common explaination of what was going on. At a press conference in New York on 10 December Granic maintained that his army was only supplying 'logistic support' to the HVO, while at the same conference Nobilo admitted there were Croatian troops operating in Bosnia in order to attract some of the Serbs away from Bihac. In his opinion this was all perfectly legal as there was a legitimate military agreement between the Sarajevo and Zagreb governments in place which covered this type of situation.[1]

General Rose on the other hand was becoming more and more frustrated as his own position and that of UNPROFOR became untenable. On his way to Bihac in order to establish just how bad the situation had actually become he found his way blocked by a Krajina Serb checkpoint. He was then berated by the local military commander who told him that if he wanted to visit Bihac he would have to obtain permission from General Ratko Mladic. 'Right,' said Rose, 'I'll have a go at that,' and promptly aborted his mission, returning instead to UNPROFOR HQ in Zagreb. 'Basically they were making some stupid political point and are destroying the peace process by acting in such an arbitrary and stupid manner,' said Rose, who had actually been forced to wait for over two hours at the checkpoint before being allowed to turn back. His trip to Bihac had been intended to rally the morale of the Bangladeshi troops and to try and re-establish a reliable supply line to them.[2] His failure to achieve these very limited objectives provided an indication of just how difficult the whole situation had become, and sadly it was about to get worse.

In the late afternoon of 12 December, as fighting for different parts of the Pocket continued unrelentingly, a Bangladeshi armoured personnel carrier was hit by a Sagger anti-tank missile just outside the UNPROFOR logistics base on the southern edge of Velika Kladusa. The Reuters report that night was full of the usual sound bites: 'rebel Serbs', a 'government enclave', and while it certainly told the story, it singularly failed to explain any of it.

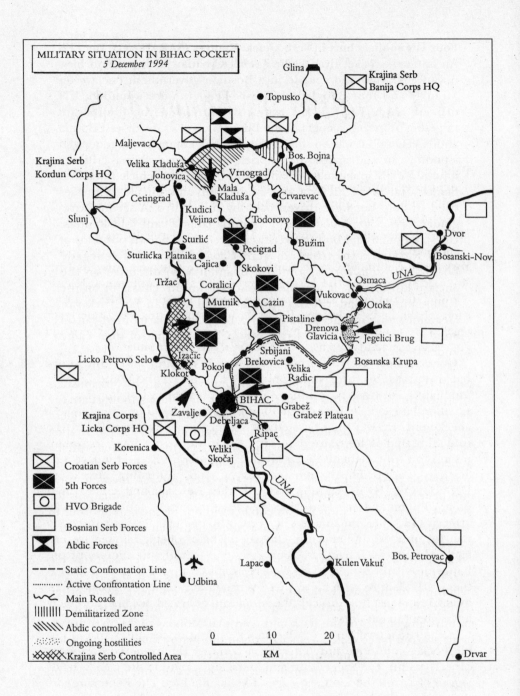

MILITARY SITUATION IN BIHAC POCKET
5 December 1994

Krajina Serb
Banija Corps HQ

Glina

Topusko

Maljevac

Krajina Serb
Kordun Corps HQ

Velika Kladuša
Johovica

Bos. Bojna

Vrnograd

Cetingrad

Mala
Kladuša

Crvarevac

Slunj

Kudici
Vejinac

Todorovo

Dvor

Bosanski-Nov

Sturlić

Pecigrad

Bužim

Sturlićka Platnika

Cajica

Skokovi

UNA

Osmaca

Tržac

Coralici

Mutnik

Cazin

Vukovac

Otoka

Pistaline

Licko Petrovo Selo

Izačić

Klokot

Pokoj

Srbijani
Brekovica

Drenova
Glavicia

Jegelici Brug

Bosanska Krupa

Velika
Radic

Zavalje

Debeljaca

BIHAC

Grabež

Grabež Plateau

Krajina Corps
Licka Corps HQ

Korenica

Ripac

Veliki
Skočaj

Croatian Serb Forces

5th Forces

HVO Brigade

Bosnian Serb Forces

Abdic Forces

UNA

Static Confrontation Line

Active Confrontation Line

Main Roads

Demilitarized Zone

Abdic controlled areas

Ongoing hostilities

Krajina Serb Controlled Area

Udbina

Lapac

Kulen Vakuf

Bos. Petrovac

0   10   20

KM

Drvar

Four UN soldiers hurt in Serb attack: Reuters (SARAJEVO), Dec. 12.
An anti-tank rocket fired from a rebel Croatian Serb position blew
up an UN armoured vehicle in a Bosnian government enclave on
Monday and four Bangladeshi peace-keepers were wounded, UN
officials said. The United Nations denounced the 'deliberate
targeting' of peace-keepers in the Bihac enclave of north-west Bosnia
and NATO said it was on standby in case UN commanders requested
a punitive air raid against the culprits. One Bangladeshi was critically
injured. A UN spokesman, Thant Myint-U, said the vehicle burst into
flames after being hit by a wire-guided anti-tank missile. Witnesses
tried to help but were driven back by sniper fire. A second wire-
guided rocket exploded nearby seconds later, Thant told Reuters.
UN spokesmen said both rockets were fired from known positions of
rebel Krajina Serbs from adjacent Croatia who, with renegade
Bosnian Moslem forces, joined a Bosnian Serb offensive on the
enclave last month. It was the second known direct assault on the
1,200-man Bangladeshi battalion. UN spokesman Jan Dirk van
Merveldt said a missile landed near a Bangladeshi armoured car on
Sunday as it approached a roadblock. The UN patrol then came
under small arms fire.

Ismail Hassain was so badly injured that he never regained consciousness
and died the following morning. It took over eight hours to evacuate the
five injured Bangladeshis by road to the American field hospital at Pleso
near Zagreb airport because, for some inexplicable reason, the Krajina
Serbs refused UNPROFOR permission to conduct a medevac by
helicopter.[3] In all probability this would not have saved Hassain's life
anyway but the fact that the UN were powerless to even medivac their
own people was lost on no one. In this, the most critical of situations for
peace-keepers, the UN was not able to act without permission in order to
save the lives of its own people. And if there had been any doubt in the
past about the scale of contempt that all the belligerents harboured
towards UN soldiers, there was none now. This was a very sad day for
UNPROFOR in more ways than one, and in effect it signalled the
beginning of the end. Later on the Croatian government would order
UNPROFOR to leave and a compromise would extend their stay a few
months longer, but in the dark and cold that Monday night, in a dreary
battle-scarred place called Velika Kladusa, the penny finally dropped for
even the most ardent supporters of peace-keeping in Bosnia. This
particular exercise had long since become a complete and utter waste of
time.

In the immediate aftermath of this attack the Bangladeshi battalion
Commander asked for NATO close air support but his higher
headquarters in Sarajevo turned him down on the grounds that it would

only serve to make a bad situation worse. Taken in context they were probably right but it sent entirely the wrong message to the people who fired the missile in the first place. From now on all the poor Bangladeshis could do was sit and watch as the conflict continued to rage all around them. Making the most marginal contribution was now destined to be misinterpreted by one side or the other, and could only lead to more casualties. Spilling more UN blood on soil already soaked with it could not be countenanced by anyone.

Twelve months later the last UN Force Commander in Former Yugoslavia, General Bernard Janvier, would write in his end of mission report that:

> The safe area policy was a military and humanitarian disaster-in-waiting. Insufficient troops were allocated to the task; air power limitations were not recognized; Security Council Resolution 836 was lacking in the deterrent effect; military advice that the areas were not defensible with the troops available was set aside; the Bosnian Muslims were allowed to use the safe areas for their own military purposes; and UH troops inside the areas became *de facto* hostages.[4]

Perhaps this provided a modicum of consolation for the Bangladeshis who had been making exactly the same points in the winter of 1994. Or then again, perhaps not.

NOTES

1. Vjesnik: 10/12/94 and WIAS 108.
2. Reuters: 11/12/94.
3. *Time Magazine*, no. 52-1994/UNMO Reports/Team Bihac Daily Report: 12/12/94.
4. Force Commander's End of Mission Report, Executive Summary, para. 9.

CHAPTER FOURTEEN

The Carter Initiative

In Sarajevo life went on more or less unaffected by events in Bihac. The last batch of detained peace-keepers were eventually released by the Bosnian Serbs and a relief food convoy was allowed through to the city, although one complete UNPROFOR fuel convoy was hijacked with the vehicles never to be seen again. When General Rose went to Pale on 12 December to complain about this he was told that from now on no humanitarian convoy would be permitted to pass through Bosnian Serb territory if it was escorted by UN tracked or armoured vehicles as these were causing too much damage to the roads! Needless to say Rose rejected these restrictions in the strongest possible terms, and in the next test case a Danish food convoy escorted by two French APCs did manage to negotiate its way through a series of Serb checkpoints without incident.[1]

In the middle of all this wrangling reports began to filter through from Serbia that President Milosevic had apparently managed to split the Bosnian Serbs to such a point that the parliament was now supposedly working independently of Karadzic and on the verge of accepting a settlement. The story went that Milosevic had enlisted the support of many rank and file Bosnian Serb politicians and had already chaired several meetings, the latest of which was now being widely covered in the Belgrade media. It was also being reported that Milosevic now supported the Economic Agreement and the Z4 Plan, proof of which could be seen in the continuing visits to Belgrade by prominent mediators from the Contact Group and ICFY. The timing of Milosevic's attempts to split the Bosnian Serbs, and the creation of a quisling grouping with whose help he was hoping to topple Karadzic, was indeed a serious development and designed primarily to facilitate removal of the remaining sanctions which in turn might quell a growing social and political unrest now evident right across Serbia.

Karadzic had been well aware of what was going on for a long time and while it was predictable that he would strike back, he still caught everyone by surprise when he appeared live on CNN on the night of 14 December and announced to the world that former US president Jimmy Carter was on his way to Bosnia to act as an honest broker in an attempt to hammer out a new and better settlement. As if to confound the world further he announced a string of unsolicited concessions which were to become effective immediately, and which were designed to prove to all the sceptics that both he and his people were operating in good faith. It sounded too good to be true and no one was sure exactly what was going on but all fair-minded people were agreed that if former president Carter was prepared to travel to Sarajevo, and put his considerable reputation on the line, then he at least deserved to be given a fair chance. His recent work in Haiti had been a tremendous success so it was not inconceivable that he might just succeed in Bosnia where all the others had failed. The only unanswered questions were how this had all come about in the first place, and who had convinced former president Carter that he actually stood a chance of producing any kind of acceptable settlement. Like everything else in Balkan politics the answers were not exactly straightforward or immediately to hand.

Apparently it all began at a cocktail party in Santa Barbara, California, in June 1994 when Borko Djordevic, a Serb then working in America as a plastic surgeon, was introduced to Tom Hanley, a partner in the Los Angeles law firm of Whitman, Breed, Abbott & Morgan. Neither of them mentioned the ongoing situation in Bosnia, and Djordevic made no reference to the fact that he had gone to medical school with the leader of the Bosnian Serbs but when Karadzic contacted his former classmate in late November, to enquire if some initiative could be started in the United States which might improve his precarious position at home, the name of Tom Hanley emerged as a potential emissary.

In early December, with a letter from Dr Karadzic in his possession, Hanley approached the White House, the State Department and the Carter Centre in Atlanta and invited them to come to Bosnia to help find a lasting settlement. Neither the White House or the State Department replied, but after a while the Carter Centre did, and on 14 December Hanley, Djordjevic and Slavko Laserevic made their way to Plains, Georgia, where some of Carter's officials met them for a preliminary meeting in a local restaurant called The Country Corner. In the course of the meeting a waitress interrupted to say there was a telephone call for Hanley. Incredibly it was Karadzic in Bosnia at the other end of the line, just wanting to confirm the message that was about to be delivered to the former president. Once that was sorted out the group departed for Carter's home.

When the former president was satisfied that the offer was genuine he phoned Karadzic in Pale and asked him to confirm once again that as a preliminary gesture all UN convoys would be permitted free movement; all detained UN peace-keepers released; all Muslim prisoners under twenty years of age released; a cease-fire honoured around Sarajevo; the airport reopened; and human rights and fundamental freedoms guaranteed throughout the Republic of Srpska. Karadzic agreed immediately, and having told CNN that this new plan could bring the fighting in war-torn Sarajevo to a halt within twenty-four hours, Jimmy Carter was on his way to Bosnia.[2]

The new development immediately drew a cool response from Western officials and diplomats. A White House spokesman said, 'while we are sceptical about the Bosnian Serbs' intentions, if the steps outlined by Karadzic are implemented, they would help reduce tensions and ease the humanitarian situation in Bosnia'. On the other hand, Lawrence Eagleburger immediately made himself available as a sort of 'unofficial spokesman', and his contempt for the initiative was flashed around the world, together with his doubts as to whether Carter actually knew where Bosnia was. This was distinctly unhelpful and NATO's Secretary General Willy Claes, in his attempts to reject Karadzic's offer, was not much better. 'I do not see any indication of a peace plan,' he said, 'this is just an elaboration of points.' French Foreign Minister Alain Juppe rejected it outright. 'There is a provocative aspect to the plan which is unacceptable', he said, and unidentified European diplomats quoted by Reuters allegedly complained that the initiative gave no details of any land to be ceded by the Bosnian Serbs, nor did it signify acceptance of the Contact Group Plan.[3]

Reaction became even colder the following morning when reports began to filter through that General Rose's helicopter had been fired upon by the Bosnian Serbs as it flew over Mount Igman, south-west of Sarajevo. These reports were *not* true, and it later emerged that Muslim troops had done the shooting, presumably so the Serbs would be blamed for it and thereby scuttle the Carter mission before it even got off the ground. Lieutenant Colonel Jan-Dirk van Merveldt, a Royal Green Jacket officer who was now operating as the UN's military spokesman in Sarajevo, was quite clear on what happened. The Sea King helicopter, arriving to fly General Rose to Split en route for a NATO meeting in Italy, took twelve rounds of small arms fire in the tail section as it flew over Mount Igman. The area around Mount Igman was controlled by Bosnian government forces and the aircraft made a forced landing near Kiseljak but none of the crew were hurt. 'The firing,' he said diplomatically, 'appeared to come from an area controlled by Bosnian government forces.' *Time Magazine*, who clearly had no faith in either Karadzic or his ability to deliver on his self-imposed pre-conditions, was only too happy to report that this attack had been launched by the Serbs. They, too, were wrong.[4]

As Carter set out for Bosnia on 18 December White House officials continued to play down the significance of what was unfolding, and some of their remarks were nothing short of appalling. To suggest that 'he might be drawn into things he does not fully understand', or 'it's more complicated than anything he has handled before'[5] did nothing but undermine the former president and whether or not this amounted to a deliberate attempt to sabotage the whole process remains a moot point. Suffice to say, legitimizing Karadzic or any of his associates was not on the Clinton Administration's agenda. As far as they were concerned there were pre-determined 'good guys' and 'bad guys' in Bosnia now, and it served their purposes best if that distinction remained intact. The fact that there were no 'good guys' in Bosnia, that all parties to the conflict had copious amounts of blood on their hands, and that at that point in time Karadzic was the only one of them even vaguely attempting to improve matters seemed to have, intentionally or otherwise, completely escaped them. And they were not alone. CNN and the Sarajevo government had done such an excellent job over the years demonizing the Bosnian Serb leadership that only a tiny minority were now prepared to be objective when it came to listening to what they had to say. The great pity here was that on this occasion Karadzic actually did deserve a hearing.

Having made their way to Frankfurt on a commercial flight Carter's group then split up, with the former president heading for Zagreb on board a US military plane while Hanley, Djordjevic and Laserevic were left to find their own way to Pale, having been inexplicably refused permission by US air force officials to travel on the same aircraft. During the stopover in Zagreb Carter met with President Tudjman, US Ambassador Peter Galbraith and Bosnian Prime Minister Haris Silajdzic, who apparently voiced the opinion that Karadzic was only interested in manipulating the situation to dilute the Contact Group Plan. Later on, across the city at UNPROFOR HQ, Yasushi Akashi refuted this suggestion and said he thought the former president too intelligent to be manipulated by anyone. What he failed to point out, and perhaps should have done, was that on each leg of the journey every single person encountered by Carter would try, by fair means or foul, to bring him around to their own particular way of thinking, and when he touched down in Sarajevo that Sunday evening Izetbegovic was the next manipulator waiting to greet him.

Meanwhile Hanley and his two colleagues were frantically trying to make their way to Pale to begin preparatory work with Karadzic for his first meeting with Carter the following day. They crossed the Serbian border with the Republic Srpska very late that night, having been delayed and questioned at several points along the way and even interrogated by Interpol agents in Belgrade, where the trio were accused for a time of being international smugglers. They arrived in Pale just after midnight and immediately set about briefing Karadzic for his meeting the next morning. Working through the night until just after 0500 hrs Hanley explained in detail what Carter could accept, and more importantly what he could not. In the latter category Karadzic was intent on trying to extract from Carter an assurance that the UN's economic sanctions on all Serb republics would be lifted as a quid pro quo for his agreement to a permanent cease-fire throughout Bosnia. The objective here was to prove to the Serb nation just who their real leader was and to achieve for all of them what Milosevic had patently failed to realize. The problem was that

Carter would never manage to deliver on this, no matter what Karadzic was prepared to concede, and it took Hanley the whole night to convince his client what the real position was. By morning Karadzic appeared to accept this and when the meeting began Hanley was confident that a comprehensive cease-fire was about to be agreed without difficulty.

However, when Carter and Karadzic went into private session and sat down with a laptop computer to put the final touches to the agreement, the matter of the sanctions raised its head again. After two hours of argument the whole process was about to fall apart on this point and probably would have done had Djordjevic and Hanley not taken Karadzic aside and warned him that if he persisted with this approach then it would be interpreted internationally that he didn't really want peace after all. This was Karadzic's last chance and he had to make up his mind whether to accept what was on offer or send Carter away empty handed. After a tense few minutes Karadzic agreed to drop the sanctions issue and agreed to comply with a cease-fire based on the provisions of the Contact Group Plan, which would reduce the Serb-held territory in Bosnia to 49 per cent. Before returning to Sarajevo to sell the deal to Izetbegovic, Carter and Karadzic went before the media circus that had descended on Pale, and it was immediately clear that something was in the offing. Praising the Bosnian Serbs for their commitment to a peace agreement Carter said that their role in the war had been 'misunderstood', and when Karadzic denied that the Serbs had been the aggressors, the former president sent shockwaves through the Sarajevo government by admitting, 'I can't dispute your statement that the American people have heard only one side of the story. The entire world is hoping and praying for peace in this country and your commitment to honour human rights.'

This also sent tremors through the White House, who lost no time in pushing Dee Dee Myers before a camera to reaffirm their official position that the Serbs were indeed the aggressors in the war. Why this outburst was deemed necessary in the middle of delicate negotiations has never been explained but it certainly had a negative effect on Karadzic who quickly became very unsure where exactly he stood between 'official' and 'unofficial' US positions. If this was designed to unnerve him it worked, and if it was a deliberate ploy then it was wholly despicable. Whatever the reality, Karadzic appeared on CNN that night and gave the impression that he had not after all agreed to a four-month cease-fire but saw this as only a possibility. 'Generally speaking we have told the Muslims we don't want any more cease-fires, we want an end to the war and not breaks for them to recover,' he said. He badly needed 'official' US support at this point and no one, from the President down, was prepared to give it to him.

The following morning Carter went back to Izetbegovic and Ganic in order to establish where they stood on the matter of an immediate cease-fire, which would allow a talks process to begin. Not for the first time the

Muslims were faced with accepting something which they believed Karadzic had already rejected, and although a lasting settlement based on the partition of Bosnia was the last thing they would ever agree to, they nevertheless agreed to come on board. After two hours Izetbegovic told reporters that his government would accept an immediate cease-fire for four months and enter negotiations on the basis of the Contact Group Plan. At this point Carter went to General Rose's headquarters and faxed a letter to Karadzic via an UNMO team who conveniently lived close to his home on the High Road in Pale. Again Carter made it clear to Karadzic that without doubt he was now going to be blamed (again) internationally if nothing materialized from this final round of talks. This was something Karadzic simply could not risk, given Milosevic's ongoing and deliberate campaign to remove him, so by the time Carter arrived back in Pale the decision had already been taken. After a brief meeting, Karadzic and Mladic looked on as Jimmy Carter announced his latest triumph to the world's press. 'The most significant achievement this morning was the Bosnian Serb leaders' agreement to a complete cease-fire throughout Bosnia to be implemented on 23 December with all confrontation lines to be monitored by UNPROFOR.'[6]

The peanut farmer from Plains, Georgia, had once again succeeded where all the rest had failed. But, as he made his way home via Belgrade and Zagreb, international reaction to his efforts could only be described as mixed at best. Sections of the British press were scathing in their remarks, with the *Independent* claiming 'his self-important piety blinds him to the fact that he has played straight into the Bosnian Serbs' hands', and while the *Guardian* was no more sympathetic it did at least recognize that 'his is the only show on the road'. French Foreign Minister Alain Juppe remained very sceptical and was adamant that 'experience in this conflict has taught everyone that the ink is never dry on agreements before they are broken', while in the US Dee Dee Myers was back before the cameras on behalf of the White House and offering only a cautious welcome to the agreement. 'If those things happen certainly that's a positive accomplishment', she told reporters, while in Belgrade Slobodan Milosevic went on the record to indicate that the deal had his full support,[7] something he reiterated on CNN's 'Larry King Live' later that night. Whether he actually meant any of this is difficult to know as the deal effectively scuttled his immediate plans to install a new leader of the Bosnian Serbs, and it all left Karadzic, at least for the moment, still firmly in control.

Meetings got under way almost as soon as Carter had departed and all sides initially appeared to be committed to the process, notwithstanding yet another attack on Sarajevo's market place in which two men died.[8] Not for the first time there was no clear indication from where the shells had been fired but it is not unreasonable to suggest that whoever ordered the attack did so in the hope of scuttling the Carter Agreement, as well as

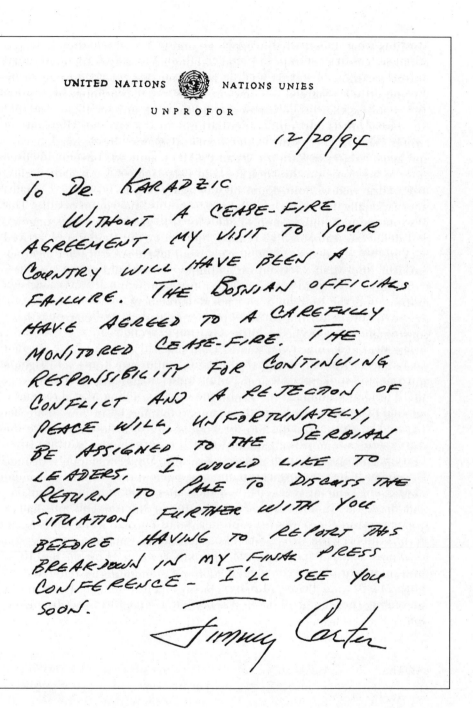

UNITED NATIONS   NATIONS UNIES

UNPROFOR

12/20/94

To Dr. KARADZIC

WITHOUT A CEASE-FIRE AGREEMENT, MY VISIT TO YOUR COUNTRY WILL HAVE BEEN A FAILURE. THE BOSNIAN OFFICIALS HAVE AGREED TO A CAREFULLY MONITORED CEASE-FIRE. THE RESPONSIBILITY FOR CONTINUING CONFLICT AND A REJECTION OF PEACE WILL, UNFORTUNATELY, BE ASSIGNED TO THE SERBIAN LEADERS. I WOULD LIKE TO RETURN TO PALE TO DISCUSS THE SITUATION FURTHER WITH YOU BEFORE HAVING TO REPORT THIS BREAKDOWN IN MY FINAL PRESS CONFERENCE - I'LL SEE YOU SOON.

Jimmy Carter

exerting some influence on Akashi. He was at that very moment deep in discussion with government ministers about the matter of the Armija's refusal to vacate the designated demilitarized area on Mount Igman. But in spite of several difficulties Akashi remained optimistic as he shuttled between Sarajevo and Pale, and at noon in Sarajevo, or 1100 hrs GMT, on Saturday 24 December, Jimmy Carter's cease-fire came into effect, and to practically everyone's disbelief it was respected by all sides.

Philip Watkins and Christopher Geidt, the EU's most senior Monitors in Bosnia at the time, assessed the implications of the Carter mission in a report filed from the dreary surroundings of their headquarters in Zenica late on Christmas Eve.[9] They accurately identified something that practically everyone else had either missed or chosen to ignore, namely that the Bosnian Croats had been completely forgotten about in the rush to shore up a peace agreement between the Muslims and the Serbs. The fact that the Croats were not demanding to be part of the process clearly established that they were operating to a completely different agenda, which had precious little in common with either of the other two. For the moment they were quite happy to continue their military operations against the Serbs near the town of Livno, especially since the Croatian army was becoming more involved here by the day. And the Bosnian Croats were not the only people 'doing their own thing'. In Croatia government spokespeople had begun indicating (leaking to the press) that President Tudjman was now on the verge of telling Akashi to remove all UNPROFOR troops from the country once the current mandate had expired in January. This was all despite the fact that the Economic Agreement was working well and that the Serbs had withdrawn their barriers and opened up the Zagreb–Belgrade Highway at 1430 hrs on 21 December. The opening ceremony had been witnessed by both Milan Martic and General Celeketic, and thereafter a procession of over sixty cars drove the 15 mile stretch from Kutina to Novska. This was a major concession on the part of the Krajina Serbs but this good will was not reciprocated by the Croats who chose instead to interpret it as a sign of weakness. Milan Babic, now the Krajina's Foreign Minister, had never been in favour of conceding anything to Zagreb, but he was overruled by both Martic and Prime Minister Mikelic. The way events were now unfolding, they might all have been far better served had they listened to him.

NOTES

1. 13/12/94.
2. Di-Mari Ricker, 'Closing a War', *ABA Journal*, January 1996, p. 69.
3. Reuters: 15/12/94.

4. *Time Magazine*, vol. 144, no. 26, p. 84.
5. Reuters Sarajevo: 18/12/94.
6. Reuters Pale: 20/12/94.
7. All Reuters: 21/12/94.
8. ECLO Sarajevo: 22/12/94.
9. RC BiH Weekly Report: 24/12/94.
10. Zubak admitted as much to ECMM in the course of the meeting with the Head of Mission on 16/12/94, and both Zubak and Prlic made it very clear that their main objective remained the continuation of CRHB, as they believed the Muslims were only paying lip service to the Federation in order to strengthen their own position.

CHAPTER FIFTEEN

Christmas time in Bihac

Back in Bihac Pocket the 'Carter Initiative' was of little interest to most of the warring elements as the fighting continued. On the evening of 18 December Michael Williams, the UN's spokesman in Zagreb, admitted that the 5th Corps appeared to be withdrawing as Abdic and the Krajina Serbs were gaining the upper hand.[1] By the 21st Velika Kladusa was back in APWB hands with Abdic ensconced once more in his medieval castle, although in fact he controlled little more than the town itself and some territory immediately to the south-west and north-east of it. His troops had not managed to recapture all that had been lost in August, effectively ensuring that most of the refugees would not be able to return to their homes for a while longer. With the town extensively damaged, and no electricity, gas, water or wood available, it was clear that apart from political considerations there was no humanitarian justification for insisting that the people vacate Turanj and Batnoga in order to return to conditions that were appreciably worse than those they currently endured.[2]

There was also the added problem of knowing that the 5th Corps had not been beaten out of the town, having chosen instead to vacate it voluntarily in an orderly fashion rather than take heavy casualties in a prolonged retrograde action. This virtually guaranteed a resumption of hostilities in the future so it became imperative for Abdic to begin creating problems for the 5th Corps further south. The Krajina Serbs duly obliged and shelled Cazin and Coralici, as well as consolidating their gains in the west. The southern confrontation line also remained active with the occasional shell landing in Bihac town although as the cease-fire negotiations made progress in Sarajevo, there was a noticeable scaling down of operations by the Bosnian Serbs.[3] In a separate development progress was made in relation to the passage into Cazin of a UN food convoy, which had at that point been held in Topusko for several days, but it quickly emerged that it had been necessary to agree a quid pro quo in relation to the supply of fuel to Abdic and the Krajina Serbs to achieve this.

On the morning of 26 December cars, trailers, tractors, trucks and buses were packed with the personal belongings of the refugees in Turanj and had been made ready for the return journey to Velika Kladusa. The problem was that none of these vehicles had enough fuel to make the trip and were dependent on the UN to provide it for them. In spite of the original promise the fuel never materialized, and by early afternoon angry refugees were returning to their previous accommodation for yet another night in the cold. UNHCR were condemned by all and sundry for exploiting the plight of the refugees but for once UN officials had played Abdic, his henchmen and the Krajina Serbs at their own game and won, albeit a very limited victory. Permission to distribute humanitarian aid, fuel and other necessities was used and abused by all belligerents, and most politicians had no qualms whatever when it came to manipulating the plight of their cold, elderly, wet, sick and hungry supporters, if that activity served to further their own causes.

UNPROFOR HQ in Zagreb had by now become completely frustrated as the Krajina Serbs continued to prevent re-supply convoys crossing through to the Bangladeshis in the Pocket, and a decision was made to by-pass them completely. In an amazing development a 'JCO Team' from Sarajevo arrived to see Francis Bonal at ECMM's offices in Bihac town looking for an introduction to the 5th Corps' Liaison Officer, with a view to sending relief convoys through the territory controlled by the Bosnian Serbs.[4] It also transpired that this team had been travelling around within the Republic Srpska and the Krajina for some time, and apparently free from all restrictions had been turning up in a variety of obscure locations. This was not the first time ECMM had come across these people; on a previous occasion they had also turned up unannounced in Knin, seeking out an EU Monitor whom they believed had managed to develop a good liaison with the 2nd Krajina Corps of the BSA. This information had been completely correct but when pressed about where they had actually got it from no explanation was forthcoming. Answerable only to General Rose these teams managed to go where no ordinary peace-keepers were permitted, and their activities, such as we know of them, remain one of UNPROFOR's most closely guarded secrets.

In any event 27 December marked the one-thousandth day of Sarajevo's siege and with only the occasional shot being fired General Rose and Minister Without Portfolio Hassan Muratovic went to Bihac in an attempt to get all sides to respect the cease-fire and be included in the Cessation of Hostilities Agreement (COHA) planned for 1 January.[5] Surprisingly, they were well received by all sides, with even Abdic agreeing to toe the line, and for the first time in years there was the prospect of a realistic countrywide cease-fire. Over the next few days the level of hostilities right across Bosnia decreased dramatically and on the morning of 29 December, having eventually obtained the necessary fuel from UNHCR,[6] between 4,000 and 5,000 refugees from Turanj began the long journey home in a convoy of 20 buses, 16 trucks, 200 cars, 200–50 tractors and 120 horses and carts. They were returning to dreadful conditions but at least they were going home, and that would provide them with some consolation.

Dzemal Ahmetovic, who had been the refugee leader in Turanj, estimated that over 2,000 tons of assorted humanitarian aid would be required urgently once the refugees had returned to Velika Kladusa as another refugee convoy from Batnoga was scheduled to arrive on 30 December. This was a conservative estimate and it would take time to organize, but for the moment the only items UNHCR and ECTF could supply were rolls of plastic sheeting for use in lieu of window panes, and small quantities of food and water. It wasn't much but at least it helped to fortify them against the worst of the wind, snow and hail. By the evening of 30 December over 6,000 refugees had returned to their vandalized, looted, broken homes in the hope that their particular war was over. They were not to know it at the time but 1995 would bring them even further tragedy – within a short time they would find themselves back on the road again and once more dependant on charitable handouts from UNHCR and other trusts and agencies.

The final days of 1994 were marked by frantic diplomatic efforts to ensure that when the COHA was unveiled on 31 December all sides would embrace it and make a determined effort to ensure it worked. ECMM's outgoing Head of Mission Ambassador von Stulpnagel, together with Philip Watkins and Chris Geidt, managed to visit Pale on 30 December and were granted a unique meeting with Dr Karadzic, General Mladic and Professor Nikolai Koljevic, at which, perhaps for the very first time, the Serbs explained some of their positions and why they held them.

In relation to the situation between the Republic Srpska and Europe, Karadzic saw the European approach to the problems in his country as one of superimposing a solution and taking no account of the Bosnian Serbs' perspective. He felt that this approach was now softening as the Contact Group appeared to recognize that all sides to the conflict had equal status. When encouraged to allow EU Monitoring Teams to operate within his territory he was hopeful that this might happen but argued that any development of this nature was likely to be linked to the Muslims' acceptance of the COHA, and Europe's recognition of the Bosnian Serbs's right to self-determination, which he claimed was guaranteed in the UN Charter.

Mladic criticized Europe for supporting the continuation of economic sanctions and for taking the side of the Sarajevo government, but he also suggested that the time was now ripe for all outstanding matters to be settled by political not military means. Both he and Karadzic expressed a wish for higher level contact with the European Union, and as the meeting concluded Karadzic pointed out that a window of opportunity now existed in Bosnia which, should it remain open, would afford ECMM the opportunity of working in his country in the future.[7]

The following afternoon Alija Izetbegovic and Rasim Delic signed the Cessation of Hostilities Agreement in Sarajevo.Then Akashi took it to

Pale where Karadzic and Mladic signed it later that night. Two days after that Krezimir Zubak and Tihomir Blaskic signed on behalf of the Bosnian Croats thereby bringing all sides on board and offering hope that within the next four months some permanent arrangement might emerge that could bring all of the suffering to an end. And the credit for all of this, whether the International Community liked it or not, went to Radovan Karadzic. If he had not approached former president Carter in the first instance none of this would have come about. It is very easy to argue that Karadzic had ulterior motives for making this move, and that had he not been under serious threat from Milosevic he would never have even considered it in the first place. Perhaps this is so but the inescapable truth remains that Karadzic set up the process, followed it through by offering a string of unsolicited concessions, managed amazingly to bring Mladic along with him, and in signing the COHA provided a very real opportunity for a lasting peace. Unfortunately neither Izetbegovic or Zubak were committed enough to take this opportunity at face value, or prepared in the longer term to set aside their own individual agendas. This would become apparent in the months ahead when it emerged who had broken the COHA first.

NOTES

1. Reuters Zagreb: 18/12/94.
2. Team Karlovac Daily Report: 22/12/94.
3. RC Zagreb Daily Report: 22/12/94.
4. Team Bihac Daily Report: 27/12/94.
5. Reuters Sarajevo: 27/12/94.
6. Team Glina Daily Report: 29/12/94.
7. ECMM Special Report: 'Meeting in Pale', Philip Watkins, 30/12/94.

CHAPTER SIXTEEN

Croatia's Gratitude to
UNPROFOR

Having concluded the Cessation of Hostilities Agreement with both the Muslims and the Serbs, on 2 January General Rose went to Mostar where he convinced Zubak and Blaskic to put their names to the document on behalf of the Bosnian Croats. Pretending to be none too pleased at having been ignored in the original discussions, the HVO eventually agreed to curtail their combined offensive with the HV against the Serbs in the Livanjsko Polje in western Hercegovina. Then, when the Armija began vacating the designated demilitarized zone on Mount Igman, the Serbs responded by opening up several of the 'Blue Route' roads into Sarajevo and the overall situation certainly began to improve.[1] As stipulated in the terms of the COHA, and indeed central to the process as a whole, the first Regional Joint Commission Meetings took place in Gornji Vakuf and Tuzla. At face value it did appear as if some progress was being made in the key areas of multiple exchange of Liaison Officers, verification of the actual confrontation line on the ground, the commencement of monitoring the cease-fire, and the establishment of military and civilian working committees.[2] With all three groups now locked into the process even the most sceptical observers were prepared to admit that a window of opportunity really did exist but it was up to the parties themselves to make use of it. What all sides had to seriously avoid was becoming distracted by unresolved issues in other places, like in Bihac Pocket, for example, where a resolution of that conflict was nowhere in sight.

Abdic had by now firmly re-established himself in Velika Kladusa and in spite of his promise to General Rose on 28 December, that APWB forces would also abide by the terms of the COHA, this never materialized. Instead his personal battle with the 5th Corps continued as before in order to grab more territory and thereby accommodate the remaining 545 refugees at Turanj, a similar number still in Batnoga, and the thousands who were now crammed into dreadful conditions in Velika Kladusa itself. In the light of this situation the official report of a French Logistics convoy which made its way from Zagreb to the Bangladeshi battalion's headquarters at Coralici on 4 January provides a unique insight into the immediate aftermath of Abdic's return to power.

4/1/95

At 2350 hrs the convoy entered Velika Kladusa. There were no lights, which allows us to assume that there is no electricity in the city. We did not notice any movement of civilians or soldiers. Only in the northern outskirts of the town and, to an even more limited degree, in the centre, could we see some damaged buildings. . . . While moving, there were some light flashes on the hills east and south-east of city (shelling with illuminating rounds?). . . . We spent the night on an exposed parking lot just south of the city centre, guarded by 2 Abdic soldiers.

5/1/95

At about 0800 hrs between 10 and 15 Abdic soldiers arrived to proceed with an inspection of the convoy load. They all looked quite young (16–30 years old) and all wore different outfits – mostly civilian clothes. The majority of them had a 'ZB' [Zapadna Bosnia: APWB] patch attached on their sleeve. I noticed at least one soldier who had an 'SVK' patch [Krajina Serb] under the 'ZB' patch. These troops gave an undisciplined and unorganized impression. I doubt if they were regular soldiers. . . . The Abdic soldiers used some 30 civilians to unload the containers. These people were all in a very bad condition, poorly dressed and not well fed. They arrived in one group from the factory building north of the parking lot and were escorted by armed men. This indicates that they were probably prisoners of war. . . . We saw a number of civilians passing the parking lot to get water We did not notice any sizeable movement of refugees. Traffic was limited to some Agrokomerc trucks. We saw at least one 'RSK' Milicija truck passing our position several times. From time to time, we heard moderate shelling approx. 5 km south-east of our position. . . . The Abdic troops were very aggressive towards UNPROFOR and UNHCR. A UNHCR vehicle that wanted to stop was harassed and sent away by pointing a weapon at the occupants. . . . There were some indications of anarchy among the Abdic people. The instructions of a member of the civilian authority to stop unloading the containers were not respected by the armed men present. At noon, the POWs returned on the double to their accommodation and were replaced by some 20–25 Abdic soldiers who surrounded the convoy. Like their colleagues already present, they wore different outfits and were armed with a wide variety of small weapons. In the afternoon, the POWs returned and the inspections of the cargo continued. . . . At 1800 hrs we could continue our movement to the BANBAT Log base in Coralici and while approaching the Confrontation Line we heard some small arms and light machine-gun fire coming from different directions but probably not aimed at the convoy. Once arrived in 5th Corps' territory, there was a remarkable change in the attitude of the population. Those who were still on the streets were extremely friendly and saluted the convoy. . . . At 2300 hrs we arrived in Coralici where the convoy was particularly appreciated because in the course of the afternoon they had run out of fuel. . . . Although the Commander of BANBAT informed us that almost every night, helicopters with supplies for the 5th Corps land [in the area] we did not hear any unusual sounds.

6/1/95
In Cazin and Bihac [town] the streets were filled with civilians and unarmed military in uniform. A number of people were selling cigarettes at local markets. We even saw somebody trying to sell two French combat ration packs. Again we noticed that, contrary to what the media reported, demolitions were rather limited. In Bihac town it was only in the immediate vicinity of official buildings, i.e., the 5th Corps HQ, the Ministry of Internal Affairs etc., that serious damage had occurred. Elsewhere there was only occasional damage such as a burnt-out flat in an apartment building, or some impacts from HMG or SA fire, or shattered windows. We did not see any people walking around with water containers so there is probably still running water available in the town.

7/1/95
While proceeding towards Velika Kladusa it was surprising to notice that none of the factories and workshops of AGROKOMERC showed signs of external damage. The transport agency was even operating, with large trucks moving around. The drive through Velika Kladusa confirmed that in a number of houses a higher number of occupants than normal were living there, with extensive amounts of laundry hanging out of the windows. Along the main road from Virginmost to Glina, we noticed a Krajina Serb soldier getting out of a UN Ukraine Battalion truck.

There was also the added problem of what was taking place further south in the Livanjsko Polje where, in spite of the Croats' declared willingness to suspend their operations, neither the Muslims nor the Serbs were quite prepared to believe them. The reason for this distrust was very simple. For months now large numbers of the Croatian army had been 'supporting' HVO operations with a tactical group based on the 4th Guards Brigade from Split; this also incorporated elements from a string of other professional units, including the 5th Guards Brigade, who had travelled all the way from Vinkovci in Eastern Slavonia to partake in what really amounted to on-the-job training.

The kind of 'support' that was involved became quite evident around Christmas time when the death notices in both *Slobodna Dalmacia* and *Vecernji List* (Croatian newspapers) recorded the deaths of six Croatian soldiers from Split who were killed on 23 December.[3] Other obituaries revealed the loss of more soldiers, including some officers, who were 'killed in action for the defence of the homeland', and other Croatian regular units were identified as taking part in the action. These included the 2nd Brigade from Dugo Selo, the 126th Brigade from Sinj, and the 132nd Brigade from Nasice. Given that most of this information was now common knowledge on the ground throughout Bosnia, Serb reservations about the combined Croats' ability to stick to the COHA seemed reasonable enough. It was also abundantly clear that both the HV and HVO, together with their political masters in Zagreb, were operating to a totally separate agenda, and if one took account of the manner in which their recent operations had succeeded, especially in retaking the town of Kupres in central Bosnia, one could estimate with confidence that their signatures on the COHA would not deter them from exploiting another military opportunity if it arose.

They could and most probably would use the Federation, the COHA or military force to further their own objectives, and ECMM's assessment at the time, that 'the Bosnian Croats' first loyalty is to Croatian unity'[4] turned out to be both ominous and accurate. But for the moment they gave the impression of supporting the COHA, and General Blaskic participated in the Central Joint Commission Meetings in Sarajevo with Rasim Delic, Ratko Mladic and General Rose. However, the continued presence of the Croatian army in Bosnia, even if they never fired another shot in anger, was guaranteed to cause problems in the longer term, and suggestions, to the effect that the Croats would now 'voluntarily withdraw into Croatia in order to comply with the terms of the COHA'[5] amounted to little more than wishful thinking. They did not withdraw and chose instead to use the lull in hostilities to prepare themselves fully for the next phase of the conflict – something that was abundantly clear to another ECMM team as they sat on top of the Karula Mountain, just north of the small town of Sinj, on a bitterly cold Sunday morning in early February, and watched a stream of Croatian army trucks, cars and Landrovers ploughing their way through the snow and ice en route to Bosnia. By the time the COHA eventually expired these troops would be ready to resume the fight with even more determination than before when they were temporarily called to a halt on 2 January.

The Muslim approach to all of this was equally predictable and within a short time it became quite clear they were simply looking for an excuse to distance themselves from the agreement completely. In an interview at the time with Philip Watkins, Rasim Delic, the Armija's Supreme

Commander, made no attempt to disguise his pessimism and expressed no confidence at all in the COHA process. Over the years the Muslims had consistently rejected any deal which would effectively partition the country and on 6 January it was clear that this new process was going to be rejected by them for exactly the same reasons. Not surprisingly Delic was only too prepared to be distracted into other areas and immediately began demanding that the Krajina Serbs get out of Bihac Pocket, as a precondition to his further participation in the whole COHA process.[6]

In tandem with this the commander of the Armija's 2nd Corps in Tuzla set about trying to wreck the Regional Joint Commission there before it got off the ground, by complaining somewhat hysterically that a Bosnian Serb Liaison Officer had been installed at the UN Sector HQ without his or Izetbegovic's permission. When he got no satisfaction from the Sector Commander he then took it upon himself to blockade the air base where the UN were garrisoned and effectively held all the troops, including the Serb officer, as hostages. This was outrageous behaviour and the failure of either Delic or Izetbegovic to sort it out at once was a clear indictment of the entire Muslim leadership. The exchange of liaison officers was specifically mentioned in paragraph 3 of the COHA, which both Delic and Izetbegovic had signed, and yet neither of them intervened to call one of their subordinates to heel. This controversy was now set to rumble on for the lifetime of the agreement and provided further ammunition for other intransigent Muslim politicians like Dzeved Mlaco, the Mayor of Bugojno, when a similar problem arose at Sector South West HQ in Gornji Vakuf and the BSA LO there, Colonel Slavko Guzvic, also found himself being held hostage.

This whole matter could and should have been resolved at the very outset but it wasn't because the Muslim leaders were merely looking for excuses to frustrate the whole process and this was the first one that came their way. They latched on to another when Karadzic produced a set of maps purporting to divide Sarajevo into fourteen parts, seven for the Muslims and seven for the Serbs, with the equivalent of a Berlin Wall running down the middle of it.[7] Screaming with indignation, and accusing Karadzic of treachery, the Muslims cited this as further evidence of Bosnian Serb bad faith when it was probably nothing of the sort. But in spite of this and other issues the COHA process did manage to struggle on. However, the only common factor between the three parties at this point was that none of them wanted to be identified internationally as the side who brought the whole thing tumbling down, and that was a statement in itself.

Meanwhile, the situation in Croatia was also about to change dramatically as rumour abounded that the government were about to express their gratitude to UNPROFOR by telling them to pack their bags and go home. This had been a possibility for months now and was described correctly by Joe Mulligan, ECMM's Senior Operations Officer in RC Zagreb, as 'the worst kept secret in Croatia'.[8] Nonetheless it still came as something of a shock when President Tudjman went live on Croatian Television (HRT) on 12 January and informed his people that he had written to Boutros Boutros-Ghali with the following message:

Excellency,

Croatia finds the present situation in the occupied territories wholly unacceptable. Moreover, given the present inefficient UNPROFOR mission, Croatia finds the continued presence of UNPROFOR in the occupied territories to be significantly counterproductive to the peace process. The Serb intransigence and UNPROFOR's reserve is *de facto* allowing the promotion of the occupation of parts of Croatia's territory. The 'freezing' of a negative status quo is unacceptable for the Croatian Government. . . . Therefore, as the President or the Republic of Croatia, I have the honour to inform you that the UNPROFOR mandate is hereby terminated, effective 31 March 1995, in accordance with Resolution 947 (1994).[9]

The tone of his personal address to the Croatian People was naturally enough a little different:

Dear Croatians and Citizens of Croatia,

I am addressing you at an historic moment that, in accordance with my constitutional powers, I have made a decision on terminating the mandate of the peace-keeping force in the Republic of Croatia on 31 March this year, in line with the expiry of the current mandate. Today I sent a letter to the UN Secretary General Mr Boutros Boutros-Ghali informing him of this decision . . . UNPROFOR's failure to fulfil its tasks and enable the implementation of the Vance Plan and all Security Council resolutions should be blamed on rebel Serb leaders in occupied areas, and even more so on Belgrade leaders who wanted to make them part of a Greater Serbia. . . . In the shadow of the peacekeeping force they continued the ethnic cleansing of Croatians and all non-Serbs, including brutal killings of defenceless people. Even today they are trying to prevent the peaceful reintegration of occupied areas into Croatia's constitutional and legal system. Taking advantage of UNPROFOR's presence, they are opposing decisions by the UN Security Council and official statements by the most responsible representatives of Governments of European and world powers, that the occupied areas are an indisputably constituent part of sovereign Croatia within its internationally recognized borders.[10]

From Croatia's perspective this decision was perfectly understandable. Tudjman was absolutely correct in his assessment of what the UN was *not* achieving in the Krajina, and he was acutely aware that the longer the situation remained as it was the greater the possibility of the confrontation line becoming a *de facto* and *de jure* border on the ground. The problem was that the Krajina Serbs still wanted nothing to do with either Tudjman or the state over which he presided, and not for the first time the authorities in Knin were quite perturbed that the Croats had completely ignored them in what was a matter of vital importance for them too. Namely the 'small' question of whether the UN stayed to protect them or went home and left them at the mercy of marauding Croatian soldiers.

Not surprisingly this move served only to further alienate those whom Tudjman wished to 're'-integrate into Croatia, assuming of course that he was ever really interested in a peaceful outcome in the first place. It also confirmed for even the more moderate elements in the Krajina that once again Croatia did not have their best interests at heart. It further provided an arsenal of ammunition for Milan Babic who, although he was the Krajina's Foreign Minister, had managed to distance himself completely from the Economic Agreement and the reopening of the Highway. He now re-emerged to claim that no matter what the Knin government was prepared to do by way of normalizing relations with Zagreb, it would never satisfy the Croats, and neither Milan Martic or Prime Minister Mikelic had any effective counter-argument with which to answer him.

International reaction to the announcement was mixed with the UN Security Council reaffirming its opinion that the presence of UNPROFOR provided the best opportunity for regional peace and security. Accordingly a formal appeal was made to Croatia on 17 January to reconsider its decision. Germany's Foreign Minister Klaus Kinkel actually admitted that he thought the decision was 'absolutely wrong',[11] and the US State Department expressed what it called 'disapproval', but other than that there appeared to be very little media interest in what was clearly perceived as just another move in the Balkan political chess game.

At a press conference in the Croatian Foreign Ministry the following day, Mate Granic announced that the termination of the mandate was not negotiable, and that the move was designed to promote further a peaceful resolution of the problem. He went on to say that the 'war option' was not being considered by his government but nevertheless he was unable to resist the temptation to make a reasonably direct threat when he said that Croatia had now amassed the military strength necessary to retake the Krajina by force.[12] This was by no means an idle remark because since the signing of a Memorandum of Co-operation on Defence and Military Relations between the United States and Croatia on

149

29 November,[13] MPRI had been deployed in Zagreb and the importation of weaponry and military equipment had commenced in clear contravention of the UN arms embargo through the Croatian State Agency 'ALAN'.[14] The Croatian armed forces were now well on their way to becoming strong enough to contemplate a new war with as many different Serbs as cared to join them in the battle.

A good example of what was going on is also reflected in a report from Hungary that outlined the story of an Iranian Air Force Boeing 747 which was forced to divert to Budapest on 20 January 1995 because of bad weather in Zagreb. When the Hungarian authorities went to search the plane the crew refused to let them come on board, claiming that all they were carrying was 'humanitarian supplies'. After high-level political intervention the flight was allowed to leave Budapest, having filed a flight plan for Tehran, but it later emerged that the Croats had convinced the Hungarian Foreign Minister to allow the plane another opportunity to deposit its cargo in Zagreb.[15] Whether the plane actually went back to Zagreb or continued on to Pula on the coast, where several similar sightings were made, is not known. Neither is it known whether the 'humanitarian supplies' in question were designated for the Muslims in Bosnia, the HVO or the Croatians themselves, or whether the Croats were just taking their cut of 30 per cent before passing the remainder on to both sides in Bosnia.[16] What does become clear is that the Iranians were sending regular 'supply' shipments to Croatia, and Ejup Ganic, Bosnia's Vice President, was making regular visits to see Alija Akbar Rafsanjani in Tehran. In 1996 *Newsweek* posed the question of whether President Clinton was actually aware of this Iranian connection but was unable to answer it satisfactorily. What they had no doubt about they printed as follows:

> *Newsweek* has learned that in early 1994 Croatian President Franjo Tudjman asked US diplomats how Washington would react to an Iranian offer to smuggle weapons to Croatia and Bosnia. That would violate the United Nations arms embargo and increase Iran's sway over the Muslim-led Bosnian government. But Washington decided that levelling the military field was its top priority – even at the expense of its own policy of isolating Tehran. Tudjman was informed that Washington had no view on the matter – a diplomatic signal to let the weapons shipments proceed.[17]

As for the Hungarians, having been involved in the very first smuggling of weapons into Croatia via Martin Spegelj in 1991, they still had apparently no difficulty cooperating with their Croatian neighbours in 1995 when it came to accepting dubious explanations for even more dubious activities of Iranian aircraft, which were flying around in their airspace. Further to this, in 1994 alone, Croatia spent almost 1.4 billion

US dollars on what were loosely described as 'Defence Affairs and Services', a figure that accounted for 31 per cent of that year's total Budget expenditure, or 10 per cent of GNP.[18] Of this, 0.7 billion US dollars was used for the illegal importation of MIG Fighter aircraft, helicopters and missiles. The remainder was spent on domestic production and development which President Tudjman confirmed on 22 December 1994 in his address to the nation, and involved ongoing contracts with 324 firms throughout the country.[19]

It was hardly surprising then that Granic was in buoyant mood and began recommending to the Serbs that they carefully consider something that was about to be unveiled at the end of the month.[20] Entitled the 'Draft Agreement on the Krajina, Slavonia, Southern Baranja and Western Sirmium', or better known as the 'Z-4 Plan', it was nothing short of a gross misjudgement by Granic to begin recommending this document to the Krajina Serbs while threatening them with military violence if they failed to do his bidding. Had he wished to ensure the Z-4 Plan would be rejected in Knin he certainly went about it the right way, and in the context of all that followed it becomes increasingly relevant to enquire whether this was his intention in the first place.

The Z-4 Plan, which purported to represent a consensus between the US, Russia, the EU and the UN, was presented to President Tudjman on the morning of 30 January, and immediately afterwards the 'Zagreb Four' – or 'Five' depending on your perspective – led by Ambassador Galbraith, set out for Knin where Milan Martic refused to even look at their proposals until the whole matter of UNPROFOR's status, and the termination or otherwise of the mandate, was sorted out. This was a valid position and, assuming that he already had an inkling of what the document contained, given that it had been floating around several agencies since 18 January, his response was wholly predictable.[21]

At face value the Z-4 Plan proposed to allow the Serbs to retain their own president, government, flag, language, radio, TV, social welfare system, police force and to raise their own tax revenue. But as one moved into chapters 4, 5 and 6 a different picture began to emerge. In the Sabor, Croatia's national parliament, the Krajina Serbs were to have only 10 out of 148 seats in the House of Representatives (6.7 per cent), and 9 out of 77 seats in the House of Counties (11.7 per cent). Access to the top jobs in central government would be on an ethnic pro-rata basis, with only one member of the Krajina government guaranteed a Cabinet post in the national equivalent. Whichever way you looked at this the Krajina Serbs were destined to remain a minority within Croatia and the insistence in chapter five that all their weapons be destroyed and the area completely demilitarized within five years simply added insult to injury, and further propagated their fear of being oppressed or, worse still, ethnically cleansed.

A little further on it emerged that the Croatian army actually envisaged garrisoning themselves all along the Krajina's border with Bosnia, while Croatian police would guard all the crossing points in an attempt to restrict free movement between the Krajina and the Republic Srpska. The real sting in the tail was saved for chapter 14 where the inevitable Croatian quest for retribution jumped from the pages. Under the supervision of a new constitutional court, a war crimes tribunal for Croatia would be set up to prosecute those considered guilty of having violated the laws of war, or having committed genocide or crimes against humanity. If by any chance the government of the Krajina declined to provide prosecutors for this exercise then Croatia was quite prepared to provide them all. Provision was made to defer all this to the international tribunal in the Hague if so requested but there was no indication as to where this latter-day inquisition might begin or, more importantly, where it was going to end.

No consideration was given to a concept of amnesty, which any fair-minded approach would have recognized immediately as central to anything the Serbs were likely to accept. So, having reduced the Serb government in Knin to the level of a town commission, or at best a county council, the proposal then envisaged disarming the people and making them sufficiently vulnerable to ensure they would raise no objection to having all their leaders tried for war crimes and then locked away for years. The only thing missing from the document was the ceremonial order for the public execution of Martic and Babic but presumably another annex covering that could be tagged on at a later date!

By any objective standard Martic was correct not to entertain either Galbraith or the Z4 Plan. It was an insult to the Krajina Serbs as a people and confirmed exactly what they feared life would become under Croatian rule. No self-respecting Serb could accept these conditions, and none of them did, but in producing such an outrageous document in the first place the International Community and the United States in particular had now firmly nailed their colours to the mast, and the pity of it was that any kind of fair and reasonable approach might actually have worked at that time. The Z4 Plan was neither fair or reasonable and, drafted in Zagreb as it was, the only real question the Krajina Serbs were left wondering about was who had actually written it up in the first place? Henceforward the Z4 Plan would be re-presented regularly as the answer to all the problems in the Krajina, and the Serb's failure to accept it as untrue further evidence of their intransigence. This particular line was, but thanks to the persistence of the Z4 group themselves, ICFY in Geneva and the Croatian government, this perception that the Serbs were exclusively responsible for the continuation of the problem gradually began to stick. Within a short few months this perception would be used against them with devastating effect.

NOTES

1. RC BiH Daily Report: 2/1/95.
2. ECMM Daily Briefing Report: 3/1/96.
3. UNPROFOR Memo, Faure to Akashi: 3/1/95.
4. Weekly Information Analysis Summary, no. 110: 13/1/95.
5. Ibid., para. 8.
6. ECMM Special Report/Meeting with General Delic, Watkins and Geidt: 6/1/95.
7. *Belgrade Telegraph*/Wias, no. 113: 3/2/95.
8. RC Zagreb Daily Report: 12/1/95.
9. HINA News: 12/1/95, 2133 hrs.
10. HINA News: 12/1/95, 2133 hrs.
11. ECMM WIAS 111: 20/1/95.
12. RC Zagreb Daily Report: 13/1/95.
13. Signed in Washington on 29 November 1994 by Croatian Defence Minister Gojko Susak, and US Defence Secretary William Perry. Source: ECMM/CAT Sequence of Events, 1st edn, 19/12/94.
14. ECMM Economics Section Special Report, no. 22: 6/10/95.
15. RC Szeged Reports 27 January–3 February 1995/WIAS 113: 3/2/95.
16. Rupert Cornwell, the *Independent*, 6/4/96.
17. 'The Balkans – Turning a Blind Eye', *Newsweek*, 15/4/96.
18. For comparison, Austria allocated 1 per cent and Germany approximately 2.5 per cent of GNP for military expenditures. ECMM Econ. Sec. Report, no. 11: 27/1/95.
19. ECMM Economics Section Special Report, no. 22: 6/10/95.
20. RC Zagreb Daily Report: 13/1/95, para. 2a.
21. My own initial reaction to the Plan was such that I remarked to both Lennart Leschley, the Head of the Danish Delegation, and Arne Nyberg, ECMM's Legal Advisor, that no self-respecting Krajina Serb could or would accept it. The two of them agreed. Unfortunately years of conditioning would ensure that the international media, the UN and ECMM would all criticize the Serbs for closing what was presented as a window of opportunity. I preferred the view that the window, such as it was, had never in fact been 'opened' in the first place. I believed that this assessment was correct at the time, and indeed remain so convinced today.

CHAPTER SEVENTEEN

'Arms Embargo! What Arms Embargo?'

When the Muslim/Croat Federation began to stagnate in the spring of 1995 a group called the 'Friends of the Federation' emerged in an attempt to revitalize the process, and a US State Department official called Robert Owen[1] was given the unenviable task of making the whole thing work. The 'Friends' turned out to be none other than the original promoters in an unconvincing economic disguise, but even promises of increased funding for much-needed infrastructural development failed to distract the Federation partners from their overriding hatred of one another. Where Muslims were in the majority they oppressed the Croats and vice versa, and while the Croatian government continued to publicly support the process in reality neither Tudjman nor his Defence Minister were remotely interested in this type of settlement. Bosiljko Misetic, Tudjman's Special Advisor on Herceg-Bosnia, was unequivocal when he said that Croats everywhere were afraid of the 'Zetra', the conceptual Muslim kingdom stretching from Turkey in the east through Kosovo, Sandzak and Macedonia to Bosnia. As far as Misetic was concerned Izetbegovic was the father of such a Zetra and would have to be removed.[2]

Meanwhile the Armija High Command, supervised personally by Rasim Delic, had begun a root and branch reorganization of their forces into divisional size units, and for the first time ever brought all their elements within one single chain of command. This was not a secret and several field commanders spoke openly about what was taking place. One such individual was General Drekovic, formerly of 5th Corps fame in Bihac but for some time now the commander of the 4th Corps in Mostar. 'The army is becoming stronger every day,' he said. 'We are now better organized. There will be soon enough heavy weapons, and the production of weapons and ammunition is very high in our territories. The structure of the army is changed to reflect the different tasks. Morale and discipline is high and we now have something to fight for.'[3] While this was all very interesting it was again quite clear that if Drekovic was to be believed the existence of the UN arms embargo and the implementation of a No Fly Zone by NATO were having no effect whatever.

The ability of the Armija to churn out ammunition for their troops from very primitive factories was presented throughout the war as a major achievement by the Muslim side. In Bihac General Dudakovic saw fit to give Arnout Van Linden from Sky News almost unrestricted access to the sheds and garages in Cazin and Coralici, where everything from mortar bombs to rifle ammunition was being produced. This was good public relations and the image relayed all around the world was one of beleaguered Muslims hanging on by their fingernails thanks to their ingenuity. The reality of course was totally different, with Croatian army helicopters flying nightly re-supply missions into the Pocket and light aircraft from a variety of other airfields in Croatia engaged in similar activities but none of this was reported in the media. Curiously there was no mention of anything to do with helicopters or other light aircraft in his daily reports. Neither was there any report in the Croatian media of a helicopter crash at Lucko airport near Zagreb on the night of 4 December 1994. An Mi-8 MTV-I, believed to be the personal helicopter of Alija Izetbegovic, filled to the brim with ammunition and explosives, failed to gain altitude and crashed to the ground in a massive explosion, killing the crew. The official Croatian explanation offered a choice – it could have been either an exploding petrol tanker or a pyromaniac blowing himself up. However UNPROFOR and ECMM knew differently.[4]

In central Bosnia the situation was similar with the majority of the civilian population employed in the production of ammunition. A case in point was the steel factory in Zenica which was no longer able to perform its traditional role and certain sections of the plant had been converted to produce artillery shells. When an ECMM team visited the area on 20 February they discovered that contrary to popular belief not all of the huge sprawling plant had been closed down. Certain sections while off limits to the Monitors were clearly in full production of 'something' and generally a hive of activity. Equally the section manufacturing industrial gases was very busy with no apparent shortage of raw materials, and close to the main exit gate a number of trolleys were clearly visible containing several hundred artillery shells obviously awaiting collection.

This discovery put many things in context but one matter that could not be easily reconciled was the deployment throughout the factory grounds of several hundred Turkish UN troops complete with their battalion headquarters, and several other support establishments as well. Admittedly these troops were there because this was the site offered to the UN by the local municipal leadership in the first instance, but by now they had become little more than human shields behind which the Muslims, on this occasion, could manufacture whatever they wanted. And all of this supposedly sanctioned and with the total compliance of both the Turks and UNPROFOR headquarters.

The manner in which the UN was being manipulated in Zenica was cynical in the extreme and a very clear indication that, no more than the Serbs, the Muslims also had little difficulty abusing the UN presence when it suited their own purposes. Someone in the higher echelons in UNPROFOR should have identified what was happening and put an end to it, but for as long as the Turkish Battalion remained where it was these UN troops could be viewed either as sitting ducks if the Serbs chose to launch an artillery or missile attack, or alternatively as partners in the proliferation of the Muslim armaments industry. Why no attempt was made to accurately report what was really going on in Zenica remains one of several unanswered questions but this paled into insignificance compared with what was happening further north around the town of Tuzla.

On the night of Friday 13 February UNPROFOR's headquarters in Sarajevo included the following paragraph in their daily report:

FINALLY, THERE IS CONTINUED EVIDENCE OF BiH (Muslim) ARMS RESUPPLY ACTIVITY. SINCE THE BEGINNING OF 6 JAN., CONVOYS OF VARIOUS SIZES HAVE BEEN REPORTED ENTERING BH TERRITORY IN THE SECTOR, CARRYING AN ESTIMATED 800–1,000 TONS OF SUPPLIES. BY COMPARISON, THE LAST PEAK IN SPECIAL CONVOY ACTIVITY WAS IN OCT. 94 WHEN 5 CONVOYS WITH AN ESTIMATED 400–550 TONS OF SUPPLIES WERE NOTED. THIS PRECEDED AN INCREASE IN ACTIVITY IN THE KUPRES (XJ 8273), CEMERSKA PLANINA (BP 9076) AND BJELASNICA (BP 7943) AREAS.[5]

Two nights previously a Norwegian UN Observer in Tuzla reported the sighting of a Hercules C-130 transport aircraft escorted by F-16 fighters, and when UN troops attempted to visit the area into which they suspected supplies were being dropped they were confronted by heavily armed Armija troops. With the entire area cordoned off the Muslim troops refused point blank to allow the UN access to the site and after a stand-off lasting several hours the UN personnel withdrew. While the official report into this incident recorded no more than that the investigation had been inconclusive, the Force Commander, General De Lapresle, nonetheless decided to cable Kofi Annan, the UN's Head of Peace-keeping Operations in New York, with his evaluation of what was going on. 'It appears that two clandestine re-supplies have taken place. The equipment being delivered is assessed to be of a high value/high technology, such as new generation anti-tank guided missiles or perhaps surface-to-air missiles – the origin of the cargo or the jets is not known.'[6]

When NATO were asked to identify this air traffic it was initially suggested that these were 'standard civilian flights and training missions'! Then it emerged that the AWACs on permanent station over Bosnia to enforce the No Fly Zone were not quite as good as all had been led to believe, and it now transpired that they were actually susceptible to 'blind spots'. In other words there were occasions within every twenty-four-hour period when NATO was unable to monitor the complete airspace over Bosnia, and if somebody flew into the area during this time then they could more or less fly around in whatever pattern they wished.

If it also happened that the AWACs were slightly off course for any reason then the size of these 'blind spots' became even bigger, and if any would-be arms supplier could get his hands on the AWAC's flight schedules the rest of it was simple. By 21 February, as more and more damning information began to emerge about NATO's inability to secure the skies over Bosnia, the issue began to take on the nature of a scandal, and one from which everyone wanted to distance themselves. In a secret memo to Kofi Annan, Chinmaya Gharekhan, Boutros Boutros-Ghali's senior advisor, indicated that within a very short time this whole matter was going to come before the Security Council and he derided NATO's 'explanations' such as they were. 'The NATO investigators would have us believe that no unauthorized activity took place. This conclusion would severely erode the credibility of UNPROFOR reporting on any air activity. The NATO report refers to "normal civilian airline traffic patterns in Serb airspace". I wonder what is this 'normal civilian Serb air traffic?'

The following day Annan sent a cable to Akashi in Zagreb which said that Thorvald Stoltenberg had confirmed to him that, notwithstanding all of NATO's explanations, including Admiral Leighton Smith's somewhat cryptic statement to Akashi and Janvier that no *uniformed* or *service* personnel were involved, the original UN reports were correct. On the evening of 19 February it also emerged that the level of Muslim air activity in central Bosnia had alarmed the UN sufficiently for Lieutenant Colonel C.A. Le Hardy, the Chief Operations Officer at Sector North East Headquarters in Tuzla, to write to General Rose's headquarters in Sarajevo outlining what was taking place and the procedures he was now implementing to monitor it properly. These measures included the deployment of TOW thermal sighting equipment, the use of a troop of Leopard tanks as mobile observation posts, and the establishment of several additional static observation and listening posts. Perhaps of most significance in the longer term was Le Hardy's comment at the end of the report in which he stated that as far as he was concerned the Norwegian officer who had submitted the original reports, Lieutenant Saetersdal, was considered to be highly competent with plenty of experience in monitoring air traffic, which he had gained while serving with UNIFIL in Lebanon.[7]

So what was really going on? Well, the answer appears to be that there was in existence a concerted covert campaign to supply arms and equipment to the Bosnian Muslims in contravention of the UN arms embargo[8] and a perusal of the *Los Angeles Times* on 5 April 1996 and the London *Independent* of the following day is very helpful in this regard. These particular newspapers indicated that during the war large quantities of illegal arms and equipment were being flown into the Croatian airport at Pula by Iranian cargo aircraft and then transported by road into Herceg-Bosna where, after all the appropriate tariffs had been deducted, what was left of the original shipment made its way to the Muslims in central Bosnia. A second and subsequently more preferred supply route involved the delivery by air of a variety of equipment directly to the Armija units on the ground.

These latter operations were apparently carried out by reserve or retired US pilots (i.e., not in uniform and not currently flying in the US forces), flying specially adapted Hercules C-130 aircraft from American bases in Britain and Europe. Landing at remote airstrips in northern Cyprus they would take on board Iranian weapons and ammunition, including artillery shells, and when all was securely bolted to pallets with parachutes attached, the pilots would set a course for the Croatian coast and onwards into Bosnia.[9] In the event that they could not complete their missions in one run Brac Island, just off the coast from Split, could be used as a staging post; and some of the local people in the island's picturesque town of Bol were adamant that American C-130s were flying in and out of their airport on a regular basis.[10] When the delivery runs were made into Bosnia they were most probably coordinated by US Special Forces personnel on the ground the presence of whom, despite complete denial by the United States, was verified by Canadian UN troops in Visoko during January 1995 and accepted as a fact by the Intelligence Section at UNPROFOR headquarters in Zagreb.[11] US special forces personnel were also operating openly in Tuzla where Major Guy Sands made no attempt to disguise either his presence or his activities. At Split airport USAF Colonel Ray Shepherd had also set up a logistics base and made no secret of the fact that US personnel scattered throughout the region were operating to specific US agendas.[12]

On the ground the local Armija units sealed off the drop zones in order to prevent the UN from wandering in on top of them and, flying low over the tree-tops with the back door wide open, pallets were quickly jettisoned as the pilots endeavoured to get out of the area as quickly as possible. Mission accomplished the pilots were then free to land wherever they wished, and again ECMM discovered one of these aircraft parked on the tarmac at Split airport on the evening of 23 February. Awaiting the arrival of a Croatian Airways 737 to take them back to Zagreb the Monitors could not fail to notice the four C-130s parked in front of the terminal building. Three of the aircraft were easy enough to account for. One was Spanish and on its weekly re-supply run to the Spanish battalion in the Mostar area. A further two were American and bore the

Identification Numbers 1620-15/1 and 1620-15/2, quite obviously belonging to the 37th ALS 'Blue Tail Flies'. The fourth aircraft was altogether another matter. It had a very small American flag on the tail, no identification number and was painted in different camouflage livery to the green or grey colouring of the other three and as dusk fell it would not have been immediately evident that this aircraft was 'different' from the others.

As the Monitors watched in silence from the viewing balcony they became more suspicious by the minute. The crew, who were all dressed in green uniforms with neither rank markings nor national flags attached, continued working on the aircraft without interference from either the airport authorities or the Croatian police, and there was neither a UN vehicle nor a 'blue beret' even vaguely associated with them.[13] While admittedly there appeared to be American personnel in one guise or another scattered all over the Split–Zadar region, and most of them were so unconcerned at being recognized that they drove around in cars with US licence plates which they had driven to the Balkans from their bases in Germany, what the Monitors had accidentally stumbled upon that night was certainly out of the ordinary. What made the whole episode even more suspicious was the presence in the airport building at exactly the same time of Colonel Kresimir Cosic, personal advisor to President Tudjman and Chairman of the Croatian Defence Ministry's committee for 'international co-operation and bi-lateral projects'. Cosic, later to become Liutenant General and Croatia's Deputy Defence Minister, was at that time functioning as Tudjman's liaison officer with the US State Department on the activities of MPRI and the implementation of the US Defence Training and Advisory Programme (DTAP).[14] It is of course quite possible that Cosic had no knowledge of what was parked in front of him on the tarmac that night but as the Monitors flew back to Zagreb that night they were quite satisfied that they had uncovered yet another piece of the clandestine re-supply jigsaw which every monitoring agency in Former Yugoslavia was trying to put together.[15]

The story of covert re-supply operations had now became 'good copy' for everyone with a story to tell, and General Mladic lost no time getting in on the act. In a letter to General De Lapresle in Zagreb and General Rupert Smith, who had recently taken over from Sir Michael Rose in Sarajevo, he outlined the Bosnian Serbs' opinion of what was going on.

ARMY OF THE REPUBLIC OF SRPSKA
No: 06/17-195
24 February 1995

On 23 Feb. 1995 at about 2010 hours, a transport plane, with weapons and military equipment, landed again at Tuzla airport's secondary runaway. It was escorted by 2 NATO fighter aircraft which were protecting it during flight and off-loading. Unfortunately, this has been repeated lately in front, within sight and hearing of NATO and UNPROFOR forces both in the air and at Tuzla airport itself. Those forces are doing nothing to prevent the violation of the relevant UN Security Council Resolutions prohibiting the import of weapons and military equipment.

Although we try not to regard this situation as an example of open partiality towards our enemies, it is difficult to avoid such an impression. Our suspicions, that senior UNPROFOR representatives had insisted on the signing of the Agreement on Cessation of Hostilities in order to enable the Muslims to have a reprieve and to gain time to regroup and supply themselves with weapons, ammunition and equipment, to continue their bloody campaign, are unfortunately becoming reality.

We expect you, as the most senior UNPROFOR representatives, to take the necessary steps to prevent the Muslims from continuing to break the signed Agreement and violate the status of the Tuzla protected area. That way, you would directly contribute to the fulfilment of the signed Agreement.

Finally I wish to inform you that henceforward we are not able to guarantee the security of NATO aircraft in the airspace of the former BH.

COMMANDER
Lieutenant General
Ratko Mladic

On the basis of this and other similar allegations ECMM launched its own investigation into the matter and despite the best efforts of Peter Erben and Roger Castle in Tuzla, and Philip Watkins back in Zagreb, it was not possible to confirm or deny that anything of this nature was taking place. Nevertheless, practically every monitoring agency on the ground remained convinced that a covert re-supply operation began in the summer of 1994 to upgrade the Armija's arsenal, and the sighting of aircraft in the Tuzla region during the spring of 1995 merely served to confirm it. In fact Akashi cabled Kofi Annan in New York on 18 July 1994 saying, 'we can confirm that the BiH has been receiving new weapons' and, listing the type and calibre of what had been discovered, he concluded by adding that 'we firmly believe that such equipment is being transhipped through Croatia for either a fee, or for part of the shipment, or both'.[16] There was also a much earlier report by the Secretary General himself, UN Doc. S/1994/300, dated 16 March 1994, which confirmed that Operation Deny Flight, begun on 12 April 1993, had not been the great success everyone thought it was and that by mid-March 1994 1,005 violations of the No Fly Zone by what were termed 'non combat aircraft' had taken place. A double game was being played on this issue and there were no other possible explanations for the manner in which the Muslims were able to recommence their war with the Bosnian Serbs at the end of March 1995, given that militarily they were a spent force less than twelve months before that. Renewed hostilities with the Serbs under more favourable circumstances had been a cornerstone of the Washington Agreement for the Muslims but to stand a realistic chance of success they had to be comprehensively supported. With their forces reorganized and the Croats now technically their allies, the lot of the Bosnian Muslims was now steadily improving. The problem was that the stronger they grew the less likely it became that they would abide by the terms of the COHA in the future.

Later on some of the main players in these covert activities were prevailed upon to tell the truth before a US Senate Intelligence Select Committee. On 21 May 1996 Richard Holbrooke admitted that he had explored the possibility of a full-scale arming of the Bosnian Muslims in 1994, in spite of the UN arms embargo, because he feared they could not survive another winter on their own. While he denied that the US was actually involved in what subsequently transpired he went on to defend the Clinton Administration's decision to agree to Iranian arms shipments through Croatia to Bosnia. Without it, he claimed, the Bosnian government would never have survived from the winter of 1994 to Dayton. However, when pressed further by Committee Chairman Arlen Specter, Holbrooke also admitted that US technical personnel had become involved in the inspection of some Iranian missiles in transhippment to Bosnia because of a report saying that the weapons in question had chemical warheads. While the source of this report was not divulged Holbrooke remained adamant that US intelligence agencies were not involved. He claimed that they had never been told of the decision in the first place, on the grounds that the whole thing was not a covert operation at all but rather a diplomatic response to Croatia's enquiry if this type of behaviour was acceptable.[17]

Two days later Deputy Secretary of State Strobe Talbott told the Committee that as far as he was aware the Clinton Administration had decided to keep its collaboration in this matter a secret, although he had informed the CIA on the instructions of Secretary of State Warren Christopher. 'Had it become public it would have stirred up further relations with our principal NATO allies which were already quite tense at the time,' he said. Talbott went on to confirm that on 27 April 1994 the Clinton Administration decided to help Iran ship arms to Bosnia through Croatia, by instructing US diplomats in the region to tell Croatia that they had 'No instructions' on what to say about such shipments.[18]

On 30 May Charles Redman and Peter Galbraith, the two US diplomats on the ground in Former Yugoslavia, confirmed the existence of the US 'No instructions' policy and of having relayed that message to the relevant personnel. Interestingly enough Galbraith was prepared to go a good deal further and stated that 'the [Clinton] Administration was convinced that the arms embargo was fundamentally an error'.[19] It is unfortunate that the US did not use the services of Madeline Allbright, their permanent representative of the UN in New York, to raise this point and explain all their misgivings to the Security Council. Instead they effectively chose to condone a gross violation of a UN arms embargo, which they had supported themselves in the first instance, as well as commencing a devious diplomatic double-game with the remainder of their NATO allies.[20]

NOTES

1. Robert Owen would later become the Administrator of Brcko pursuant to the Dayton Agreements.
2. In an interview with Tim Clifton, Political Secretary, ECMM HQ, 23/1/95.
3. ECMM Weekly Information Analysis Summary, no. 114: 10/2/95.
4. Jane's Sentinel Newsletter, vol. 7, p. 4.
5. ECLO Sarajevo Daily Report: 13/2/95.
6. Night and Day/The *Mail on Sunday*: 24/9/95.
7. UN Sector North East Report, no. 1,020, 19 2123 B, February 95.
8. UNSC RES. 713: 25/9/91.
9. Night and Day/The *Mail on Sunday*: 24/9/95.
10. While there is no disputing the fact that the United States was using Brac as a base from which to launch RPVs, or 'drones', on high-tech reconnaissance flights over Bosnian Serb positions, the reporting of so many C-130 flights is not consistent with this operation. Accordingly one can conclude that something else was on in Brac as well, and this is supported by the reaction of the detachment of Croatian special police who were visibly perturbed when an ECMM investigation team attempted to visit the airport there on 12 January 1995. See also 'Heading off War in the Southern Balkans', Misha Glenny, *Foreign Affairs*, vol. 74, no. 3, pp. 101–2.
11. 'Defence and Foreign Affairs Strategic Policy' of 31/10/95 also reported the deployment of US Special Forces personnel 'on active duty' in support of both the Bosnian Croats and the Bosnian Muslims.
12. Jane's Sentinel Newsletter, vol. 7, p. 4 and 5.
13. ECMM Special Report – Vinuesa/O'Shea: 15/1/95.
14. Interview with General Cosic, *Jane's Defence Weekly*: 19/11/97, p. 32.
15. Misha Glenny was adamant that all EU Monitors were military intelligence officers who, because they were dressed in white uniforms, looked as though

'they were emissaries from outer space who had been sent to save the human race from itself', *The Fall of Yugoslavia*, pp. 158–9. One wonders what he might have said had he come across two monitors, resplendent in their white attire, standing for over an hour in the bitter cold on an airport viewing balcony, as they observed the antics of some loosely disguised American aviators.

16. Cable: Akashi to Annan 'BiH Violations of the Arms Embargo': 18/7/94.
17. Reuters (Washington): 21/5/96.
18. Reuters (Washington): 23/5/96.
19. AFP (Washington): 30/5/96.
20. See November 1996 US Senate Select Committee on transfer of Iranian arms to Bosnia.

CHAPTER EIGHTEEN

The Serb Stranglehold on Bihac Recedes

With attention firmly focused on air activity around Tuzla,[1] the helicopters that were operating in and around Zenica,[2] and the ongoing attempts by Akashi to keep the COHA on the rails, the Serb stranglehold on Bihac began to look as if it might now be coming apart at the seams. This had begun in late January when reports filtered through that General Manojlo Milovanovic, the Bosnian Serb army's Chief of Staff who had been coordinating all Serb operations around Bihac, had apparently resigned. This was allegedly a pre-emptive strike against Radovan Karadzic whom it was rumoured was about to dismiss Milovanovic for the recent series of losses that the BSA had incurred, the last of which had been suffered on the night of 13 January 1995. In a clear breach of the COHA the 5th Corps had launched an attack on Serb positions near the hospital in Bihac town and, unprepared for this development, the Serbs were believed to have suffered up to 120 casualties and lost significant ground.

On the other hand, Milovanovic was quoted as saying that his soldiers were cold and hungry, had received little or no pay for months, and that he could no longer continue to operate in this environment. It also emerged that he was about to dismiss several of his field commanders in order to make one last attempt to cut the Pocket in two, but apparently Karadzic had ordered him to stop in order to comply with the terms of the COHA.[3] Two days later a Bosnian Serb press release denied that Milovanovic had attempted to resign because he had been refused permission to capture Bihac town, insisting instead that he was on regular duty and had in fact been 'recently decorated for his outstanding work in the field'.[4] The real story would appear to be that Karadzic certainly wanted to sack Milovanovic because of his reluctance to abide by the terms of the COHA, that the 5th Corps did attack, and that Karadzic refused permission to counter it. Milovanovic then attempted to resign but *Mladic* would not accept it.

Artillery battles also continued in and around Bihac town, this time with the Serb positions significantly shifting in both the south and west. As people began returning to the villages from which they had fled before the Serb onslaught in November, Bill Foxton, a British EU Monitor operating in the Pocket, went along to see how they were getting on. His Special Report is a unique and fascinating eyewitness account of the miserable circumstances he came across that cold February morning.

Today Team Bihac visited the recently liberated villages of SOKOLOC, ZAVALJE, ZEGAR and PRIVILICA. Scenes of devastation were expected but the sheer scale of the vandalism was not. Without exception, every house had been systematically looted and smashed. All the internal electrical fittings and sanitary ware had been ripped out, or simply smashed. The damage of war was of a moderate scale compared to the damage caused by the successive units of troops which had occupied the villages since November 1994.

The streets were littered with the contents of the houses. The Catholic church in the centre of ZAVALJE had received several hits from shells and had been set on fire, whether deliberately or not is difficult to say. However, what was clear was that the altar and stations of the cross had been systematically destroyed. The church had contained an ossary and this had been ripped open and its contents spread about the floor. All forms of religious symbolism had been mutilated or defaced.

We were invited by an old lady to visit her house. The house could be described as a poor village house and the lady, who was in her late seventies, pleaded with us to tell her how she should begin to rebuild her life. The small wood burning stove had been wrenched from the floor and smashed along with all her furniture. It would be difficult to imagine a more pathetic sight.

When we arrived in SOKOLAC one house was still burning. In the centre of the village what remained of the mosque minaret lay across the road. It had been brought down in three parts by controlled explosions. The desecration of the main prayer hall was made complete by the inscription of the 4 Cyrillic S's in the Hebrab which points to Mecca. The calling card of 1 Krajina Corps (BSA) was evident, with the graffiti daubed on the walls proclaiming their own villages of Bosanska Gradiska, Doboj, Prnjavor, Knezevo, Vlasic, Bos Dubica, and those of the 2nd Krajina Corps, Grmusa and Racic.[5]

Such was the situation in the villages immediately south of Bihac town in the spring of 1995 and similar scenes of devastation were to be found wherever a front line had been established. However there was another side to all of this and some very strange arrangements were also entered into.

In February 1995, for example, between ten and fourteen trucks belonging to the 5th Corps made daily excursions into Krajina Serb territory and loaded up with a variety of goods, some of which could loosely be described as 'surplus humanitarian supplies'. For example a tin of canned beef, which could not be sold in the Krajina for 2 Deutschmarks, because the people had no money, would make its way into the Pocket and end up retailing for 8 Deutschmarks. Of course this wasn't happening accidentally. Several ECMM reports from that time were quite clear that the whole operation was strictly controlled by both the 5th Corps and by a man, known locally as the 'Head of the Smugglers', who allegedly coordinated the entire black market. He was also alleged to have a 50 per cent stake in Bihac town's infamous discotheque, The Galaxia, which amazingly defied the Serb gunners by continuing to operate right throughout the war. The other 50 per cent, not surprisingly, went straight into 5th Corps' coffers.[6]

For most people survival was now their only focus, and the story of the old lady who traded her curtains, two bath towels, a table cloth and some bed linen for 17 kg of flour was the rule rather than the exception. The predicament of these ordinary people was not about to improve either if the spring planting of corn seed and potatoes did not take place. UNHCR was ready to buy the necessary 900 tons of seed but there appeared to be no prospect whatever of the Krajina Serbs allowing a convoy of over ninety trucks to pass unhindered into the Pocket.[7] Clearly it would be of no advantage to the black market or its operators on any side of the confrontation line to have the people growing food for themselves so, not for the first time in this political and military quagmire, the ordinary people remained at the mercy of those who were supposedly orchestrating their protection.

This particularly convoluted picture became further confused with the return of some 5th Corps soldiers who had been taken prisoners of war by the Serbs and were now released as part of an exchange programme supervised and organized by UNMOs and Red Cross Officials. The brutality allegedly associated with the incarceration of this group was recounted to Bill Foxton shortly after their release, and while accepting the subjective nature of the interview, their stories remain a terrible indictment of the manner in which the Bosnian Serbs conducted this detention, and their complete rejection of the basic rules of the Law of War. Their story is perfectly consistent with other accounts from other people who suffered and survived these savage regimes and while they may never have heard the term post traumatic stress disorder before their captivity, they certainly know all about it now. The mental and physical torture endured by Zlatko Juricic and Sevad Veladzic, two Privates in the 5th Corps' 502 Brigade, provides a graphic explanation of why the International Community found it necessary to establish a War Crimes Tribunal in the first instance.

STATEMENT MADE BY ZLATKO JURICIC

I was captured on the 9th of September 1994. I was in civilian clothes and I had been doing some purchasing on the black market. I returned to where I had hidden my uniform and got dressed. I had been drinking more than was good for me and I wandered off in the wrong direction and was captured. I had eight hundred Marks on me and after my capture the Serbs fought each other over who should have the money. They even cut open the seams of my uniform to see whether I had other money concealed. They stripped me to see whether I was circumcised and they beat me on the head with a hammer.

I was then taken to Slunj to the 'Polygon Area' and I was subjected to a very special interrogation because of my wrist-watch. My captors, it seems, had captured two Croatian Special Forces soldiers who had been trying to sabotage a bridge and they imagined because of this watch that I was the third member of the team. They broke my teeth with a pair of pliers and badly beat me.

I was then taken by Gazelle helicopter to Omarska, 25 km north of Banja Luka. I was again beaten by officers and ordinary soldiers. At a certain moment General Manojlo Milovanovic appeared and accused me of being an instructor in the Tudjman army, charged with training soldiers of 502 [Brigade] for Special Forces work. They kept calling me 'Ustasha'. After being forced to eat some tainted food from the floor I was again beaten and I fainted twice. The General then ordered them to stop. I was given some water and then transported to Bosanski Novi, 50 km north-east of Bihac.

Here I was kept in the cellar of the fire brigade building. There I met Nazif from 505 Brigade who had already been there for twenty-two months. I also met Ibrahim Halkic from 511 Brigade who was exchanged with me among these thirty-one. I was forced to confess on radio to all kinds of crimes including lies about 5 Corps that we were hanging Serbs in the trees.

I was then asked to defect and whether I was willing to return to Bihac and kill Dudakovic, Hambdu Abdic and Sarganovic. My file was marked 'Birch 94'. [This was an operation in 1994 in the Buzim area.] I was then transferred to Kamenica in the area of Drvar, 70 km south-east of Bihac. I was put in solitary confinement in a cell measuring 1.80 m. by 0.80 m. There was no window. The cells were numbered 1, 2, 3 and 'floor'. The difference was that it had a wooden floor while the others were concrete.

There was a prisoner there called Dizdarevic from APWB. The APWB prisoners were treated equally badly by the Serbs. They were each given two blankets and a mattress as thick as a cigarette box. I was then taken out to pick up cigarette ends but every time I bent down to pick one up they beat me. When I stood up, unable to pick one up, they beat me on the hands for failing to do so. In the prison [also] were Serb criminals and deserters who were allowed to move around. They also beat us on the orders of the guards.

There was only one rule which was to bow our heads and put our hands behind our backs. I was kept in solitary for forty-six days. Dolic was in the next cell and he was forced to sing the whole night, despite being wounded. Musadinovic had at this time just arrived and his screams kept us all awake at night. On one occasion we were divided into two groups. One group would sing while the other group were beaten in shifts of half an hour. The beating would only stop if those being beaten could spit blood before the guards. Some were unable to produce the bloody spit and were beaten to death.

From the 9th of November I was assigned with two other Croats to a work detail. Our task was to bury the dead. Their names were Cavar, aged twenty-two from Tomislavgrad, a driver in the Croatian army, and Davor, also from Tomislavgrad. We buried in total thirty-two bodies in a grave measuring 5 m by 5 m. They were not all prisoners. The depth of the grave was only 0.40 m deep. While we were digging we would find skulls and bones from previous times. I remembered one skull that had a hole in the forehead the size of an ashtray with no exit hole.

Twenty days before my exchange I witnessed the execution of a 5 Corps soldier Fikret Begic, by the prison's chief administrator. I know that this murderer was a former JNA Security Officer at ZELJAVA. [The Former JNA Airfield west of Bihac town.] He shot him from a distance of one metre in the head with a 7.65 pistol. Because Fikret Begic was incapable of standing they had propped him against the wall. The bullet came out the back of his head and ricocheted into a window breaking the glass. There were two other witnesses to this murder, both APWB prisoners called Omer and Ibrahim. They had to carry Fikret Begic to the place of execution. I never saw them again. After the execution I was given Rakia [plum brandy], bacon and bread, as though nothing had happened. . . . I am having nightmares about this murder now. The officer who killed Begic had dark hair and blue eyes and had a limp in his right leg from an old wound. He drives a red Lada car (without a number-plate) and he is known by the Nickname of 'Dronjak'. . . . I am sure ICRC Banja Luka must know who he is.

I was in a cell with Marjan Niksic, a Croat civilian who was systematically beaten to death by a guard who must have weighed 100 kg. This guard knew karate by the way he jumped in the air and kicked Marjan repeatedly in the chest. Marjan Niksic died in my cell on New Year's Eve. I am ashamed to say I did not report it. Instead I took his blanket because it was so cold. In the morning the guards realised that Marjan had died in the night and gave me a terrible hiding for not reporting the death. I ask my colleagues to forgive me for what I did. The next day I was put into cell no. 1 with 6 APWB prisoners. . . . They were also beaten to death because I had to bury some of them.

Zlatko Juricic

STATEMENT MADE BY SEVAD VELADZIC

I was captured on 7th November [1994] near Gorjevac, together with my Company Commander Captain Hazim Toromanvic, and with Fikret Hajrulahovic who was killed on the spot. I was interrogated together with my Company Commander and they kept beating us with shovels, chains and a rake. They beat my Company Commander so badly that he died on the 4th of December [1994].

We were forced to beat each other with chains. I believe in total we were twenty-seven prisoners. Even wounded people were beaten. They would even carry them out of the cells to beat them. I know for sure of six who died of beatings. I never knew their names except for my Company Commander. They would leave the dead for some days in the cells. We were in our underwear and it was winter with extreme temperatures. We had to walk in the snow in our stocking feet.

According to the shift would depend on when we got our beatings. Some shifts would beat us one hour after lunch and the others would beat us at night. As for food we got three loaves for twenty-seven men and a bowl of soup between two men for twenty-four hours. We always had to move in groups of three so that there would always be two to carry the one who had been beaten senseless. Two of my companions had to carry out the dead body of my Company Commander. They were immediately isolated from the others. Even ICRC did not see all of us. We only came out to be beaten and they even brought in local people to beat us. I was mainly beaten by the Chief Administrator 'Dronjak' who told me I would die slowly like my Captain.

We then had a visit from ICRC and told we would be moved to Pasjak (near Drvar). We were told what we may say and told never to mention Kamenica. Only twenty-three of thirty-one on this recent exchange were seen by ICRC. Only three of those here today had a visit from ICRC. Six 5 Corps soldiers are still there with ten APWB, and seventeen Croats. We never knew we were going to be exchanged. We were split up and even just before the exchange they put in three and took out three. I was lucky to get out because ICRC never knew about me. They keep moving you, in order to keep everything secret. If somebody dies they cut off their heads or put three legs with one body. The families can never be sure to have the right body. Bodies never have names. They pin on a number or they just give a certain body a name. We know there are three mass graves in the area of Kamenica.

Sevad Veladzic[8]

While these stories are undeniably shocking and sickening it must be pointed out that no one side in any phase of the Yugoslav conflict ever had a monopoly when it came to brutalizing the enemy, and this was as true in Bihac Pocket as it was anywhere else. In a confidential report to ECMM's Regional Centre in Zagreb, Monitors on the ground confirmed that they were equally concerned that war crimes were being committed by elements of the 5th Corps as well as by the Serbs.

> These crimes will be difficult to prove conclusively but we feel that HQ ECMM should be made aware of what we already know. At body and prisoner of war exchange meetings each side tries to discover how many of each (dead or alive) the other side has. Neither side wishes to admit to more dead bodies that the other side. Usually when an exchange is agreed both sides pitch up with comparable numbers of bodies and prisoners. In some cases the bodies have been buried in shallow graves and the faces are quite green. However it has been reported recently to us that one body was delivered which was so fresh that rigor mortis had not yet set in. In another case a body had been decapitated so cleanly at the neck that it was in itself suspicious.[9]

And then, as if the presence of these traumatized returnees and their accounts of incarceration at the hands of the Serbs were not having sufficient negative impact on the ordinary citizens of the Pocket, another unsavoury situation began to raise its ugly head which without doubt had the potential to set Muslims and Croats at one another's throats yet again.

NOTES

1. The *Sunday Times,* 5/3/95 also reported the involvement of Turkish aircraft in the resupply operation at Tuzla with the equipment dropped allegedly supplied by Saudi Arabia. While this could not be confirmed at the time it eventually transpired that this is indeed what happened but was only the tip of the iceberg. See Defence and Foreign Affairs Strategic Policy, 30/4/96, p. 3.
2. Special UN Report/Sector North East HQ: 19/2/95.
3. RC Belgrade Special Report, Marcel Cintelan: 31/1/95.
4. Reuters Belgrade: 2/2/95.
5. Team Bihac Special Report, Bill Foxton: 14/2/95.
6. ECMM Investigation Report, 'The Economy in Bihac Pocket', Bill Foxton and Oscar Meyboom, 1/3/95.
7. Team Bihac Special Report, Bill Foxton: 1/3/95.
8. Team Bihac Special Report, Bill Foxton/Luc Vermeulen: 23/3/95.
9. ECMM/Team Bihac Special Report: 5/3/95.

CHAPTER NINETEEN

General Vlado Santic Disappears!

On the evening of 10 March the HINA News Agency in Zagreb reported that a statement had been issued by the Bosnian Embassy in which the 5th Corps in Bihac were quoted as having no reliable information on the alleged arrest, and/or disappearance of the HVO officer Major General Vlado Santic, who had recently resumed command of the 101 HVO Brigade in the Pocket, and was also theoretically Deputy Commander of the 5th Corps. By contrast a HVO spokesman asserted that Santic had disappeared, following his arrest by members of the 5th Corps' 502 Brigade, as he left the Sedra Hotel in Bihac town at 0120 hrs on the morning of 9 March.[1] Before long rumours began circulating that in fact Santic had been killed by some members of the 5th Corps and some commentators began forecasting the renewal of widespread Muslim–Croat conflict right across Bosnia. This uncertainty was further exacerbated by the ambiguous answers Dudakovic insisted on giving to Bill Foxton when he visited the General's headquarters to find out what was going on. As the Monitors left the meeting they may not have had any better idea as to the whereabouts of Vlado Santic but they had unwittingly obtained a unique insight into the world of Atif Dudakovic, from his perspective as a beleaguered, encircled, embattled soldier, doing his best to hold his command together in the face of overwhelming odds and other factors apparently beyond his control.

Q: Do you know where General Santic is?
A: *Yes.*
Q: Did you have him arrested?
A: *No.*
Q: Is he safe?
A: *No.*
Q: Where is he now?
A: *I don't know.*
Q: What happened to him?
A: *I do not know, I can only guess. It was a personal vendetta between members of 5 Corps and General Santic. They have been arrested. There is an investigation*

going on which will prove whether or not he is dead. This incident has nothing to do with HVO and 5 Corps. It also has nothing to do with Croats and Muslims. It was not planned and I am not involved. Yesterday evening there was a meeting of the Regional Presidency Council and after that meeting they issued a communiqué which will only be of interest to our enemies and extremists. At the moment all international organizations are trying to investigate this matter. It is ridiculous. The truth is that there was an incident with Santic, people were drunk. I personally do not want the situation to deteriorate, but anything is possible.

Q: Do the Croats want to go to Croatia?

A: *Yes, because they feel they are no longer safe [here]. I asked the Croatian delegation to send professional officers . . . the HVO Bde is [has become] a private army. It has to be reorganized. This would be good for us and the Croats . . . what I need is a well-organized HVO to be used against the Chetniks and to protect their own people. My main problem at the moment is Santic. There is a deeper meaning behind this. It was SANTIC's behaviour against Croats and Bosnia which finally escalated. It was done by MPs and members of 502 Brigade. What had to happen happened. The perpetrators were military but it has nothing to do with the army. Santic has been arresting members of the HDZ Party and others in Bihac. What good has he done here? These are the reasons but the consequences are not good. I have no obligation to do anything about this. I could leave it to the legal system. That's life. To do everything without the legal system would be easy.*

Q: How long before we can learn the fate of General Santic?

A: *The law states that we can hold them for three days before they have to appear before a judge. We must follow the law. We suspect a limited number of persons. Experts appointed by me are investigating. According to the law we need proof. I can't get around the law. I must get to know what is behind this but according to the law. Every miracle lasts three days [local saying]. My friends, this is a difficult period for me, someday someone will write a book about it. It is a very special responsibility to command an encircled unit. It is special because at the same time you have to live with the surrounded population. The army [5 Corps] was created during the war. A lot of them are drunks, criminals and without education. It's not like building an army in peacetime where you can select capable people. It's a problem when you have traitors in your own unit. Like Fikret Abdic [much laughing].*

Q: Does the General know the relationship between Milosevic and Tito?

A: *No, please tell me.*

Q: Tito had a mistress called Zdenka who died of TB aged twenty-seven on 1 May 1946. Her cousin Vera Militic had a daughter out of marriage by Moma Markovic (one of Tito's Partisan Commanders). The daughter was named Mirjana. Vera Militic was arrested by the Gestapo and tortured. She was released and immediately arrested by the Partisans, tried and executed. The baby was adopted by Zdenka's parents and grew up in a grace and favour house, gifted by Tito, in Pozarevac. This fifteenth-century house is still owned by Mirjana. It is Milosevic's country house now because Mirjana Markovic married Slobodan Milosevic. [The General then left the room and returned with some photographs of Fazilla Abdic. There were five in total and could be best described as family album shots. One photograph was her with a girlfriend both in bikinis on a beach and the others were of her at meals and functions. Two of the photos also included Fikret Abdic. The General then removed two books from his library shelf].

A: *These books are about tactics [but], nowhere does it tell you how to function tactically from a position where you will always be surrounded.*[2]

As Muslim and Croat politicians mounted a determined campaign to prevent the 'Santic Affair' turning into another blood bath, a commission was established to investigate the whole matter, and within a short time three members of the military police unit attached to the 502 Brigade were arrested and arraigned before Judge Fikret Hodzic in Bihac town.[3] This seemed to satisfy most people concerned but it made no attempt at all to explain why Santic was killed in the first place. The Mayor of Bihac certainly had no sympathy for him.

We found the bodies of two Serbs buried in Vedro Polje. These two Serbs were captured alive by the 501 Brigade during the liberation of Vedro Polje. At that time they were in the process of advancing to retake Zavalje. They handed the prisoners over personally to General Santic. He took them to HQ HVO and tortured them and shot one in front of the other to make the other one talk. The Serb who saw his friend shot to death said 'I will never tell you anything'. Santic immediately shot him dead. The bodies were then taken back to Vedro Polje and buried but not before Santic had personally hacked off their heads. . . . Are you surprised that such a man has many enemies? There were ten witnesses to this atrocity . . . I want to kill Serbs on the front line [too] but not like this. In half a year he went from a Corporal to a General. His rank was not recognized in Croatia or here.[4]

But ethnic savagery alone could never have justified Santic's liquidation. There had to be more to this story – and there was. Santic had been one of Franjo Tudjman's key personnel in Bosnia-Hercegovina and had been promoted from the rank of 'building contractor' to Croatian Army General by the Croatian President himself. In return for this elevation Santic had the responsibility for keeping the HVO out of direct hostilities with both the 5th Corps and Abdic until such time as Croatia had decided which way to jump. This was by no means an easy task as there were HVO encampments in both sections of the Pocket, and while supporting Dudakovic against the BSA was fine in the south, and even in line with Tudjman's overall military strategy, in the north his only option was to promote a line of strict neutrality and hope that everyone else left the HVO alone.

Santic never agreed to an incorporation of the Bihac HVO into the 5th Corps, when such a move would have made perfect strategic sense, because to have done so would have brought both him and his forces into Izetbegovic's chain of command and Zagreb would have lost its excuse to continue meddling in the affairs of the region. Equally, in relation to Abdic, the fact that the HVO never took up arms against the APWB suggests that Tudjman was not prepared to assist in the removal of this thorn from the side of the Bosnian President, and with Santic commuting regularly between Bihac, Zagreb and Velika Kladusa the suggestion emerged that his relationship with Abdic may have been far closer than had originally been suspected. The death of Santic may well have had more to do with sending a message to Tudjman to desist from interfering in the affairs of the region by continuing to offer covert support to the APWB, than any individual hatred or vendetta relating to Santic himself.

NOTES

1. HINA News: 10/3/95.
2. Team Bihac Special Report, Meeting with General Dudakovic: 12/3/95.
3. RC Belgrade Special Report: 4/2/95–20/3/95.
4. Team Bihac Daily Report: 24/3/95. Also contained in this daily report is an interesting insight into some of the risks that EU Monitors are prepared to take in order to find out what exactly is going on in remote areas. Bill Foxton's good humour disguises in large measure the actual dangers involved, 'Team patrolled to Grabez [Bosnian Serb Front Lines], left our vehicle, and patrolled on foot to collect wild flowers. Team patrolled as far as WK744644 and began to attract the unwelcome attentions of BSA. However, 5 Corps immediately retaliated with mortars and we were able to return to our vehicle at walking pace, after some undignified running.'

CHAPTER TWENTY

A New Military Alliance

One of the more dramatic developments in the overall scheme of things occurred in Zagreb on 6 March when the Chief of Staff for the Croatian army General Janko Bobetko, together with the HVO's General Tihomir Blaskic and the Armija's Supreme Commander Rasim Delic attended a meeting at the Presidential Palace, with Tudjman, Ganic and Zubak, and announced to the world's press that all three armies had entered into a formal military alliance and established for the first time a joint headquarters. The ink was barely dry on the paper before the Muslims began refuting Croatian assertions that there was now also a single chain of command, but whatever the reality the mere fact that it happened at all was hugely significant.

Bobetko would assume chairmanship of the Joint Command, whose objectives would include the development of closer links with one another in pursuance of the 'Washington Agreement' and 'The 1992 Agreement on Friendship and Co-operation between Croatia and Bosnia', as well as mutual self-defence against the threat of renewed aggression by the Serbs. Of equal importance was the fact that this announcement came hot on the heels of a number of rabble-rousing statements from both Gojko Susak, Croatia's Defence Minister, and Borislav Skegro, Croatia's Deputy Prime Minister, to the effect that Croatia was now ready militarily and economically to crush the Krajina Serbs once and for all. While all this was in some measure a response to the announcement two weeks previously in Banja Luka of a formal military and political arrangement between the Krajina and Bosnian Serbs, it was also designed to increase the pressure on Knin to reconsider the relative merits of the Z4 Plan. Clearly Tudjman had lost all respect for the international efforts trying to solve the problem by peaceful means, preferring now to rely on Croatia's new found friendship with the US and his belief that Clinton and his agents would come to his assistance whenever the going got tough. In all of this, however, one thing was certain. The marriage of convenience that was blessed in Zagreb's Presidential Palace on 6 March would prove to be *the* major turning point in the conflicts of both countries. Equally, the decision of both the US and Germany to permit and probably encourage it ensured that from now on not all parties to the conflict could expect to be treated equally either. The West, or rather those elements who called the shots economically and militarily, had finally decided who the 'good guys' were. The rest would have to live with the consequences of that decision.

A new German initiative was then launched almost immediately when Klaus Kinkel arrived in Belgrade hoping to convince Milosevic to recognize Croatia and thereby appease the Croats sufficiently to call off Tudjman's newly trained and up-gunned troops. Unsurprisingly Milosevic was not interested so Kinkel summoned Zubak and Ganic to Bonn on 8 March and the Contact Group began advocating a Summit Conference lest the situation prematurely detonate. But the mediation process had now become a farce and an ECMM report at the time vividly captured the confusion.

At present it appears that if the meeting [Summit] goes ahead the only invitees will be Milosevic, Tudjman and Izetbegovic, and therein lies the problem. According to UN Resolution 942 Bonn cannot invite Karadzic to political discussions unless Pale accepts the Contact Group Peace Plan. The Resolution does not prohibit UNPROFOR, UNHCR, ECMM or President Carter from having political talks in Pale but at the moment that is as far as it goes. The comparative success of the Carter Initiative was to bring Karadzic and Mladic on board and make them sign their names to the document. If the COHA breaks down, and the Serbs are responsible, then it is these two who must answer the difficult questions, not somebody who signed on their behalf. Making all the parties accountable for their actions is central to the resolution of the conflict but for as long as [one of] the main protagonists can hide behind their 'official representatives' they remain detached and can always blame someone other than themselves for the situation which they have created.

If any real progress is to be made the technical difficulties which currently prevent the International Community from dealing directly with Karadzic and Mladic must be overcome. With firing levels so low [across Bosnia] it is possible to say that the COHA is still holding, just! While a permanent cease-fire looks as far away as ever it must be said that the Carter Initiative definitely saved lives and has allowed political dialogue to develop. Sadly a new impetus is urgently needed if there is to be any meaningful extension of the COHA and it remains imperative that technical difficulties do not prevent Karadzic and Mladic from taking their [rightful?] place at the conference table.[1]

Meanwhile in Croatia confusion continued to reign in relation to UNPROFOR and whether its troops were staying or going. This uncertainty was compounded by reports from Knin that an internal power struggle had begun between the moderate Mikelic and the combined forces of Babic and Martic. Save for the relative success of reopening the Zagreb–Belgrade Highway through Sector West the Economic Agreement of 2 December was all but dead,[2] and the omens for the immediate future were anything but good. It was in this uncertain and volatile environment that another American mediator began operating, as he introduced a somewhat novel approach to the business of Balkan politics which he called 'knocking heads together'. Richard Holbrooke, the new US Assistant Secretary of State, who interestingly enough had spent the previous few years as the US Ambassador to Germany, had arrived to save the Balkans. After several rounds of discussion in Copenhagen, on 12 March Tudjman announced that the UN could stay for the time being, as long as a new mandate was worked out that physically placed UN troops on Croatia's internationally recognized borders with Bosnia-Hercegovina.

Tudjman then flew off to New York to talk all this through with Boutros Boutros-Ghali on 17 March and while attending the ceremony to mark the anniversary of the Washington Agreement, both President Clinton and Madeline Allbright were wholesome in their praise for Dr Tudjman's apparent U-turn. A White House communiqué went further and said that President Clinton had expressed his personal gratitude to Dr Tudjman and his admiration for Croatia's decision to accept the further presence of UN forces, thereby avoiding a possible renewal of the war and a widening of the conflict in the region.

Armed with this endorsement and whatever additional under-standings he had managed to extract in Washington Tudjman returned to Zagreb. He was immediately confronted with considerable dissatisfaction from elements within the Sabor, and also from the refugee and displaced population who were still crammed into every spare hotel room, private house, flat, bed-sit, apartment, camp site and guest house across the country.[3] As details of what had been agreed began to emerge it became clear that the main stumbling block had been ensuring that the word 'Croatia' was included in the UN mandate, as well as an agreement to reduce the size of the UN force, and the deployment of a civilian police force to monitor the twenty-five to thirty crossing points between the Krajina and Bosnia along the international border.[4]

All of this came as something of a shock to the Krajina Serbs who, although it was of direct relevance to them, were again the last to be informed. Not surprisingly they totally disagreed with these developments but this worried neither Tudjman, Holbrooke or Akashi as the major diplomatic initiative concentrated exclusively on appeasing the Croats. Eventually, after much haggling, some amendments were made to the report which Boutros Boutros-Ghali submitted to the Security Council on 26 March, and on the 31st there were three new resolutions, 981, 982 and 983, which established three separate but interlinked missions and extended their mandates to 30 November 1995.[5]

In Croatia there was now UNCRO: the United Nations Confidence Restoration Operation. In Bosnia there was still UNPROFOR while in the Former Yugoslav Republic of Macedonia (FYROM) there was UNPREDEP: United Nations Preventative Deployment. In actual fact nothing much was about to change at all and the contentious issues like the size of the force(s), and who exactly was going to sit on the international border would all be worked out later on. After a few days' silence Babic released a statement in Knin in which he specifically pointed to the absence of any 'confidence' between the citizens of the Krajina and Croatia, recalling that while both had been able to develop some confidence in one another in the post-Second World War period, he seriously doubted that anything of that nature could happen again. The Krajina Serbs' lack of confidence in their neighbours was what had caused them to resist Croatian rule in the first place, and from their perspective nothing had happened in the meantime which indicated that they would ever be treated as anything other than second or third-class citizens in a state dominated politically by Tudjman's HDZ and socially by the Catholic Church.[6]

While these reservations had no impact on the likes of Holbrooke, Galbraith or Stoltenberg, somewhat amazingly Babic found support from a totally unexpected quarter. On 3 April the Croatian Human Rights Committee issued a statement in which it claimed that ordinary Croats could only have 'confidence' in their own judicial system if all current members of the State Judicial Council and the President of the Supreme Court resigned from their positions because the method of their appointment had been illegal in the first instance. Apparently they had all been appointed by Prime Ministerial Decree, something which was not permissible by law, and this left the whole procedure open to the suggestion that they were appointed because of their political dependability and reliability as distinct from their individual or collective competence.[7] This particular story was actually covered by HINA News in Zagreb making it perfectly reasonable to suggest that quite a number of Croatians themselves had precious little confidence in the manner in which their country was being run by the HDZ. If one were to place what Babic was actually saying in that particular context, and read it in conjunction with the 'Charter on the Rights of Serbs and Other Nationalities in the Republic of Croatia', where Serbs in Croatia had already been singled out for special treatment, one might well have been able to understand his reservations when it came to the matter of a forced coexistence in one state, with Franjo Tudjman in charge of it. Unfortunately very few people were in any way interested in this particular perspective.

While the world focused on events in Croatia the general situation in Bosnia was deteriorating dramatically as each new day passed. UNHCR convoys continued to be denied access to the eastern enclaves of Zepa, Srebrenica and Gorazde, which in turn led to increased suffering by the population and generated even more correspondence between the Pale authorities and Akashi. Karadzic's letter on 5 March provides an unique insight into how the overall picture looked from the Serb perspective.

РЕПУБЛИКА СРПСКА
ПРЕДСЕДНИК РЕПУБЛИКЕ
САРАЈЕВО

REPUBLIC OF SRPSKA
PRESIDENT OF THE REPUBLIC
SARAJEVO

To: H.E. Yasushi Akashi, SRSG

5 March 1995

Excellency,

I am glad that you mention 'a major effort to effectively implement the 31 December 1994 Cessation of Hostilities Agreement'. But just how 'major' has this effort been on your part? Why have you not objectively and fully informed the Security Council and in particular the world media about the incessant breaches of the COHA by the Muslims? You know perfectly well, for example, that the Muslims are completely ignoring the Central Joint Commission, thereby undermining the entire Cessation of Hostilities Agreement. What pressure, if any, have you brought to bear on the Muslims in this crucial respect? And why is UNPROFOR pretending not to know anything about arms supplies to the Muslims via Tuzla airport? May we expect you to take urgent action over this matter in the Security Council? I am sorry to observe, Excellency, that UNPROFOR has not faced up to the real issues and problems concerning the implementation of the Cessation of Hostilities Agreement, and we are fed up with the double standards which the international community persistently maintains in this conflict.

We wish to pinpoint the major problems, to see who is responsible for those problems, and to find ways of resolving them. Clearly, the Muslims are hell-bent on shattering the COHA but we shall be generous: we shall give them several days, maybe ten, after which we shall expect them to start behaving in accordance with the letter and spirit of the COHA. If, thereafter, no significant progress is recorded, I am afraid that our patience will have run out. Moreover, Excellency, we shall hold UNPROFOR partly responsible for the calamity that is bound to ensue if the Muslims do not abandon their obstructionist policy.

Believe me to be,
Yours sincerely,

Dr Radovan Karadzic
President, Republic of Srpska

On the military front the situation was bleak and best summarized by the fact that when Akashi went to Sarajevo on 12 March in an attempt to keep the COHA on the rails the plane in which he was travelling was fired upon as it landed, leaving a rather large hole in the rear section of the fuselage. The Serbs were immediately blamed for the attack but it later emerged, and was confirmed separately by Greek EU Monitors on the ground, that the shots were fired from Butimir – a Bosnian Muslim [government] controlled area. Akashi first met Izetbegovic and then went on to Pale the following day to see Karadzic but little was achieved, with both sides doing little more than continuing to hurl abuse at one another.

NOTES

1. ECMM WIAS, no. 118, 10/3/96, para. 10/Assessment.
2. It should be pointed out that the Krajina Serbs were not exclusively to blame for this state of affairs. In relation specifically to the reopening of the Obrovac power station in the Krajina it had been agreed that the Croats would provide the necessary new parts to enable the resumption of some production and thereafter the plant would be linked into the overall Croatian electricity grid from which both communities could benefit. However, there being little or no electricity available in the Krajina at this time, the Croats understood very well the value of the parts in question and began to use them as an additional bargaining tool in the overall negotiations. This was wrong, it was contrary to both the letter and spirit of the Economic Agreement, and the longer the containers remained stationary in Zagreb airport the more frustrated the Serb authorities in Knin became. Viewed from this perspective it becomes a lot easier to understand why neither Martic or Babic wanted anything to do with Croatians pretending to bear gifts!
3. Total number of registered displaced persons/refugees in Croatia on 12/1/95 = 383,039. Another 56,887 Croats had relocated themselves to other countries with over half of this figure now resident in Germany. (Source: Croatian Government official figures.)
4. WIAS 119: 17/3/95.
5. UNPF Chronology of Events, p. 34.
6. WIAS 122: 6/4/95, para. 5.
7. WIAS 122: 6/4/95 and HINA News: 6/4/95.

CHAPTER TWENTY-ONE

A Muslim Offensive
Shatters the COHA

With Zubak and Ganic celebrating the anniversary of the Washington
Agreement with Tudjman and Clinton in the United States, Izetbegovic
next travelled to Bonn where he made the most amazing statements. He
began by effectively advocating renewed conflict as the only means to
solve the problems in Bosnia. 'If the Serbs do not accept the Contact
Group Peace Plan,' he announced, 'then we must fight, we have no other
choice.' The very next day he apparently decided to revoke this statement
and declared that the Muslims would not launch an offensive against the
Serbs, even if the Serbs failed to accept the CGPP by the time the COHA
expired at the end of April. 'We will not start an offensive on 1 May but
we will not agree formally to extend the cease-fire,' he confidently told
reporters. He concluded by saying that his motto still remained, 'when it
is a question of war or peace we will negotiate when we can, and fight
when we must'. The problem now was which version to believe – but it
did not take long to find out.

As UNMOs and Monitors on the ground across Bosnia plotted and
reported the redeployment of thousands of Armija troops, it was clear to
even the most ill-informed observers that something was about to
happen. And it did. At 0500 hrs on the morning of 20 March Bosnian
government troops launched a huge offensive in north-central Bosnia in
an area known as the Majevica Hills. Beginning with an infantry attack
and supported by artillery and mortar fire, the government forces set
about trying to change the configuration of the confrontation line in
order to take Tuzla out of Serb artillery range. It did not work and two
hours later Serb shells began raining in on Tuzla town. As the morning
wore on the attack began to peter out, helped no doubt by some very
heavy snow falls, and during the next two days both sides settled into a
pattern of minor skirmishing and reciprocal shelling.

At precisely the same time that morning a second attack was also
launched by Izetbegovic's troops in the area of Vlasic Mountain. Again
the objective was to shift the confrontation line sufficiently to take Zenica
and Travnik outside the range of Bosnian Serb artillery, but this proved
too ambitious and before long Serb shells were crashing down on Travnik

too. By Wednesday this assault had evaporated and the Muslims were left licking their wounds, with precious little to show for their efforts. Attacking uphill against well-prepared defensive positions is difficult enough at the best of times but attempting it in daylight and in heavy snow surely bordered on the suicidal. If the Muslims were seeking to record a psychological victory of some description there were several easier targets which they could have opted for without suffering as many casualties as they did. Clearly the Bosnian government had now adopted a dual approach to the ongoing situation, but there appeared to be no co-relation at all between the international face of Bosnian politics and the military activity of Izetbegovic's generals on the ground. Either the military commanders were acting independently, which was highly unlikely, or the recent political statements were designed for international consumption only and a hidden agenda was in operation with which all of the key personnel were familiar.

These attacks were a clear, unambiguous and deliberate breach of the COHA and the International Community should have immediately condemned the Sarajevo government for them. This did not happen, and the absence of any formal rebuke effectively gave a clear signal to the Muslims to carry on. Worse still it then emerged that Generals Bobetko, Delic and Blaskic were all in Travnik at that time and coordinating what had now become combined HV, HVO and Armija operations against the Serbs. Bobetko then appeared on TV explaining what a great job they were all doing, and while this provided clear unequivocal evidence that both Tudjman and Izetbegovic were willing conspirators in breaching the COHA, not a single reprimand was forthcoming from the International Community.[1]

In the context of everything else that subsequently happened in 1995 it is vital, if not in fact critical, to understand that it was the Muslims and *not* the Serbs who bore the responsibility for shattering the comparative peace which Karadzic and Carter had managed to cobble together less than three months previously. The Muslims had never wanted to be part of it in the first place and their behaviour in relation to the presence of BSA liasion officers in Tuzla and Gornji Vakuf typified their overall approach. An example of the Muslim attitude is illustrated by the findings of an ECMM team who visited the town of Bugojno in central Bosnia in February 1995. The entire place had the appearance of an armed encampment as hundreds of Armija troops thronged the dirty battle-scarred town. There was no evidence that anyone was preparing for peace or even making any attempt to harmonize relations with the local Croat minority.[2] Instead there was only overwhelming evidence of military preparation for the next phase of the war, an integral part of which had involved the desecration and demolition of the Partisan graveyard in the centre of the town where

Serbs, Croats and Muslims had previously all been allowed to rest in peace together.[3] Even the dead had become targets for Izetbegovic's troops as they psyched themselves up for the next battle and the local SDA Mayor in the town, Dzeved Mlaco, went right along with them. From the Muslim perspective the COHA was just an opportunity to re-group and re-arm – nothing more, nothing less.

As the days began to stretch into weeks the Armija continued their attacks with unconfirmed reports suggesting that the Stolice communications relay tower, north-east of Tuzla, had been captured from the Serbs. However, apart from other small gains around Lukavica, there was nothing to indicate that any major changes to the confrontation line had actually taken place. In the Travnik/Vlasic Mountain area shelling continued unrelentingly as the Armija continued to press home their First World War style frontal attacks but this time the line was moving significantly, with the Serbs vacating anything up to 60 square km. In retaliation the Serbs shelled Konjic on 24–5 March as well as the supposedly 'safe area' of the Gorazde, and locations to the north and east of Mostar, causing civilian casualties in all three areas. Then, to confuse matters even further, it emerged that a meeting had taken place between President Milosevic and Muhamed Filipovic, Izetbegovic's special envoy,[4] where it was apparently agreed that in return for Belgrade's recognition of Bosnia's territorial integrity and sovereignty, and promotion of the principles in the Contact Group Peace Plan. The Sarajevo government would be prepared to agree to the abolition of economic sanctions, and permit closer economic links between the Republic Srpska and Serbia/Montenegro in a similar manner to the proposed monetary and customs union between the Federation and Croatia.

The Croatian media immediately began speculating that yet another 'secret agreement' had been concluded, this time between Milosevic and Izetbegovic, which would result in mutual recognition and the acceptance of a 'special status' for the Bosnian Serbs. While there is little doubt that the meeting took place it is highly unlikely that any deal of this nature was actually agreed. A more realistic interpretation would suggest that this was yet another double-cross by Milosevic who was solely interested in putting further pressure on Karadzic to accept the CGPP, which in turn would facilitate the lifting of sanctions against both Serbia and Montenegro. The only positive aspect of the meeting was not that anything had been agreed, because in reality nothing had, but rather the fact that for the first time in years Serbs and Muslims had actually managed to sit down together in the same room and talk to one another. It wasn't much progress but at least it was a start.

Meanwhile Yasushi Akashi spoke of his grave concern that the parties appeared determined to plunge Bosnia into a new war, with incalculable consequences for the region as a whole. The offensive actions of the

Armija, he said, were a clear breach of the COHA and the retaliatory actions of BSA had contributed to an escalation of violence that was rapidly getting out of control. Eventually he singled out the Bosnian government for their lack of cooperation in implementing the provisions of the COHA, and appealed for restraint as renewed diplomatic efforts got under way. The German Foreign Minister Klaus Kinkel finally spoke out and publicly reminded Izetbegovic that it was he who had endorsed a peaceful resolution of the conflict during his recent visit to Bonn and that he was now in breach of that endorsement.

All of this fell on deaf ears and at the 7th Session of the SDA's Main Board in Sarajevo on 27 March it became clear just where Izetbegovic and his followers were coming from and, even more importantly, where they thought they were going to. It transpired that they were under the impression that they were conducting a diplomatic offensive abroad and a simultaneous military counter-offensive at home. Conveniently oblivious to the fact that it was the Muslims themselves who had initiated the recent round of barbarity, Izetbegovic's address makes very interesting reading.[5]

> The current situation in Bosnia-Hercegovina is characterized by a diplomatic offensive and our military counter-offensive. Our aim remains an integral democratic BiH. A federal organization is possible and desirable, but as a federation of cantons and not national territories. The latter would engender a further tendency of ethnic cleansing. . . . Our aim is a democratic state, a multi-national and multi-party one. This commitment gives to our political model a striking advantage over the obviously retrograde one-nation, one-religious, one-party concept of Karadzic's SDS or Boban's HVO. Our democratic concept is a condition for our political and also military victory in this war. Without this concept there is no integral Bosnia. . . . Unacceptable are the requests for us to return in kind everything to the enemy. Why? The first reason and difference is of principle nature: we are Democrats, they are Fascists. The second difference is that they want a tearing apart of Bosnia, they ask for themselves one part of such a broken Bosnia, and we want an integral Bosnia within its internationally recognized boundaries. Such a Bosnia is only possible as a democratic state. . . . We cannot have our objective and their political philosophy. . . . When it comes to war and peace, we will continue sticking to our motto: to negotiate wherever we can, to wage war where we have to. . . . When it comes to the military point of view, there is a different situation depending on whether we have only Karadzic's forces against us, or we have Karadzic's forces and Serbia, or we have Karadzic's forces, Serbia and Russia. These are the three options which are possible. . . . One should bear in mind that

Milosevic has probably cut off his relationship with the political leadership of the Bosnian Serbs, that is with Karadzic, but not with the military structure . . . Milosevic may give up on Karadzic, but, by doing so, he does not necessarily give up the idea of the Greater Serbia. The two need not be linked. One should be cautious and distinguish between the two.

We will not consent to an extension of the cease-fire, for an extension of the cease-fire legalizes the occupation of the country. We will not, of course, accept it unless the Serb side in the meantime accept the CG Plan in the course of April, or an acceptable political settlement is offered. . . . If the West want peace in the Balkans, we wish it success, but it cannot achieve that to our detriment. This requires the following as a minimum: we ask for two things, for the Bosnian Serbs to accept the CG Plan, and for Milosevic to recognize BiH. These are the minimum conditions if they want peace talks. . . . If the international community for any reasons does not succeed [in these areas] we will ask from all our friends in the world to help us in realizing our right to self-defence, in which the lifting of the arms embargo is the most important measure. . . . The arms embargo against BiH is legally and morally untenable. Legally because it is contrary to the right to self-defence which is a natural right and explicitly recognized by article 51 of the UN charter. It is practically untenable because it maintains the existing unbalance in arms by which the war is extended. Finally the embargo is immoral because it is for the benefit of the one who attacks and to the detriment of the victim.

In the end I would only say that this is a difficult and glorious age of Bosnia. Difficulties are enormous but chances are greater than they have ever been in the history. We believe that light will win a victory over darkness, and life over death.[6]

Haris Silajdzic in his address to the same meeting alleged that more than 70,000 Muslims had fled the area of Sandzak which straddles the border between Serbia and Montenegro within the past year as a result of Serbian persecution. This was a total exaggeration on the Prime Minister's part but such rhetoric virtually ensured that the proposed 'Declaration on the Violation of Human Rights and Freedoms of Bosniac Muslims in Sandzak and other parts of Serbia and Montenegro' would be accepted by a large majority.[7] The deliberate reintroduction of the Sandzak issue and the attempt to label those who lived there as 'Bosniacs' defied logic unless the Muslims now believed that either they were sufficiently well armed to take the fight to the Serbs, or they knew the United States and Germany were about to enter the equation on their side – or both. Certainly most independent observers were baffled at the arrogance of their new positions when there did not appear to be anything there to back it up. In a confidential report to all EU Foreign Ministers, ECMM HQ in Zagreb identified that the Sarajevo government had now begun using the Armija as a political tool and the prospects for the immediate future were considered to be anything but good.

> The offensive actions launched by the Armija before the period of the COHA had expired demonstrates, and represents, a more robust posture from the Muslim politicians. Therefore having previously been seen as the compliant party with regard to International Community initiatives, this position has now been challenged. The reasons given for the abandonment of the COHA, i.e., non compliance [by the Serbs] in Bihac; are less important than the fact that the politicians were confident enough to breach it [in the first place] and face the consequences of International Community condemnation [if it materialized]. . . . The prosecution of diplomatic ends by military means is obviously enhanced by an army capable of applying effective pressure. Previously the immaturity of the Armija, and the distraction of the war with the Croats, had placed a limit on its usefulness as a political tool. Two factors have altered this: the Washington Agreement, which has allowed the Armija to focus on their primary aim of regaining territory from the BSA, and [secondly] the development of the Armija with regard to weapons, training, and organization. . . . With Muslim politicians using the Armija to signal its frustration with the International Community, a degradation of relations might be expected. There are tangible indications that UNPROFOR relations with the Sarajevo government are becoming increasingly difficult, the tone of whose attitude was recently set by General Rasim Delic when he described UNPROFOR as 'a stone around his neck'.[8]

NOTES

1. UN SRSG Weekly Situation Report: 5/4/95.
2. ECMM Special Report, 'No Surrender – No Compromise': 24/2/95.
3. UN G2, Sector SW, Special Report: 19/2/95.
4. UN SRSG Weekly Situation Report: 5/4/95.
5. I once accused Dzeved Mlaco, the SDA Mayor in Bugojno, of operating on the basis of 'no surrender and no compromise'. Clearly he learned that particular philosophy from Izetbegovic.
6. Izetbegovic's address to the 7th Session of the SDA's Main Board in Sarajevo, 23/3/95.
7. ECMM WIAS, no. 122: 6/4/95.
8. ECMM Coyug 1/1 April 1995: 'Use of Armija for Political Ends'.

CHAPTER TWENTY-TWO

Political Unification of the Krajina and Bosnian Serbs

Across the border in Croatia trouble was now brewing on a number of fronts with the Krajina Serb leadership apparently split down the middle on how far they should trust the Croatian government. On 2 March twenty delegates to the Krajina's Assembly tabled a motion of 'no confidence' in Prime Minister Mikelic. This was followed abruptly by a public denunciation of Mikelic by Milan Martic who also called for his dismissal on the grounds of incompetence and corruption. Mikelic, one-time friend of Fikret Abdic and the current advocate of closer links with Croatia proper, then began his own defence by launching a stinging attack on Martic, claiming that it was he who had been the responsible minister during the Krajina's worst period of lawlessness. This apparently did the trick because when the Assembly reconvened six days later Mikelic survived by thirty-seven votes to twenty-five, thanks to an amazing U-turn by the Serbian Radical Party, who, notwithstanding the fact that it was they who had called for the vote in the first place, now walked out of the Assembly before the vote was taken.

Secure for a while longer, Mikelic set about removing those he considered to be a direct threat to him within the administration, but ironically the net result of his purge turned out to be a strengthening of Foreign Minister Babic's position. Whatever Mikelic chose to do the best he could hope for was to generate a situation where Babic and Martic would begin fighting between themselves. In that scenario it was just conceivable that he might survive politically but if a crisis should develop then it became an absolute certainty that he would be identified as the 'voice of Milosevic' and thereafter sidelined as the other two united to oppose him. In this scenario his future tenure would be a short one,[1] and an issue which could put all of this to the test was now looming on the horizon. On 21 April Boutros Boutros-Ghali was due to publish his report that would attempt to reconcile both sides in relation to UNSC Res. 981 and at the same time confirm the ongoing presence of the UN in the Krajina. In reality it would matter little what he proposed because one of the parties involved was virtually guaranteed to find fault with some part of the plan.

Tension began to grow in anticipation of what the Secretary General might propose, and one aspect of this was the appearance of articles in Western newspapers claiming that Croatia would only accept 'White Battalions' in whatever force the UN decided to replace UNPROFOR with. This was immediately refuted by the Croatian government and on 13 April the Foreign Ministry vehemently denied accusations that Croatia had ever expressed racist or chauvinist attitudes towards members of UN forces from Asia and Africa. Their only objection to the UN operation, which had been repeatedly mentioned by the Croatian government, was related to the ineffectiveness of the UN Forces through their inability to perform their tasks according to the [UN] Resolutions. 'The Republic of Croatia repeats that there has not been any manifestation of racism in State policy or among the Croatian people. This can be testified to by many UN officials and members of international organizations operating in the territory of the Republic of Croatia. These members have always been dear guests to whom the Croatian state gave all the possible assistance in the performance of their duties.' While the denial may well have been emphatic not everyone was convinced and an ECMM report on 20 April threw a totally different light on the matter.

> Non-European units of the UN contingent in Croatia have repeatedly been targeted in the Croatian government-controlled media as being 'lazy, incompetent and stupid'. The hostile attitude of the Displaced Persons during the blockade of the crossings to UN units in the summer of last year, as well as the insensitive and often brutal behaviour of Croatian government officials and soldiers towards UN peace-keepers, makes it hard to believe that while these may not have been expressions of chauvinism, they are certainly not acts of a host towards 'dear guests'. If Croatia had planned to influence the composition of UN personnel, then the publication of the REUTERS story in Western media has made it void. Even the late denial of the Ministry of Foreign Affairs will not help to repair the political damage for Croatia.[2]

Seemingly undeterred by all this bad press Croatia's Foreign Minister Mate Granic continued to lobby the UN to ensure that the end product turned out to be acceptable to him. The key issue remained an insistence by the Croats that UN troops be deployed along the international border with Bosnia and thereby physically confirm to the world the sovereignty and territorial integrity of Croatia. Bearing in mind that all of these aspirations had been contained in previous UN Resolutions it became very difficult to envisage how UN Res. 981 was now going to be effective, given that the Serbs were unlikely to cooperate. When one then took account of the fact that under the new resolution UNCRO would actually have less troops available to perform these tasks than had previously been the case with UNPROFOR, and that the Croatian army was adopting threatening postures all along the separation zone, it quickly became apparent that for all the political debate that was supposedly taking place the prospect of anything concrete emerging was nil. In his analysis of the situation on 20 April ECMM's Jochen Kramb proved himself to be one of the most perceptive Balkan commentators and he got it absolutely right. 'However, should the implementation plan be completely unfavourable for Croatia one could expect HV [Croatian Army] to move into Sector West [thereby] demonstrating that Croatia is not willing to accept every decision of the UN Security Council [which is] contrary to her policy.'[3]

While the Croats continued their public campaign to influence the Secretary General's report, the Krajina Serbs, in anticipation of being sold out by the International Community, sent a delegation to the fiftieth session of the Bosnian Serb's Assembly which, conveniently enough, was taking place just across the border in Sanski Most between 15 and 17 April. It quickly became clear that this was no ordinary meeting when Milan Martic turned up, accompanied by the leaders of both the Krajina army and church. On the Bosnian Serb side Karadzic presided over the entire proceedings with General Mladic also in attendance, as indeed were the leaders of the Serbian Orthodox church.

On the outset Karadzic launched into a blistering attack on Mladic for his failure to hold the line against both the Muslims and Croats in recent weeks,[4] and some initial reports suggested that Karadzic had actually tried to relieve him of his command.[5] In reply Mladic attempted to shift the blame to the political authorities for failing to supply him with much-needed fuel and equipment and proclaimed that the continuing rift between Belgrade and Pale was the greatest tragedy for all Serbs. He then delivered a very pessimistic prediction for the future admitting that in his opinion the BSA did not have the capability to achieve an overall military victory, nor could they count on retaining indefinite control over 70 per cent of Bosnia. At the end of a very bitter debate Mladic demanded that the politicians establish optimal war goals so that his soldiers would at least know what objectives they were dying for.

This was not well received by the politicians, and for many it looked as if the ghost of the 49/51 division of Bosnia was now being advocated by their own military supremo. If that were the case, and it is not beyond the bounds of possibility that Mladic may well have been delivering this specific message on behalf of Milosevic, the members of parliament were not prepared to entertain him. Their problem now was that they could no longer trust their top general, or the advice he was offering, and all of this seemed to vindicate the attempts made by Karadzic at Prijedor on 14 March to curtail his power and influence. To compound matters further it then emerged that Mladic had recently been having regular meetings in Zvornik with General Perisic, Milosevic's obedient JNA Chief of Staff, and had also been making regular visits to Belgrade[6] – as indeed had several of his top commanders. Mladic was *not* operating on the same wavelength as Karadzic but there did not appear to be any obvious or immediate solution to the problem. Irrespective of what agenda Mladic was really following the Bosnian Serbs still needed him and his army to protect them from massive retribution on several fronts. For all the wrong reasons he was allowed to remain in power. As the meeting continued Karadzic's contempt for his general became even more evident and eventually the Assembly voted that Mladic should begin to push for a final military victory if an overall political solution were not reached within a short time.

The delegates next turned to the more volatile matter of uniting the military and political resources of both the Bosnian and Krajina Serbs, and after the required debate they agreed to begin a unification process almost at once. If this arrangement became a fait accompli it would in all probability be far easier for both groups of Serbs to consolidate their current positions, and this was bad news for a large number of people. It was certainly not good for the Croatian government, who immediately recognized that any attack by them into the Krajina might now bring the Bosnian Serbs down on top of them as well. It was even worse news for Bosnia's Croats and Muslims who were now set on a course to try and take back whatever land they could grab in central Bosnia, and it was particularly bad news for the international mediators who condemned the new alliance as a further obstacle to an overall settlement. What none of these people made any attempt to understand was *why* the Serbs had found it necessary to band themselves together in this manner in the first place. No one had made any attempt to see the situation from the Serb perspective because had they done so they would immediately have recognized that the Serbs genuinely believed their backs were to the wall, and that the whole world was set against them. And there were compelling reasons for harbouring these beliefs.

In Croatia President Tudjman and his government had become completely indifferent to and intolerant of the genuine fears and aspirations of the Krajina Serbs. They got away with this because neither the United States or Germany were prepared to put a stop to it, and were now in any case aligned with the Croats in pursuit of their own long-term objectives in the region. The UN organization on the ground had become totally impotent and served only as a target for mockery and ridicule, and the occasional bored sniper in and around Sarajevo. Karadzic's attempts to stabilize the situation in Bosnia continued to be rubbished and the relative success of the Carter Initiative received no recognition from anyone. The BSA were not the ones who broke the COHA, and they were not the ones in daily violation of what remained of it, but the Bosnian Serbs, both militarily and politically, continued to be painted as the villains. In this scenario it mattered little what Martic, Karadzic or any other Serb politician tried to say or do, and they were all acutely aware of this. They decided to band together in what really amounted to nothing more than a measure of mutual self-defence, but the world condemned them for it.

Karadzic was again accused of promoting the notion of 'Greater Serbia' when nothing of the sort was the case but it suited other bigger agendas to tout that particular line. In this context the UN too bore some responsibility because Akashi knew the real story, and in writing to Kofi Annan on 26 April he identified clearly what had really been going on in Sanski Most.

> Reports from the session indicate a serious rift having developed between the military and political leaderships in Pale, aggravated by the ongoing economic blockade and the struggle for limited financial and material resources. It would appear that Karadzic and the Bosnian Serb political establishment face the prospect of a further erosion of authority; a process tacitly encouraged by Milosevic. The meeting between Milosevic and Mladic in Belgrade on 21 April, which was allegedly convened without Karadzic's knowledge, would support that contention. It is therefore likely that Karadzic will mobilize his own political support to counter the machinations of the military.[7]

Later in the same document Akashi identified that those aligned in opposition to Karadzic had been meeting secretly in Belgrade and now included Milosevic, Mikelic, *Fikret Abdic* and Mladic,[8] so it can hardly have come as a great surprise to anyone that Karadzic, Martic and Babic decided to join forces to ward off the potential threat that a military alliance of that quartet would pose. But this was never explained properly in the media and before long it became quite clear that the West had abandoned its neutrality. Bearing all of this in mind it was hardly any wonder that when Karadzic went with Mladic to tour the front line near Vlasic Mountain at the conclusion of the Assembly meeting, he confidently announced to the press that he was addressing them as the Supreme Commander of the Serb forces, and that since the Muslims had opted for war, 'things will be the way war brings them; it will be a war to the end, the end of the Muslim army'.

This vain attempt to reassert his authority – because essentially that's all it was – also went down very badly with the Western media who, deliberately or otherwise, chose to misinterpret him and then proceeded to compound matters further by conveniently ignoring the fact that huge numbers of the Croatian army were actually fighting their way up the

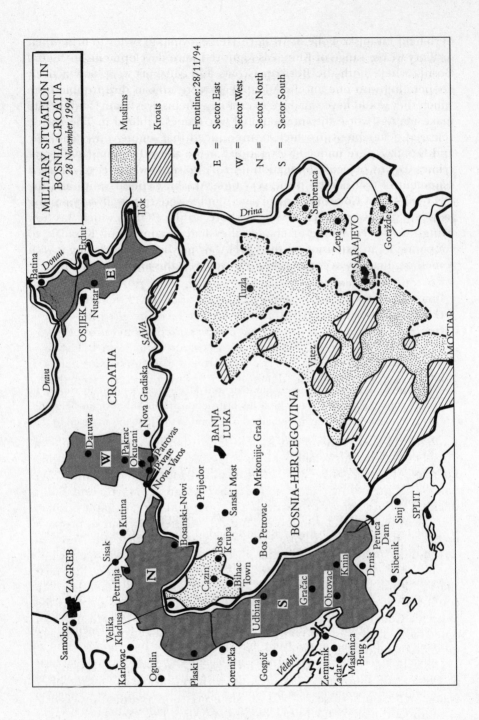

MILITARY SITUATION IN BOSNIA-CROATIA
28 November 1994

Muslims

Kroats

Frontline: 28/11/94

E = Sector East
W = Sector West
N = Sector North
S = Sector South

Serb-held Livanjsko Polje in Western Herzegovina, in order to bring their artillery within range of Knin. Also ignored were developments in central Bosnia where both the Bosnian Croats and Muslims were now actively cooperating with one another. The Serbs were now in dire trouble from which they would never manage to extricate themselves again[9] and then to make matters worse the international war crimes tribunal in The Hague released a statement in which it announced that among others, Mladic and Karadzic were under investigation for the alleged commission of war crimes. By any objective evaluation it made no sense whatever to release a statement of that nature at the very time Akashi, General Smith and the UN Civil Affairs Co-ordinator Enrique Aguilar were frantically commuting between Sarajevo and Pale trying to shore up the COHA, which was now dying on its feet. Whatever chance they had of convincing Karadzic to cooperate in an extension of the COHA, or maybe even replacing it with something better, was completely destroyed with this announcement.

NOTES

1. RC Knin, Special Report: 21/3/95.
2. ECMM/WIAS: 20/4/95.
3. ECMM/WIAS, no. 124, 20/4/95, para. 5.
4. The ongoing dispute between Karadzic and Mladic was continually rooted in suspicions that Mladic was taking his instructions from Milosevic in Belgrade. This was largely because he remained a general in the JNA and was paid in that capacity from Belgrade, as indeed were several of his subordinate commanders.
5. RC Belgrade, Special Report: 24/4/95.
6. Ibid. Mladic made two visits to Belgrade in April 1995, neither of which were authorized by Karadzic.
7. UN SRSG, Weekly Report: 26/4/95.
8. Also reported in Nasa Borba and VIP News in Belgrade: 24/4/95.
9. The level of distrust between Karadzic and Mladic had by this point become so bad that the police, who had always been completely loyal to Karadzic, were now reorganized along military lines and those whose loyalty was considered suspect found themselves 'cleansed' in the process. A popular story at the time suggested that the police had effectively been turned into a 'praetorian guard' to protect Karadzic *from* Mladic, and while no doubt this became one of their functions, special police units of up to 700 men actually ended up fighting on the front line around Stolice Tower in March in an attempt to halt the Muslim advance in that area. One can surmise that these units were thrown into the line because Mladic was either unable or unwilling to commit his own personnel to the battle, and this goes a long way to explain why Karadzic attempted to bring Mladic to heel first at the assembly meeting in Prijedor, and later again in Sanski Most.

CHAPTER TWENTY-THREE

The Croatian Army
Invades Sector West

Back in Croatia toleration of any Serbs, be they Krajina or Bosnian, had once again hit an all time low after Dubrovnik airport was shelled on 19 April. What made this attack different to previous ones, however, was that it took place at the very moment Croatian Prime Minister Valentic, two of his cabinet colleagues, the British, American and French military attaches, the local ECMM team, and a throng of media personnel were actually lined up on the tarmac for the official reopening of the airport. As they were about to begin the ceremony a 122-mm mortar shell came whistling through the air and impacted near some parked aircraft about 200 m from the terminal building. Undeterred the ceremony continued amid the singing of patriotic Croatian songs and Valentic eventually declared the airport open.[1] The significance of the interruption was lost on no one and merely confirmed to the Ministers present that it was a matter of urgency to dissuade the Serbs from continuing with this policy.

One way of frustrating the Serbs was to make it almost impossible for them to travel along the Highway between Sectors East and West, even though the Economic Agreement expressly permitted them to do just that. Almost immediately the Croatian police began taking several hours to clear each individual Serb vehicle through their checkpoints. Technically the Croats were still permitting the Serbs freedom of movement along the road. The problem was actually getting access to it, and before long huge tailbacks developed on the Serb sides which made a mockery of the whole process. This was a calculated provocation by the Croats, designed to achieve nothing except a further deterioration of relations between the two sides, in the expectation that some incident might occur which would provide President Tudjman with an excuse to send his army across the confrontation line.

By Monday 24 April Milan Martic had almost given them that excuse. Speaking on Radio Knin the previous evening he said that he was tired of writing warning letters to Boutros Boutros-Ghali and other officials in charge of the negotiating process. 'Since we cannot bring our fuel to the Krajina, or any other material, I have informed the UN that I have ordered the highway to be closed for twenty-four hours commencing on

24 April [at] 0600 hrs. If this measure does not improve the situation then the RSK leadership will decide on the suspension of the economic relations with Croatia, because we do not want the RSK to be underestimated.' And indeed Martic had a point because on Saturday about 400 Serb cars had been lined up queuing for petrol at the Croat service station in Nova Gradiska but were unable to buy any fuel.[2] Then, on Sunday, about seventy Serb trucks on the highway at the Lipovac crossing point in Sector East were left waiting for clearance to travel onwards as the Croatian police began implementing a 'go slow' policy, which essentially frustrated the whole agreement.

The Croatian response was totally predictable and a government statement was issued immediately to the effect that the Serbs had 'permanently' closed the road. No mention was made of the fact that the closure was only to have effect for twenty-four hours, nor was any explanation given of the Serbs' reasons for taking this action in the first place.[3]

Both sides had now raised the stakes considerably and it was in this context that on the morning of 24 April, Martic found himself chairing a session of his Supreme Defence Council that had to address, among other things, the matter of whether or not the Krajina Serbs could live with the terms of the latest offering from the UN Security Council, namely Resolution 988. After prolonged discussion they concluded that UN Peace Forces, whatever they were actually called, should continue to be stationed in Krajina in pursuance of the Vance Plan (1992), the Cease-fire Agreement of the 29th March, and the Economic Agreement of 2 December 1994. While the name 'UNCRO' was totally unacceptable the Knin government remained nonetheless ready to cooperate with the UN to find a peaceful solution but only for as long as the UN was prepared to continue treating the Republic Srpska Krajina as a state of the Serbian nation. With that out of the way, Martic, Babic and Mikelic then met with the ICFY co-chairman, Thorvald Stoltenberg, who had just arrived in Knin to discuss the matter of reopening the Highway.[4] No doubt the four of them were very impressed by the 'diplomatic' and conciliatory statement issued that afternoon by Hrnjvo Sarinic on behalf of President Tudjman which said, 'If the Serbs do not open the highway at 0600 hrs on Tuesday, the Croatian police will do it for them'.

In any event logic finally prevailed in Knin and at 0500 hrs the following morning the barriers on both sides of the dual carriageway were removed. At the subsequent press conference Martic denied that he had capitulated in the face of the Croatian ultimatum, preferring instead to make another attempt at explaining why he had closed the road in the first place. In a rare conciliatory gesture he concluded by saying, 'we will stop the Economic Agreement completely if Croatia blocks the highway [but] on the other hand, if the situation improves, we will develop our relations with Croatia'.[5] What he did not know, and Stoltenberg did not mention either, was that the Croats had already decided how the matter of the Highway was going to be resolved and their preparations were already well under way. For weeks the Croats had been moving personnel, tanks, artillery, mortars, communications equipment and a plethora of other hardware into positions all around Sector West, allowing them to mount an offensive on the UNPA if and when they got the green light from Zagreb. They had also taken a series of measures to defend themselves from any Bosnian Serb incursion from across the Sava river which might materialize in support of the 18th Krajina Serb Corps in Okucani. And this was not done secretly. Everyone operating in the area was completely aware of what was going on and to his credit Henrik Markus, who was now operating as ECMM's Liaison Officer at the UN's Sector West HQ in Daruvar, sent a detailed report to ECMM HQ on 24 April in which he catalogued exactly what was happening, down to the number of troops involved, where they were deployed, what they were actually doing, and the number of tanks and guns deployed in support of them. 'The HV [Croatian Army] seems to be ready to take the northern part of the UNPA at any time,' he wrote. 'The overall picture of HV deployment shows the UNPA is completely surrounded from the east, west and north. The biggest strength is located exactly at Pivare for obvious reasons: to avoid [prevent] any reinforcements from the BSA side.'[6]

With Croatian activity as blatant as this the question arises as to why no international pressure of any kind was applied to encourage them to stop. The answer to that is very simple, nobody wanted them to stop and the prevailing strategy demanded that the Serbs receive a bloody nose, and the sooner the better. The problem now was that Martic had taken the wind out of all their sails by backing down so another pretext would have to be found before the serious action could begin. And as luck would have it the Highway provided that opportunity once again.

On the evening of 28 April an incident took place at the INA petrol station on the Nova Gradiska side of Sector West which caused an already tense situation to escalate out of all proportion. A fracas broke out when a Croat called Sugic claimed to have identified a Serb called Blagijevic, whom he immediately accused of killing his brother at some point during 1991. Sugic then produced a knife and stabbed the Serb to death. The Croatian police arrested Sugic and took both him and the corpse away, but when they refused to release Blagijevic's remains to his family for burial his brother hijacked two Croatian vehicles (which were travelling along the road at 2140 hrs) in an attempt to force the Croatian police to comply with his family's wishes. They ignored him completely, apparently oblivious to the growing tension. Later, at 2230 hrs, someone opened fire on a white VW Golf as it passed through Sector West and one of the occupants received two bullets in the head. A minibus travelling immediately behind crashed in the confusion and one passenger died instantly, having been crushed beneath the vehicle, while a second died on the way to hospital. The five who were unhurt were taken away for questioning, this time by the Serbs. At 2230 hrs UNCIVPOL then decided that it had now become too dangerous to carry out patrols so at midnight the Highway was officially closed again, although several people decided to ignore this development and drove up and down it regardless.

By 0700 hrs the following morning ECMM, UNCIVPOL and UN Civil Affairs were all actively involved in trying to bring both sides together and were eventually rewarded for their efforts when at 1215 hrs the Croatian police and Serb authorities sat down together to iron out their differences. An agreement was reached that all personnel and vehicles involved in the incidents would be handed back at 1600 hrs. By 1800 hrs this exchange was complete but the highway, which should have reopened one hour later, remained closed.[7] HINA News reported that the road would be open on Monday 1 May 1995 and Tuesday 2 May between 0600 hrs to 2000 hrs, and from Wednesday 3 May on a round-the-clock basis,[8] but the Serbs were far from happy. This was clearly reflected in the advice Colonel Babic, of the Serb's 18th Corps in Okucani, was now giving to his people. 'Those Serbs who want to go to the petrol station again can do that,' he said, 'but they expose their throats to Croatian blades.'[9]

The Krajina Serbs were also well aware of what the Croats were up to just across the Bosnian border in the Livanjsko Polje, and in his report from Knin on the night of 30 April, Irish EU Monitor Jim Fitzgibbon reported on HV build-up activities at several points along the entire confrontation line. Fuelling what now amounted to collective paranoia Radio Knin began broadcasting a statement by Prime Minister Mikelic which was not designed to promote compromise. 'Attempts from the Croatian side to attribute responsibility to the Serbian side, when the incident has been provoked by the assassination of a Krajina Serb citizen, have to be rejected without reservation,' he said. 'The highway will remain closed for safety reasons, and a further escalation [of the situation] cannot be excluded.'

In tandem with this the radio station then reported that the Croatian army was continuing with combat operations in the Livanjsko Polje and that between 60 and 70 122-mm mortar rounds had landed in the village of Unitsa, while 30 HV vehicles had been spotted in Dabar. This amounted to very bad news but what very few Krajina Serbs really understood was that the Croats had been operating to a completely different agenda for a considerable time now and were only in need of an excuse to begin a huge new offensive. Equipped with an arsenal of new weapons, which had been pouring into the country since 1991,[10] Susak, Bobetko and the HV Generals had been eagerly looking for an opportunity to use them, and the closure of the Highway, while understandable from the Serb perspective and perhaps even justified by objective analysis, provided them with the opportunity they were looking for.

Sometime after 0200 hrs on the morning of 1 May, ironically a United Nations Holiday, a Croatian car was travelling between Pozega and Pakrac along the infamous Dragovic road. Why anyone would risk this particular journey at night, and especially when the overall situation was so volatile, is beyond comprehension, but the fact remains that two Croats took it upon themselves to make this journey along what surely must rate as the loneliest most eerie stretch of road in the entire world. This was where hundreds of Serbs used to live before the war but when the fighting started in 1991 they were routed by the Croats, who systematically destroyed their homes and burned their property to ensure they would never come back. If one ever wished to see the effects of ethnic cleansing without risking a trip to Bosnia then this was the place to visit. In any event, on this, the first morning of a brand new summer, the Serbs high in the hills overlooking the road opened fire on the car and the two occupants were injured.

At 0230 hrs the Commander of the Croatian army's Operational Zone in Bjelovar contacted the United Nations Sector HQ in Daruvar and announced that a 'Special Police Action' to reopen the Highway was about to commence. By 0430 hrs all UN troops in Sector West were on full alert and at 0500 hrs Hrvoje Sarinic made contact with the UN's Deputy Force Commander in Zagreb and admitted that a major Croatian attack on Western Slavonia (Sector West) was about to commence in order to reopen the Highway, but he insisted that this would be a 'limited police action', whatever that was supposed to be. By the time Roddy de Normann, ECMM's Deputy Head of Regional Centre Zagreb, which had responsibility for monitoring life in Sector West, was activating his operations staff, at 0515 hrs the first Croatian troops were already on their way into battle with 500 of them supported by 12 tanks pushing eastwards from Nova Gradiska. On the western side of the Sector an unspecified number of troops were on the move across the separation zone, while 600 special police, a full infantry battalion and an artillery regiment were deployed around Lipik and Pakrac. Before long Bosnian Serb artillery south of the Sava river began engaging the Croatian guns supporting the attack and by 1030 hrs over 360 shells had landed in the general vicinity of Nova Gradiska.[11]

Whatever else this attack might have been it certainly was not a 'limited police action' and neither was it an impromptu response to the most recent incident on the Dragovic road.[12] This was a pre-planned, pre-meditated, deliberate escalation of the conflict, which displayed no regard whatever for the plethora of international treaties and agreements into which the Croatian Government had supposedly entered in good faith. Now they reverted to nothing more than 'jack-boot diplomacy' and 'negotiation at the point of a gun' on the very day that the COHA expired in Bosnia, and with a very real possibility of dragging the Bosnian Serbs into the fighting in Croatia as well. Once again the Croats had chosen to express their gratitude to the contributing countries of the United Nations by treating them with contempt, and by 0900 hrs the Jordanian battalion had begun taking casualties as Croatian artillery and small arms fire rained down on top of them. What this was supposed to achieve is anyone's guess but clearly the UN were no longer to be treated as the 'dear guests' Franjo Tudjman had been so keen to label them back in January.

By 1100 hrs, when Mate Granic arrived to brief the Diplomatic Corps in Zagreb, Croatian forces had advanced up to 3 km into the Sector on its eastern side, with another 2,000 of them on their way from Slavonski Brod in order to cut the road between Okucani and Stara Gradiska. This would prevent any possible link up between the shell-shocked 18th Corps and the Bosnian Serb army south of the Sava river. In his statement Granic persisted with the line that what was taking place was a 'limited police action in pursuit of terrorists', who had provoked the situation in the first place by attacking vehicles passing along the Highway and the Dragovic road. He continued to insult his audience by telling them that the aim of the operation was to reopen the Highway and provide security for those using it, not to overrun the entire Sector, and that Croatia remained committed to a peaceful reintegration of the occupied areas and continuation with the Economic Agreement.

He got away with this preposterous explanation because none of those present knew enough to contradict him but by lunchtime the truth was beginning to emerge, thanks largely to the presence of ECMM on the ground and some UNMOs operating in the area. For the first time a government statement admitted that the Croatian army were indeed involved and closing in on the Serbs from all sides. By mid-afternoon it became clear that the operation had three objectives: firstly, to secure the perimeter of the sector; secondly, to secure the pontoon bridge at Jasenovac and the Sava river bridgehead at Bosanska Gradiska; and thirdly, to push along the Highway. At this point the Croats began claiming that Jasenovac had fallen that morning, and that HV artillery was now within shelling range of Bosanska Gradiska and the Stara Gradiska bridge. If this was true then the 18th Corps were in dire trouble but UN reports suggested that much of this was propaganda and that in fact the Croatian advance was proving far more difficult than first reported.

Contributing in large measure to this was the revelation by UNCRO that fifteen members of UNCIVPOL, their two interpreters and eighty-nine members of the Argentinean and Nepalese Battalions had been taken hostage by the Serbs in order to provide a human shield against the advancing Croats. In response to this the Croats commandeered several UN vehicles and as a convoy of tanks pushed west along the Highway towards Okucani, a white UN APC and a white UN Landrover appeared at the head of the HV column.[13] In tandem with this Radio Knin broadcasted a general mobilization of all Krajina Serb reservists. Following the removal of their heavy weapons from the various UN monitored weapons storage sites, and a meeting of the Supreme Defence Council in Knin, matters took a turn for the worst just after 1600 hrs when five artillery shells were fired at the city of Karlovac and another four impacted in Sisak. In retaliation two Croatian Air Force MIG 21s took off from Pleso and just after 1715 hrs attempted to destroy the bridge over the Sava at Stara Gradiska. They failed, succeeding only in dropping two bombs on top of the 18th Corps personnel who were minding the bridge, but the introduction of combat aircraft into a 'police action' left no one in any doubt as to what Tudjman's intentions really amounted to at this time.

When ECMM's Roddy de Normann eventually got to see Brigadier General Plestina, the Croatian Army's Senior Liaison Officer, at 1900 hrs that evening, he did admit that Croatia was worried about international reaction to this unprovoked attack, but continued none the less to promote the official line that this was an operation of 'liberation'. He managed to persist with this argument while simultaneously admitting that the Croatian strategy was to squeeze the Sector from all sides, leaving a narrow corridor in the south through which all the Serbs could escape to Bosnia.[14] Obviously one man's ethnic cleansing is another's operation of liberation.

In any event, while Plestina was trotting out the HDZ party line, another meeting was under way out in the UN's Pleso Camp near Zagreb airport. Akashi was frantically trying to cobble together a deal which would at least freeze the situation on the ground and thereby enable some discussion to take place. Having rushed back from Sarajevo where the COHA now lay in tatters, he began what would amount to over six hours of mediation between the Knin and Zagreb governments and, notwithstanding a UN Security Council condemnation of what the Croats were doing, no progress was made. At 2130 hrs Akashi eventually put forward a UN proposal which contained three essential elements: an immediate cease-fire, the release of all UN personnel held by the Serbs, and a return by all parties to the positions they occupied on the ground as of 30 April.

The Serbs, represented by Mikelic, Prijic and General Loncar, immediately accepted but Sarinic, on behalf of the Croatian government, rejected it. Instead, and knowing the Serbs would not agree to it, he demanded that the Highway, together with a 2 km strip either side of it, be put under exclusive Croatian control. This was totally unacceptable to the Serbs as the loss of a land link to the Republic of Srpska would create a Serb enclave right in the middle of Croatia which would become little more than a large open prison. In that context, and bearing in mind the geographical proximity of Sector West to the Second World War concentration camp at Jasenovac, the Serb delegation could never agree to what was, from their perspective, little better than herding their people once again into captivity. Sarinic was well aware of this, which of course leads one to suspect that was why he made the suggestion in the first place, and at that point, not surprisingly, the talks broke down. As towns and villages throughout Croatia and the Krajina observed a blackout that night, and Croatian radio stations continued to appeal to the Serbs to 'lay down their arms' and 'join in normal life' in Croatia with the full rights guaranteed to them under constitution, both sides regrouped and reorganized to face what the morrow would bring. For the Serbs it would just be more bad news and Foreign Minister Babic knew this only too well. In a statement issued on his behalf that evening he accused the UN of becoming little more than 'an instrument of Croatian foreign policy', given that they were unable and unwilling to take any action to protect the Serbs living in the so-called UN Protected Area of Sector West.

When dawn broke the next morning it became obvious that the Croats were intent on starting where they had left off the previous night, as MIG 21 fighters swept up and down the length of the Highway. By 0645 hrs Croatian artillery was back in action at the rate of five rounds per minute in order to soften up the Serb defences before the next push by the infantry, who were now arriving from a variety of bases across Croatia.[15] By 0800 hrs the squeeze on Sector West had recommenced with the position of both the 18th Corps and the civilian population becoming more untenable by the minute. At 1010 hrs the Croats unleashed an intense shelling of the Sava Bridge at Stara Gradiska (across which over 5,000 civilians had already moved into Bosnia) as well as launching two airstrikes against the nearby 18th Corps headquarters. The situation had now come to a head and the Serb commander in Gavrinici had already looked for a cease-fire which would be supervised by the UN, but all he got in response was a demand from the Croats to surrender. Then, at 1025 hrs, a number of explosions rocked the centre of Zagreb. Dr Jan Gallus, an EU monitor from Slovakia working with RC Zagreb, was one of the first on the scene.

After the shelling of the centre of Zagreb I went to monitor the situation in town. All target areas were protected by police, special police, and police officers in civilian clothing. At the beginning they were not cooperative, however, after explaining my role, I was allowed to see all areas. The school yard (Krizanicova school) was hit by an 'Orkan' rocket projectile, the diameter of the crater was approx. 1 m, and approx. 0.75 m deep. All around there were exploded small bomblets. There were two pupils and one teacher injured. In the area of Strossmayer Square a projectile exploded probably in the air (near the building of Ministry of Foreign Affairs). There were a lot of bomblets unexploded all around. One or two rounds landed at the corner of Vlaska and Draskovicova Streets. I saw three dead bodies (two men, one woman in the area). The medical doctor in the hospital at Draskoviceva told me that there are more than fifteen wounded, mostly heavily (in his hospital), two have to be operated on. The prognosis is very serious. The situation is similar in all hospitals. According to the unofficial info. passed by the policemen and doctors there are many wounded, the number is not known for the time being (more than fifty). There were five Orkan rockets exploded in the centre of the town. There are three dead and at least fifty wounded, approx. thirty per cent seriously, and a lot of material damages (mostly cars). All is under investigation by police and specialists (there are a lot of unexploded bomblets). The situation in the town is normal, though people are in shock, they cannot believe what has just happened.[16]

In Pakrac a surrender was now being negotiated for the 800 Serb troops who found themselves totally surrounded by the Croats and only able to survive because they still held the high ground in the area. By 1400 hrs Okucani had also fallen as thousands of civilians grabbed what few possessions they could carry and fled southwards into Bosnia rather than take their chances with their conquerors. Just before 1600 hrs President Tudjman appeared on television to announce that the action to retake the Highway was complete and that western Slavonia had been 'liberated'. In using the term 'liberated' the President clearly chose to indulge in another bout of historical revisionism because had he been bothered to consult either the 1981 or 1991 census he would have discovered that this area had always been overwhelmingly Serb since the days of the Vojna Krajina.

This point was actually made to Sarinic the following day by ECMM's Head of Mission, Ambassador Albert Turot, when he asked whether some of the concepts in the Z4 Plan which pertained to areas with a Serb majority population might now be implemented in Sector West. The answer he got made it absolutely clear that no local political autonomy whatever would be granted to the Serbs, and that the priority now was to identify 'war criminals' and try them either before a tribunal in Croatia or else defer proceedings to The Hague.[17] What Tudjman, Susak, Granic, Sarinic and the HV had actually been involved in for the past two days had been nothing short of 'precision ethnic cleansing': they had imposed their collective will by military force on a Serb minority who genuinely feared for their very lives if compelled to live in the same jurisdiction as people whom they believed to be post-Communist neo-Fascists.

At 2100 hrs Haram Basik agreed to surrender his 600 troops in Pakrac to the UN, as well as handing over all heavy weapons within forty-eight hours and all other lighter equipment within four days, while over 5,000 Serb civilians continued to flee across the Sava bridge into Bosnia. As another salvo of rockets descended on Zagreb the following morning, pictures of Peter Galbraith visiting the wounded in hospital were flashed around the world, and with Sarinic in close support, the US Ambassador launched into a reprobation of the Serbs for perpetrating these attacks. There was, of course, no condemnation of the Croats for starting this latest round of bloodletting in the first instance; as always that would have been expecting far too much. But Galbraith was correct in so far as he was prepared to go. The indiscriminate shelling of civilian targets is always wrong, it is a breach of International Humanitarian Law, and can never be excused no matter what the circumstances, but he could very profitably have addressed the matter of why it had happened in the first instance had he been even remotely disposed to look at the overall situation from the Serb perspective. He wasn't, and once more the world was treated to another round of Orwellian diplomacy.

While this was dominating every international news bulletin Akashi was frantically trying to obtain agreement between the Croatian government and the Knin authorities which would facilitate a permanent cease-fire. Throughout the night Akashi's officials hammered out the details of a plan that would allow UN troops to escort those remaining Serb civilians who wished to leave as far as the Sava river, but these efforts were rewarded on the morning of 5 May with renewed Croatian airstrikes, which in turn sparked off a fresh battle in and around Pakrac town.[18] The UN Security Council responded to this, at last, by condemning all violations of the old Cease-fire Agreement of the 29th March 1994, and demanded an immediate cessation of hostilities in the Sector. Akashi and General Janvier then set out for Daruvar but their helicopter was denied permission to land in Sector West by the Croats.

In the midst of this confusion UN troops who thought they were going to be involved in a peaceful separation of the forces now found themselves caught in the middle of renewed fighting, and in order to save their own skins they battened down the hatches of their armoured vehicles and left the area as quickly as they could. This was the correct decision but unfortunately their withdrawal was captured on video by several TV crews who had also wandered into the area and the UN's battered image took yet another punishing body blow.[19] Later that evening the first pictures emerged of lines of Serb fighters being marched away as Croatian troops waving flags were seen 'liberating' several towns and villages in the area. Perhaps the most interesting aspect of this triumphalism was the complete absence of the people who had been supposedly liberated – there were absolutely none. As the Croatian army rolled into each town and village with their clean-up teams right behind them, literally washing the blood off the streets, painting white lines on the roads, erecting road signs in Latin script and clearing away all war debris before the international media were allowed into the area, the streets were empty save for a few elderly people who were either too old or sick to embark on a journey into exile. By any stretch of the imagination this was not 'liberation'. This was conquest and a land grab; it was precision ethnic cleansing.

The maltreatment of the new Serb POWs seemed to pass almost unnoticed too. ECMM's Gunter Barron appeared on several international TV reports to tell the world that these Serbs were being treated well and that no human right had been violated, and while from what he saw he probably genuinely believed this to be true but the reality was altogether different. Later that evening more video footage was released that showed prisoners being publicly humiliated as they were forced to strip to their dirty soiled underwear and then remain standing for questioning by Croatian policewomen, who nonchalantly blew cigarette smoke into their faces while admiring their discomfort.[20] Corralled now into football stadia and gymnasiums at Varazdin, Bjelovar and Pozega over 1,100 members of the 18th Corps began a period of contemplation in which they would ask themselves how all of this could possibly have happened so quickly, and why neither Martic or Karadzic had come to their rescue. Sector West had fallen to the Croats without any real resistance and had left the Croatian army buoyant and euphoric. Tudjman's gamble had paid off handsomely and having gained the tacit approval of the International Community, the Croatian President was fortified in his belief that having got away with it once, he might well be able to do so again in the future. It was obvious that the balance of forces had now shifted significantly in favour of the Croats and this would dramatically influence events from now on. But there was also the matter of hidden agendas, and the rumour factory began to churn out endless stories which suggested that Sector West had in fact been sacrificed by Milosevic in order to have the economic sanctions lifted in Serbia and Montenegro. This was certainly close to the truth and the full story would emerge later on but the significant aspect of the whole saga was that the fall of Sector West would ultimately mark the beginning of the end for the Republic of Srpska Krajina. Within a very short time, the whole deck of cards would come crashing to the ground and the flames of 'Pan-Serbian Nationalism', as kindled by Milosevic and Babic in 1989, would soon be extinguished.[21]

NOTES

1. ECMM Team Dubrovnik, Special Report: 19/4/95.
2. ECMM Daily Briefing, no. 9872 for 22/3 April 1995: 24/4/95.
3. A further example of Orwellian doctrine at work. The Serbs were the bad guys; the bad guys had closed the road; therefore the closure was further evidence of just how bad these people were. Too simplistic to be true? Alas, no!
4. ECMM Daily Briefing, no. 9873 for 24 April 1995: 25/4/95.
5. ECMM Daily Briefing, no. 9374 for 25 April 1995: 26/4/95.
6. ECLO West, Special Report: 24/4/95.
7. ECMM Reports, a.) RC Zagreb Special Report: 30/4/95, b.) ECLO Highway Daily Report: 29/4/95, c.) ECLO West Daily Report: 29/4/95, d.) Team Slavonski Brod Daily Report: 29/4/95.
8. RC Zagreb Daily Report, Sunday: 30/04/95.
9. RC Zagreb Weekly Assessment 23–9 April 1995, dated 30/4/95.
10. Defence and Foreign Affairs Strategic Policy, Oct./Nov. 1992, p. 10–11.
11. ECMM Coyug no. 1: 1/5/95.
12. ECMM Daily Briefing, no. 9879: 2/5/95.
13. RC Zagreb Log: 1/5/95.
14. RC Zagreb Log: 1/5/95, 1900 hrs.
15. For example, at 0715 hrs that morning, the 104 Brigade had just arrived from Varazdin and were busy forming up in Novska, while the 81st Independent Guards battalion had moved into Pakrac. RC Zagreb Log: 2/5/95.
16. Humanitarian Cell RC Zagreb/Special Report, Jan Gallus (Slovakia), 2 May 1995. At 1215 hrs a statement issued on behalf of the Chief of Police in Zagreb confirmed that six Orkan rockets had hit the city, killing two people and wounding fifty others. Another three rockets landed near the airport, one on the runway, and Lufthansa suspended its operations.
17. Meeting between Sarinic and Ambassador Turot: 3/5/95.
18. UNPROFOR Sequence of Events, 1995.
19. ITV News report by Paul Davies.
20. ECMM's presence at the POW processing centre in Bjelovar, and the manner in which some Monitors were unwittingly or otherwise manipulated by the Croatian media handlers who were present throughout, was the subject of a stiff rebuke by Senior Monitor Roger Bryant. He thought it necessary to circulate two Special Reports on 7–8 May in which he drew the attention of all members of ECMM to the provisions of International Humanitarian Law and the role of individual monitors in upholding that law.

CHAPTER TWENTY-FOUR

The Beginning of the End for the Krajina Serbs

As the Krajina Serbs struggled to come to terms with the loss of Sector West and the fact that neither of their ethnic brothers in Belgrade or Pale had raised a finger to help them, it quickly emerged that this might well be only the first phase of a larger Croatian offensive. However, thanks to the continued intervention of Akashi, and several complaints by UN officials that the Croats had been involved in a number of human rights violations,[1] Tudjman was persuaded to call his troops to heel for the moment. The last thing Tudjman or Susak needed now was bad international press so in order to keep their sponsors on side Sarinic paraded before the media to insist again that Operation Flash had been nothing more than a police action to reopen the Highway; that really Croatia's relations with Knin had not been damaged at all; and that he hoped both sides could now get on with the business of implementing the Economic Agreement. As outrageous and ridiculous as all of this was, the more Sarinic touted it the more convincing he became, and within a relatively short period this lie became accepted internationally.

In Knin the leadership was now split into several different political camps with the government, police and the military all in complete disarray, and the inevitable in-fighting between Martic, Mikelic and Babic erupted on a grand scale. The first target turned out to be Mikelic himself, who was berated by his colleagues for having gone too far with the Croats in the first place when he signed the Economic Agreement. Next to suffer was General Celeketic, who was blamed for the collapse of the 18th Corps and the failure of other units to come to their support. He decided to offer his resignation rather than wait to be fired and in the course of his final statement he attributed the fall of Sector West to 'the lack of political and military support from outside the Krajina, which [he] had expected to materialize because it had been previously agreed, and also because of the dirty political games being played [now] by certain individuals'.[2]

Martic then turned to Karadzic for support and a joint session of both the Krajina and Bosnian Serb parliaments was called for 31 May, as in excess of 10,000 refugees from Sector West were now squabbling between themselves over what pathetic accommodation and shelter they could find. In apparent revenge for the Croatian attack and subsequent ethnic cleansing several Catholic churches in Banja Luka were destroyed and many Croats still living there were harassed and killed.[3] In a letter to the Bosnian Serb authorities the Catholic Bishop, Franja Komarica, reported the discovery of the charred remains of both a priest and a nun in the ruins of one church and declared that this was the fifth priest from his diocese who had been murdered in the past three years.[4] In the towns of Tovarnik and Ilok in Sector East Croats were expelled from their homes and around Knin ECMM's Jochen Kramb, a remarkably perceptive Monitor, once again identified another very significant phenomenon taking place.

> The Croatian minorities in the southern half of Sector South are also harassed with the purpose of cleansing in the area. But on the other hand the more 'wealthy' Serbs in this part of the Krajina are aware that the last months have been a period of gradual adaptation to reality, namely that the dreams about an independent Krajina state are as good as flown away. Therefore they have begun to leave this area really spontaneously, because it has no future, for other parts of the 'real' Serbia. The distribution of the available space will thus be a 'poor people issue' with on the one side local Serbs without means and on the other old age Croatians who want to finish their lives in their small properties. Croatia and Krajina have no longer land and people to exchange, either by force or by negotiations: the only possible alternative to 'conquest' or 'liberation' is perhaps money.[5]

Those Krajina Serbs who understood the real politics of the situation were now packing their bags and heading for the relative safety of Belgrade and beyond, but for the remainder, who comprised the vast majority of the population, nobody was telling them anything. Then to compound the confusion it was announced in The Hague that Judge Richard Goldstone had evidence in his possession which established that Dario Kordic, the HDZ leader in Bosnia, and General Tihomir Blaskic, his military counterpart,[6] had committed war crimes in central Bosnia in the course of the war.[7] Two days later the international tribunal applied to the Sarajevo government to defer jurisdiction to The Hague in connection with these serious violations of international humanitarian law in the Lasva Valley in 1992 and 1993,[8] and when Goldstone then arrived unexpectedly in Croatia to examine events surrounding the 'liberation' of Sector West[9] a sense of panic gripped Zagreb. All posturing and obstructionism immediately ceased, which allowed the long overdue Status of Forces Agreement to be signed between the Croatian Government and the UN.

In the short term UN troops would remain in the Krajina but even the most optimistic observers realized that it was just a matter of time before the Croatian army were unleashed by Tudjman again. Having flexed their muscles and got away with it they continued to receive all the wrong signals from their main sponsors, and almost immediately preparations began for the next offensive with a huge military parade in Zagreb on 30 May[10] Tudjman's conviction that he would not be prevented from beginning a second attack on the Krajina had a lot to do with his ongoing communications with Peter Galbraith. Having received the famous 'No instructions' instruction in relation to breaking the arms embargo, he now received a 'message' from Washington which expressed 'concern' over the on-going HV build up. While ever-grateful for American concern, the Croatian President took this as yet another green light to proceed with his plans as Galbraith neither said nor did anything further to dissuade him.[11] In relation to anything the UN might hope to achieve at this time General Peeters, Deputy Force Commander of UNPF, was quite clear when he wrote that, 'the presence and action of the UN Force in Croatia has become irrelevant to both sides. We should recognize and admit the situation and we should assess if our present way of thinking is still valid.'[12]

In Bosnia both sides were also busy getting back to business in preparation for yet another summer of ethnic violence and atrocity. On 6 May Sarajevo's five months of comparative stability was shattered when several artillery shells landed in the Muslim suburb of Butimir, near to the famous tunnel entrance under the airport runway,[13] which had provided a lifeline to the city in its darkest days.[14] In the context of a return to violence it was hardly surprising that this economic and military lifeline should once again become a target and on this May morning eight people died and another forty were wounded as the Serbs began to strangle the city one more time. With the airport closed to humanitarian flights the Serb's objective was clearly to close the tunnel as well but as so often in the past this attack only ensured that the besieged citizens of Sarajevo continued their lives with even more determination than before.[15] General Smith apparently requested NATO airstrikes in the aftermath of this latest atrocity but Akashi turned him down on the basis that the overall situation was now too delicate and tense, and any escalation caused by the intervention of NATO might only serve to put UN soldiers at greater risk than they already were.[16]

With the whole fabric of the Balkans now crumbling around him Akashi set out for Belgrade and a meeting with Milosevic, Martic, Mikelic and Babic, during which they discussed among other things the 657 Serbs from Sector West who were still detained in Varazdin and Bjelovar at the pleasure of President Tudjman's investigators.[17] They also addressed the matter of the UN's perceived culpability in failing to prevent the Croatian attack and Milosevic said all he had expected was that the UN would 'implement their peace mission, no more, no less'. He went on to say that he wanted a demilitarization of western Slavonia, with the UN in place to enforce it, and this in turn would allow Serbs to continue living in the area. Knin's position, Milosevic said, could not be properly defined until its leaders stopped fighting with one another. In a public reprimand of the Krajina's President, Milosevic told Akashi that he had vehemently opposed the shelling of Zagreb, and blamed Milan Martic exclusively for it.

With Milosevic and Mikelic apparently speaking as one voice, Martic now found himself marginalized and isolated as Babic kept his mouth shut. As the meeting broke up it was clear that as far as Milosevic was concerned two factors had contributed to the fall of Sector West. The first had been the ineptitude of the UN troops garrisoned in the Sector. The second was Milan Martic who by his excessively hard-line attitudes had provoked the Croats into this course of action, and who had now successfully alienated all Serbs from international sympathy by indiscriminately firing rockets into the centre of Zagreb city.[18]

With Martic and Babic sidelined in the Krajina, and Karadzic unable to effectively make any decision without Mladic's agreement in Bosnia, Milosevic had convinced himself that he was once again pulling all the strings in the 'Pan-Serbian Nationalist orchestra'. As the Krajina leaders made their way back to Knin they were in no doubt where the key to their survival lay but the problem was how to reconcile that with the certain knowledge that if they adopted a more moderate approach Tudjman would see this as a sign of weakness and roll his HV troops right in on top of them. Caught between a rock and a hard place these two die-hards were well aware that whichever route they took now, in the longer term they were virtually guaranteed to lose everything.

But the situation was getting steadily worse in Bosnia too and although rumour abounded that Karadzic was on the verge of making a new proposal to the Contact Group, there was no evidence on the ground to support this. Instead, on 7 May, eleven people died and fourteen were injured in Sarajevo,[19] while over 2,200 firing incidents were recorded in the city on 10 May as fighting intensified in the Posavina corridor where the Serbs in Brcko and Bosnian Croats in the Orasje Pocket hurled tons of ordnance at one another and succeeded in shifting the confrontation line only marginally.[20] With the situation now going from bad to worse Akashi, General Janvier and General Smith flew to Paris for a meeting with the ICFY co-chairman Thorvald Stoltenberg, but nothing new emerged. While they were away, however, the Serbs once again decided to begin curtailing the flow of gas into Sarajevo and the level of sniper activity was also stepped up. One of the first casualties here was a French UN soldier who was shot while on duty in the city as a member of an anti-sniping patrol, and the refusal of the Serb military to allow his immediate evacuation probably cost him his life. He was eventually flown to Paris but died four days later from his injuries.[21]

The very next day a full-scale artillery battle erupted in the suburbs of Sarajevo when, following a Muslim mortar attack on the Serb barracks at Lukavica, over 1,500 assorted shells rained down on the city in reprisal. In addition to this the situation in Posavina was steadily getting worse and fighting now spread to areas like Gradacac and the Majevica Hills north of Tuzla, while a new Muslim offensive got under way around Sarajevo itself and actually succeeded in bringing Pale within Armija artillery range for the first time. From the sanitized environs of UN HQ in New York Akashi condemned this escalation of violence,[22] and expressed all kinds of pessimism for the future but clearly no one had any interest in what he had to say. Certainly General Dudakovic was not concerned with this current round of international diplomacy. The only type of diplomacy he had any immediate interest in was that variety enforced at the point of a gun, and once again he now felt confident enough to launch the 5th Corps on another offensive to the south-east of Bihac town, which immediately sent hundreds of Serbs scurrying off to the relative safety of Banja Luka and Sanski Most.

With a total of 4,643 violations of the No Fly Zone recorded by UNPROFOR at the beginning of May[23] and a sharp increase in military activity by all sides clearly evident, every monitoring agency in the region was now waiting for events to enter a downward spiral – and on the night of 25 May they were not disappointed. As hundreds of people gathered outside cafes in the centre of Tuzla, a salvo of artillery rained down on top of them, leaving seventy-one dead and over 130 wounded.[24] Three days later, in retaliation for several NATO airstrikes, the Bosnian Serbs seized 377 UN soldiers and held them hostage at a variety of locations in order to ward off further punitive attacks. This was immediately effective as pictures of UN soldiers handcuffed to ammunition bunkers were flashed around the world, and it took three full weeks of negotiation, and the establishment of a Rapid Reaction Force, to eventually secure their release. Now it was quite clear that for all parties the Carter Initiative and the COHA had achieved little more than the provision of a period of calm during which they could re-group and re-arm. This was particularly true in the case of both the Muslims and the Bosnian Croats where, although the Federation was in serious political difficulty at this time, both armies appeared to be benefitting dramatically from continued foreign intervention, which we now know to have been primarily of American and Iranian origin.

The US engagement in this area has become more and more obvious and US diplomats seem to have become the favourite supporters of ABiH [Muslims] and HVO [Bosnian Croats] . . . US General (Ret.) John SEWAL (special envoy of the US President for co-ordinating the process of establishing the Federal Army) met the ABiH Chief of

Staff, the ABiH Supreme Comdr [General Delic], the Comdr of the 2 Corps, and Vice President Ejup Ganic, in Mostar. In the press statement the US General explained that his mission is just *a part* of the political, military and economic support of the USA to the Federation of Bosnia Hercegovina. He also stated that the Federal Army should be considered as a final goal but his impression was that neither Armija nor the HVO were ready at this moment for it. The main purpose of his visit was to find a way for more close co-operation between Armija Comdr Delic and the HVO Comdr Blaskic.[25]

ECMM's Daily Monitoring Activity Report on 17 May went even further.

The American presence in Bosnia is increasing. Members of the American Embassy sit on most Municipal and Cantonal Assemblies. Last week ECMM met unexpectedly three American Military Advisors. The American Charge d'Affaires is a preferred interlocutor of the Bosnian [Muslim] Government. This growing American influence is likely to encourage the Bosnian government to opt for a military solution in order to retake the territories lost in 1992 and 1993.[26]

Nevertheless the prospect of a final solution in Bosnia appeared to be as remote as ever and the Clinton administration struggled to find a policy they could have any policy in. Eventually, at the end of June, the President's National Security Advisor, Anthony Lake, came up with his 'endgame strategy', which involved bombing the Serbs to a compromise if they refused to go there voluntarily.[27] Once this was officially accepted the writing was on the wall! Day by day in July tons of military hardware made its way to the HV, HVO and Armija troops on the ground.[28] The political die had been cast and the necessary military action would follow on now in due course. General Delic even set about visiting all his front-line troops in order to make sure they understood that the war had been transformed from a defensive action into what he now also called 'a war of liberation'. He was no doubt also influenced in his thinking by the decision of UNPROFOR Commander Rupert Smith to begin withdrawing his troops from the eastern enclaves as soon as possible, on the basis that neither the UN nor NATO could actually defend them there anyway. Under pressure on all front lines and watching his enemies grow stronger by the day, it was in this scenario that Ratko Mladic decided to unleash the BSA on the eastern Muslim enclaves of Srebrenica and Zepra.

Over the next two weeks some of the worst atrocities of the modern Yugoslav conflict were perpetrated by the Bosnian Serbs as first Srebrenica and then Zepa crumbled before a relentless BSA onslaught. Why General Mladic permitted what happened to take place will perhaps never be explained, until perhaps he is forced to answer that question to save his own skin if he ever appears before the International Criminal Tribunal in The Hague. No doubt he will try to suggest that he was only responding to a known UNPROFOR decision to get its own troops out of the enclaves that summer anyway, and he will probably attempt to tell us that the actions of his troops were merely a measured response to Muslim terrorist provocation over the years. The reality, of course, is that whatever explanation he comes up with can never justify the summary execution of nearly 3,000 Muslim men and the hunting down of another 4,000 as they fled in terror across the hills and valleys of eastern Bosnia in a futile attempt to make their way to safety at the Armija's front line near Tuzla. The ICRC figure for those still missing following the BSA's attack on the UN safe area of Srebrenica still stands at 7,079 – 38 per cent of the total number of people missing in the entire Yugoslav war.[29]

The UN would also bear the brunt of severe criticism for their perceived failure to protect the enclave from Mladic and his thugs but the truth of that is very simple. The Dutch UN Battalion was neither mandated, empowered or equipped to go to war with the Serbs. Mladic was well aware of this, as indeed he was of Akashi's and Janvier's reluctance to call in close air support, lest it make an untenable situation (from the UN perspective) appreciably worse. He knew their misgivings and he understood their reservations, and he exploited them all to the full. The story of Srebrenica is a sickening litany of barbarity, atrocity and murder. The responsibility for it lies exclusively in the hands of Ratko Mladic and his political and military masters in Belgrade who paid his salary at the time and who continue to do so to the present day. In an oft-cited TV interview given long before the horror of Srebrenica unfolded, Mladic boasted that his preferred military tactics were to shell people out of their minds and to shoot all his prisoners of war. Certainly no one in the International Community took this kind of bravado seriously at the time, and that was a very serious mistake.[30]

NOTES

1. ECMM WIAS, no. 127: 11/5/95.
2. ECMM WIAS, no. 128: 18/5/95.
3. UN Sequence of Events, 7 May 1995.
4. ECMM Daily Monitoring Activity Report, no. 9,892 for 13–14 May 1995.
5. ECMM WIAS, no. 129, 25/5/95.
6. ECMM Daily Monitoring Activity report, no. 9,882 for 6–7 May 1995.
7. 9/5/95.
8. 11/5/95.
9. 15/5/95.
10. Brigadier General P. Peeters, 'The Aftermath of Sector West', 13/6/95.

11. Marcus Tanner, *Croatia – A Nation Forged in War* (Yale University Press), 1997, p. 296.
12. Brigadier General P. Peeters, 'The Aftermath of Sector West', 13/6/95, para 4, p. 5.
13. Asim Metiljevic, 'Digging a Lifeline for Sarajevo', *Transition* magazine/OMRI, 31/5/96.
14. In January 1993 work began to connect Butimir with the other Muslim suburb of Dobrinja, and digging in both directions simultaneously, using only shovels and pickaxes, forty people worked four shifts per day in order to claw their way beneath the concrete overhead. At 0107 hrs on the morning of 13 July 1993 a hole big enough for a handshake appeared and soon thereafter a stream of people began to flow in both directions. In the years that followed the Sarajevo authorities continued publicly to deny the existence of the tunnel but everyone knew it existed, the Serbs, the UN and ECMM included.
15. ECMM Daily Monitoring Activity Report, no. 9886 for 6–7 May 1995.
16. Ibid., no. 9,888 for 9/5/95.
17. Ibid., no. 9,889 for 10/5/95.
18. ECMM Daily Monitoring Activity Report, no. 9,889 for 10/5/95, para. 9.
19. RUSI International Security Review, 1996, p. 119.
20. The Bosnian Croats admitted that they had lost about 200 square metres of ground at a cost of 3 dead and 35 wounded: ECMM DMA Report No. 9889 for 10/5/95.
21. 15 May 1995: UN Sequence of Events.
22. 16 May 1995, ibid.
23. UN Doc S/1995/5–9/5/95.
24. Postmortem on UNPROFOR, Richard Caplan, London Defence Studies, No. 33, p. 17. Published by the Centre for Defence Studies, King's College and Brasseys's UK (1996).
25. ECMM WIAS: 25/7/95.
26. ECMM Daily Monitoring Activity Report: 17/7/95, para. 7.
27. Woodward, Bob, *The Choice* (Touchstone: Simon and Schuster (US)), 1997, p. 254.
28. Yossef Bodansky, 'Some Call it Peace' (ISSA), 1996.
29. David Rohde, *A Safe Area* (Pocket Books), 1997, p. 350.
30. See also Official Dutch MOD Debriefing Report on Srebrenica; Honig and Both, *Srebrenica, Record of a War Crime* (Penguin), 1996.

CHAPTER TWENTY-FIVE

Operation Storm and the Fall of Fikret Abdic

After the flood of refugees had finished pouring into the Krajina from Sector West and then dispersed further afield into Bosnia it became quite clear that the overall situation in the Krajina was once again impacting significantly on the ordinary citizens of Bihac Pocket. Here normal life, such as it was, had all but come to a standstill although routine body exchanges between the 5th Corps and the Krajina Serbs continued as before.[1] UNHCR convoys remained barred from travelling through the Krajina as the Knin authorities continued to insist that if the International Community could not be bothered to distribute adequate tonnage to them then no deliveries were going to reach Bihac either, notwithstanding that people were beginning to starve. Many of the older people were now openly begging for food in the streets, something which up to that point in the conflict had never been seen before and was anathema to the whole Muslim culture.[2] None of this affected the black market of course, which continued operating as happily and successfully as before at Trzacka Rastella near the international border. The main commodity changing hands now was grain and the convoys involved experienced no difficulties making their way into the Pocket through several 'hot' confrontation lines. In real terms, however, the quantities in question were totally inadequate and did not significantly improve the overall situation.[3]

The HV conquest of Sector West had however provided a modicum of comfort to the beleaguered commander of the 5th Corps. Hosting a dinner for General Dudakovic at the ECMM house in Bihac town on 5 May the Monitor team there also invited along Colonel Hamdu Abdic, Commander of the 502 Brigade, and UNPROFOR's Bihac Area Commander Colonel Helsoe to see what information they might be able to discover. Having first established that the General was delighted with the gift of a bottle of champagne, which he then proceeded to polish off rather quickly, he went on to confirm that the 5th Corps now had a twelve-barrel multiple rocket launcher, and were planning a raid on the town of Korenica in the Krajina, which had recently come within range of their 82-mm mortars. It also transpired that they were planning raids on several other positions which the Krajina Serbs held around Bihac town but, according to Hamdu Abdic, this was not as easy as one might think as the Serbs kept moving their tanks around now that fuel had become more plentiful. It also transpired that for the first time Dudakovic had managed to set up a proper infantry training school in the 5th Corps and with each brigade now releasing a company for training at any one time, a lot of progress was being made, as well as enabling the Corps to use this group as a mobile reserve when required.

Dudakovic also admitted that a 'Special Unit' had been established and if he managed to obtain the radios, ear pieces and throat microphones that he was waiting for, then this unit could be deployed immediately. Interestingly the General stated that he envied the 7th Corps in the Tuzla region because of the excellent equipment they had been receiving, and he believed that if he got his hands on similar hardware then he could finish the war in Bihac within a week. In relation to the 'unresolved' disappearance of Vlado Santic Dudakovic laughed it off and said that he was waiting for a postcard from Australia.

> General Dudakovic made a very confident impression. He is well aware of his strong and weak points. Team assess that it is not very likely that an attack will be made in the North towards Velika Kladusa. However the possibility of an attack towards the S/SE is there [because] the General and everybody else in the Pocket, especially in Bihac town, are fed up with the daily terror of shelling, killing, and/or the wounding of innocent civilians.[4]

A few days later the 5th Corps returned the hospitality and invited ECMM to visit them in Cazin but on the way to the function the Monitors found themselves trying to evade a creeping artillery barrage as 155-mm shells landed in nearly all of the villages they drove through. Unable to determine the reason for the ferocity of the Serb shelling, especially since the targets were all civilian, the Monitors sought out Colonel Helsoe at the function and discussed yet again the status of the Bihac 'safe area'. Asking whether NATO airstrikes could now be justified to dissuade the Serbs from repeating this level of indiscriminate shelling against civilian targets, Helsoe replied that he had clear guidelines and when he felt it was politically and militarily expedient airstrikes would be requested. But for the moment his main objectives were not to do anything that could make a bad situation worse. Later on, when Bill Foxton was speaking with Hamdu Abdic, a drunk senior NCO began to engage his Brigadier Commander in conversation. 'Brigadier Abdic, while still talking to Monitor Foxton, head-butted the NCO who was then summarily dealt with by the Brigadier's bodyguards. There was a twenty second demonstration of gratuitous violence which was extremely unpleasant. General Dudakovic became involved and demanded to know what it was all about. The party came abruptly to an end and all those attending went home.'[5]

The following day the Monitors visited the UNMOs in Coralici and having examined their operations map with all the recent artillery impacts plotted on it, formed the opinion that the Serbs were actually trying to send a message to the UN and ECMM by the manner in which they chose to shell the Pocket. If they traversed their guns and rockets 10 degrees towards the north their shells would fall right in the middle of the UN Camp in Coralici. As the Monitors and UNMOs downed another cup of tea they were all agreed that while NATO airstrikes might be warranted as a result of shelling during the past few days, if that option were exercised a retaliatory strike by the ARSK would now take out the UN HQ at Coralici, and the BSA would have little difficulty demolishing Cazin.[6]

So from the UN perspective the primary objective was non-escalation, while Dudakovic was content for the moment to concentrate on low-intensity raids into Krajina. On the night of 9 May a 5th Corps 'Special Unit' managed to penetrate the Serb lines and conducted a short sharp operation to the outskirts of Slunj, capturing some valuable equipment and twenty POWs in the process.[7] This now became the offensive pattern of the 5th Corps who were clearly content to absorb the daily retaliatory shelling in the south and to leave Abdic to his own devices in the north until circumstances were more favourable.

In the middle of this the civilian population continued to suffer. Feed the Children's representative in the Pocket, Beverly Koski, estimated that there were many children who, although not undernourished, were physically underdeveloped. She believed that this was a product of unbalanced diets which had not allowed these children to reach the normal physical heights and weights that one could expect to find in similar children in Europe. She was also convinced that most children in Bihac got little or no milk and the standards of dental care were abysmal. Most of the programmes run by NGOs in the Pocket were focused on expectant mothers and babies from one to three year of age. From three years onwards all children were expected to eat adult food, without vitamin supplements or enough fresh fruit and vegetables. When the Monitors asked some of the children how old they were they were also surprised to find they were so small for their age, and with no improvement in the food situation in sight their plight was not about to get much better.[8]

Then, on the morning of 17 May at 0515 hrs, the Bosnian Serbs began to shell Bihac town yet again, but this time in a defensive action. Thanks to further successful raids to the south-east and east of the Pocket by the 5th Corps, the Serbs were now being systematically beaten back and forced to concede large tracts of ground. Dudakovic had made an attack towards Ripac village, retaken it, and in the process managed to surround the 17th Kljuc Brigade (nearly 200 men). On top of that the 15th Drvar

Brigade, the 3rd Petrovac Brigade and 11th Bosanska Krupa Brigade all withdrew, and the Kljuc Brigade was expected to attempt a breakout in order to join up with them once it got dark. Orders were given to accept their surrender or annihilate them but no prisoners were to be taken if they did not surrender. The ECMM assessment was that the 5th Corps would be in the village of Gorjevac by nightfall and when that was achieved Bihac town would be out of range of BSA artillery. 'There is an immense feeling of relief among the community at large. The daily shelling has been an enormous strain on the citizens of Bihac.'[9]

At last, on the evening of 18 May the UNHCR convoy, which had been expected for weeks, finally arrived bringing 124 tons of basic food to the Pocket. Unfortunately, when this was distributed, there was not a lot to smile about. In a general distribution babies born in 1994 and 1995 each got 2 kg of baby food while each adult got just 0.5 kg of beans and 1.5 kg of seed potatoes, which most people would probably eat because it was now far too late to plant them. On the medical side MSF also received a two-truck supply of medicines, but these would really make no appreciable difference either.[10]

As the month wore on the 5th Corps managed to further consolidate its position in the south and east, although a row broke out between Colonel Helsoe and Dudakovic when it emerged that Serb houses in the recently retaken Ripac area had been set alight.[11] Skirmishing continued on all front lines with minor alterations being affected but in some cases there was a price to be paid for these limited gains. There was the case of the two 5th Corps Military Police personnel who were captured on the Srbljani plateau on 18 May and having had their ears, noses and fingers cut off, they were then impaled on two stakes. Both were found naked on the 22nd with their genitals removed. Such was the barbarity of the conflict that a video was made where they were found, and of their condition later in the mortuary, would be used to spawn even greater reciprocal savagery in the future.[12]

And so it went on. The black market continued to thrive with 9 tons of cooking oil, 12 tons of sugar, 15 tons of washing powder and almost 5 million cigarettes all managing to find their way across several front lines on 25 May alone.[13] But the most interesting piece of scandal by far in Bihac in May 1995 was the disclosure, by supposedly reliable sources close to ECMM, that a case was being prepared against two senior 5th Corps officers by General Dudakovic, based on allegations that both had been with General Santic on the night he was killed and that one of them was believed to have fired the first shot while the other finished the job.[14] According to the source, when Hamdu Abdic was told about this he immediately went to find the General and a fist fight ensued between the two of them.[15]

Of far more immediate importance however was the news that UNHCR were about to terminate their operations in the Pocket, and when ECMM caught up with Monique Tuffeli she was all packed up and ready to go. It was part of an overall programme of downsizing across Bosnia, she said, but that explanation did nothing to allay the fears of the ordinary people who had come to believe that as long as the international agencies were present among them, they would somehow or other manage to survive.[16] But, at 1430 hrs on 2 June, in a state of total disarray and only following intervention by ECMM with the 5th Corps, UNHCR departed Bihac Pocket at the Licko Petrovo Selo crossing point.[17]

Life in Bihac became even more difficult throughout June and July as all along the separation zone between Croatia and the Krajina a constant and barely disguised build-up of the Croatian forces got under way. Abdic forces supported by the Krajina Serbs also began to make some headway against the 5th Corps, as a push southwards from Velika Kladusa and Vrnograc got under way. Dudakovic had, however, managed to consolidate his position to the east of the Pocket, having successfully evicted all remaining Bosnian Serbs from the west bank of the UNA river. At this time groups known as the 'Visivubus' were also mobilized. Comprised of people less that sixty years of age, they were called up for ten-day training periods and employed near the front line in observation roles. In other measures taken all telephones were disconnected, with the exception of those belonging to the 5th Corps and senior politicians, and when people went to purchase food on the black market there was none available because everything had been commandeered by Dudakovic. Continuing with limited aggressive operations in the west and holding the line with Abdic in the north the 5th Corps, knowingly or otherwise, were successfully keeping large numbers of RSK troops tied down all around the Pocket when realistically they might now have been better redeployed elsewhere.[18] In fact UNCRO HQ in Zagreb estimated that over 100,000 professional Croatian troops were now fully combat-ready and if one also took account of their Home Guard and Reservists the total number probably exceeded 140,000. In the Livanjsko Polje the combined HV/HVO offensive continued to gather pace as well and when the town of Bosanska Gravaho eventually fell on 28 July, the Knin authorities declared a state of war. Within hours over 50,000 troops had been mustered but at least 7,000 of these were totally bogged down in the conflict around Bihac. An EU report at the time analysed the situation extremely well.

The HV is now in an extremely strong position to launch a massive attack against the 'RSK'. It is able to attack Sectors North and South at the same time. It also has the option to decide when and where to attack. Because of the deployment of the bulk of [HV] forces around Sector North the main thrust could be aimed at the 'ARSK' surface-to-surface missiles [in the Petrova Gora/Polygon Area] in order to eliminate the threat to Zagreb, Karlovac and Sisak. The 'ARSK' has a long front line to defend and also has only limited mobility because of the lack of outside support. The fact that a significant number of troops are still engaged in the Bihac Pocket and in the area of Grahovo and Strmica [in the Livanjsko Polje] adds to the operational difficulties.[19]

On the political front the temperature was now at boiling point as President Tudjman began issuing warnings that Croatia would solve the 'Krajina problem' once and for all unless serious peace talks got underway immediately. Yasushi Akashi, who by now had effectively given up trying to exert any further influence on the Croatian government, warned again about the danger of a full-scale war in the region, but he too understood that time had run out for the Krajina Serbs. In Geneva a meeting chaired by Thorvald Stoltenberg went into session but as the delegations present did not represent the highest political level in either the Krajina or Croatia the best that could be achieved was agreement to begin 'talks about talks'. On 1 August the Joint Defence Council of the Bosnian and Krajina Serbs met in Drvar and called for immediate military intervention by Belgrade to balance up the situation. Martic declared that he had been given 'assurances' by Milosevic that Serbia would not remain neutral if the Croats attacked Knin but this was not the message which independent observers understood was coming from Belgrade. The head of the Serbian Bureau office in Zagreb, Mr Knezevic, was openly suggesting for the very first time that the duty of the Krajina Serbs was to be loyal citizens of Croatia and seek their democratic position as a national minority in line with the relevant provisions of the Croatian constitution. This philosophy was not well received in Knin where Milan Babic had once more become Prime Minister on 28 July.[20] Recognizing that the Krajina could not survive without Serbian support he left immediately for Belgrade to seek out his old sponsor Milosevic.[21]

Within the Pocket the situation remained the same, with the exception of the northern confrontation line, where limited offensives continued to be mounted daily against the 5th Corps by Abdic forces who of late were having a reasonable degree of success. By the end of July assistance had also begun to pour in to Dudakovic, with cargo aircraft from Croatia constantly unloading at Coralici airfield. This, when taken in conjunction with a significant reduction in Krajina Serb activity on the western side of the Pocket, now indicated that the tide was at last turning for Dudakovic, and the more the Serbs were forced to disengage and re-deploy to face the Croats the more vulnerable Abdic and his followers would become in Velika Kladusa. It was also significant that at this very time, when the plight of the citizens of Bihac was about to improve, the Sarajevo government decided to keep the case of the enclave right at the top of the political agenda, in a determined effort to justify Croatian and/or international intervention in the overall conflict. Foreign Ministers Sacirbey and Granic both appeared before the media and announced that if the International Community failed to do anything to 'save Bihac' then the Armija, with the help of HV, would do something about it themselves. What they failed to mention was that pursuant to the Split Agreement of 22 July, the Croatian army now had an open invitation from Sarajevo to commence operations in Bihac anyway, and all they were looking for was the appropriate excuse.

Through good media management both the Sarajevo and Zagreb governments had continually pumped out the story that Bihac was about to fall and that strategically this could not be tolerated, nor could the lives of the male population of the Pocket be sacrificed in the same manner as had happened a few weeks previously at Srebrenica. But it is important to note that while admittedly the situation was quite bad, it was not as bad as that, and ECMM reports of the time confirm this.

Date: 21/7/95
General Situation: Tense but quiet. At 0330 hrs this morning 4 ORKAN 268 mm Rockets impacted east of Bihac town.
Military Situation: In the late afternoon yesterday the RSK launched 4 ORKAN rockets on Cazin, UNMOs were investigating a previous MRLS attack when they heard the ORKANS heading in their direction. They took cover and miraculously were unharmed. However the whole area is now strewn with unexploded anti-personnel mines from these Rockets and UNPROFOR have cordoned off the area. The mines are in the shape of small handbells and cannot be neutralized. 5 Corps will try to destroy them by shooting at them. The situation is only slightly better for 5 Corps now than it was in July 1994.
Humanitarian Issues: The ICRC House was attacked last night by three armed and masked men. They entered the sleeping accommodation and tied up the Head of ICRC (Suzanne Fiscbach) and a British Nurse, and taped their mouths. They then systematically searched the house for 50 minutes. They stole money, jewellery and selected items.
Economic Situation: Dire. Flour now 550DEM per 50 kg bag, Oil 35 DEM per litre, Salt 40 DEM per kg.

Date: 23/7/95
General Situation: Fighting has decreased. RSK attacks seem to have stopped temporarily. Sporadic shelling is ongoing. There are however 130 wounded 5th Corps soldiers in Cazin hospital since 0700 hrs this morning. 25 other soldiers with more serious wounds have been

transferred to Bihac Hospital. Work still continues on the runway at Coralici to extend and widen it. Team can only speculate that Croatia will airlift troops and equipment in if 5 Corps cannot hold the present confrontation line.

Date: **24/7/95**
General Situation: Calm and quiet
Political Situation: The pact between Croatia and Bosnia, although signed, has so far produced nothing tangible.
Military Situation: It has become clear that at certain times during the battle yesterday there was hand-to-hand fighting. A young soldier described how the only distinguishing feature of APWB was a white ribbon on the epaulette. He claimed that 5 Corp captured two tanks definitely and immobilized another seven or eight others. Team can confirm 1 × M84 which we were allowed to inspect this morning in Cazin. It is significant that there has not been a single shell fired by the BSA into Bihac town and we believe this is a deliberate policy lest it generate another NATO airstrike.

Date: **25/7/95**
General Situation: A calm and quiet day in Bihac town with no incoming shells.
Military Situation: Team heard what appeared to be 2 SA-2 Missiles heading in the general area of Cazin. They were fired from the BSA side (unconfirmed). The full-scale fighting which has been widely predicted has so far not materialized. Team also learned that Colonel PRSA of HVO has now been confirmed in his post as the Comdr of 501 and is now a brigadier.
Other Matters: Bihac police have arrested the three 'culprits' who broke into the ICRC House. We understand that they have been receiving an 'organized' beating. Our source told us it is an experience they will never forget for the rest of their lives and it is thought they will also get 3 years hard labour.

Date: **26/7/95**
General Situation: Calm and quiet in Bihac town but very active in the west and north.
Military Situation: At approximately 0200 hrs this morning there was a tremendous firefight in the area of Bugar. This is the feature still held by 5 Corps. At the same time a Hercules C-130 landed on Coralici airfield, stayed for five minutes and unloaded its unknown cargo. (Team assume it was ammunition.) It then took off. At that moment the RSK Forces fired everything they had at the plane but it was not brought down. Shortly after this a small light aircraft that had accompanied the Hercules took

off, heading for Croatia. A helicopter also landed two days ago but not at Coralici. This is the first indication of the resumption of helicopter flights since the downing of Ifran Ljubankic's aircraft on 28 May. A reconnaissance aircraft was observed flying extremely high and in a cross-grain flying pattern over the general area of hostilities.

Date: **28/7/95**

General Situation: Calm and quiet in Bihac safe area but vigorous fighting in the east and north since the early hours of this morning. Today over 4,000 shells have been exchanged by the warring factions.

Military Situation: The military situation has been extremely active with both warring factions really slugging it out. In the north and east there have been no significant infantry attacks but the most deafening artillery duels. At one stage outgoing shells from Mala Kladusa were at the rate of 600 per hour.

Humanitarian Issues: We estimate the refugee figures will be around 4,500–6,000 by the end of this week.

Economic Situation: Dire with no convoys in the forseeable future.

Most commentators in the region now began to realize that the Croats were going to go ahead and launch their offensive to 'liberate Bihac' one way or the other, and this was subsequently confirmed by US Ambassador Peter Galbraith when he admitted in an interview with Tim Ripley that, 'they [the Croats] told us they were going to do it. . . . Given the attacks on Bihac we did not dispute their right to intervene militarily. We warned them about human rights, POWs and mistreatment of the civil population. It was not an agreement, just a "no objection". . . . It was "no light" at all.'[22]

As the Geneva peace talks chaired by Carl Bildt ground to a halt because the Croats present were not remotely interested in anything other than a military solution, Milan Babic appeared on television in Belgrade on the evening of 3 August and announced to the world that the Knin authorities would now accept the Z4 Plan. Clearly his talks with Milosevic had failed completely and this was his last attempt to convince the Croats to stand down their armed forces, lest the entire region be plunged into turmoil. The problem was that any statement of this nature would only confirm to the Croats that Milosevic was not about to commit the JNA to save the Krajina and in fact served to spur them into action. Unable to resist the temptation any longer Deputy Interior Minister Sarinic contacted UN HQ in Zagreb and at 0320 hrs on 4 August and informed General Janvier that Tudjman had decided to unleash the entire HV in an operation to retake the Krajina by force. Offensive action would commence one hour and forty minutes later. Notwithstanding that this was in breach of the Cease-fire Agreement of 29th March 1994, and in complete disregard the fact that UN peace-keepers were occupying positions through which the main attacks were designed to go, reports from both the UN and ECMM identified the first Croatian artillery shells as impacting in the Krajina at 0505 hrs. This was not another false alarm, President Tudjman had kept his word, and his US and Germany sponsors stood back and allowed him get on with it.

Attacking on two fronts simultaneously the 1st and 2nd HV Guards Brigades began a drive through the northern part of the Krajina in a planned attempt to link up with the 5th Corps in Bihac Pocket, while in the south the 4th, 7th and 9th Brigades, supported by a plethora of other specialist groupings, drove into the Krajina in a three-pronged attack on Knin. Dudakovic then launched his own attacks westward in the first instance, in an attempt to link up with the 119th and 123rd HV Brigades by attacking through Plitvice. In order to punch a hole in the Serb defences some of the 5th Corps' initial targets became UN observation posts, then occupied by Polish troops, and four such positions were easily overrun, with the occupants then held captive for a time. In response to all of these attacks the initial Serb reaction, while somewhat disorganized in the south, proved very determined in the north with both the Kordun and Banja Corps putting up fierce resistance. As day two dawned with ever-increasing Croatian shelling it quickly emerged that the Licka Corps were frantically withdrawing into Bosnia on a route which took them to the south of Bihac Pocket, and they were also destroying their equipment and ammunition storage dumps as they left. Further south the Serb defences were now crumbling at an unprecedented rate as the Croats poured into the Krajina via the back door from the Livanjsko Polje, and without much prompting the Knin authorities packed their bags and abandoned the town to whatever fate lay before it. By 1700 hrs 90 per cent of the Krajina was back in Croatian hands, with only small pockets of resistance still holding out around the northern towns of Topusko and Glina.

As the Croats advanced on Knin, burning and looting all before them, UN troops again found themselves subjected to assorted ill-treatment. One of the worst examples occurred when Danish peace-keepers were forced to march in front of advancing HV infantry and tanks in order to provide what essentially amounted to a human shield. That this was an unequivocal breach of International Humanitarian Law bothered none of the HV commanders on the ground and this set an unfortunate tone for even worse atrocities to follow.

By now several thousand civilians were on the move as they fled before the incessant HV artillery bombardment and by 0200 hrs on 6 August over 20,000 people had gathered near Topusko. A few hours later the town of Petrinja was captured virtually unopposed after the entire population had fled and although both military commands recognized an impending humanitarian disaster, they were unable to agree to terms of surrender which would allow the Serbs to lay down their arms with honour. The fighting went on, and in retaliation for a Serb artillery attack on the chemical works at Kutina the Croats targeted an area west of Topusko that night. This coincidentally happened to be the location of what had now become one of several huge refugee convoys awaiting a chance to leave for Bosnia and beyond. The following day another convoy of refugees, which was trapped near Glina, was targeted directly by the HV artillery, while another was strafed by the Croatian air force. When the BSA eventually launched five aircraft against the HV, two of which were shot down, the Croats took it upon themselves to vent their anger at this development by again firing in reprisal on the unfortunate refugees, who were simply trying to escape the madness of a situation they barely understood in the first place. Defence Minister Susak later accepted that what he called several 'incidents' had occurred but incredibly he described them as 'minor' in nature. Taken in this context his apology on behalf of Croatia to the Kingdom of Denmark and the Czech Republic for the deaths of their UN peace-keepers, as the HV ploughed through their UN positions, must surely rank as inadequate.[23]

The 5th Corps however were euphoric following their speedy link up with the HV near Rakovica and buoyed by this success Dudakovic decided to launch his troops one more time against Velika Kladusa and Fikret Abdic, while simultaneously pushing north-eastwards in an attempt to cut off the Serb withdrawal along the Glina–Dvor road. By now UN and ECMM estimates put the refugee figures at well over 40,000 in Topusko alone, with countless others scattered all over the place. The absolute confusion which reigned was best exemplified by a frantic radio transmission received by the UN just after 1800 hrs, in which an ARSK officer begged for help from the village of Donji Zirovac where a refugee column of women and children were dying all around him. His pleas went unanswered and the shelling continued regardless.[24] Shortly afterwards the 5th Corps converged on Dvor and became embroiled in vicious hand-to-hand fighting on the outskirts as the Serb rear guard struggled to keep them at bay. At this point it was also alleged that some elements of the 5th Corps actually launched a depraved attack on a convoy of civilian refugees but in the confusion of the mass exodus positive proof was hard to come by. Nevertheless it remains quite probable that this barbarity was in fact a reprisal for the death of Brigadier Izmet Nanic, commander of the 505 Brigade, who was killed in the same area a few hours previously. Intense mediation followed and at 0700 on 8 August a cease-fire was agreed, which allowed the Serbs to hand up their weapons and then depart for Bosnia unhindered. In order to facilitate this development the 5th Corps were ordered to withdraw from the Dvor–Glina road and thereby allow the pitiful convoys to proceed into exile without further acrimony or loss of life.

Within the space of five days the Krajina region of Croatia had been subjected to an unprecedented and systematic ethnic cleansing, with over 300,000 people, whose ancestors had first pacified the Vojna Krajina in the late sixteenth century, now condemned to face life as refugees in either Bosnia or Serbia – two places marginally less hospitable than where they were now leaving. Milan Babic remained in Belgrade and would be instrumental in obtaining agreement from Milosevic to resettle large numbers of his people in both Vojvodina and Kosovo. Those who decided to resettle in Bosnia, however, were set to face a much more volatile future, the origins of which were now plain to see in the public power struggle that erupted between General Mladic and Radovan Karadzic.

But the Krajina Serbs were not the only losers as a result of Operation Storm. Certainly Croatia had solved some of her strategic problems but victory also involved the unwanted arrival of tens of thousands of people loyal to Fikret Abdic, who once again had chosen to abandon their homes in Velika Kladusa rather than take their chances with Izetbegovic, Dudakovic and the 5th Corps.[25] On previous occasions they had taken refuge in what until recently had been the Krajina. Now this was Croatia, the situation had changed dramatically and 35,000 people were now camped by the side of the road to Vojnic or living crammed into filthy conditions near a place called Kuplensko, determined not to return to their homes no matter what agreement was reached or what guarantees were given.[26]

20/8/95: The refugees from Velika Kladusa are now living in Kuplensko under miserable conditions [and] they refuse to return home. They need food, especially baby food, and sanitary items. The Abdic refugees are jointly accommodated in the primary school and empty houses. The Croatian military commander in Vojnic stated that these refugees who formerly lived in Turanj and Batnoga were looting and stealing from properties [in the area]. To prevent this a joint Croatian police/military presence had been strengthened and [ominously] ECMM and the ICRC were asked to leave the area. For the last twenty days, no meeting between the [Sarajevo] government and Mr Abdic has taken place. Despite the difficult conditions there have been no particular incidents in the camp. No refugees have left by force or voluntarily. Food is the major problem despite recent UNHCR convoy. A major problem is pregnant women, the location for current deliveries and the care of new-born babies. UNHCR, the ICRC and medical teams from HQ SN are present in the camp and providing medicines, flour, bread, water and protective covers for cottages and, among other things, the toilets have been reconstructed. Help is getting organized: messages are taken by the ICRC, registration has begun and aid is distributed on fixed points throughout the camp. The medical centre is working properly. People in the camp look tired and dirty. ECMM was told by some refugees that Muslim civilians were taken into custody [by the 5th Corps] in at least to two places in Velika Kladusa with about 150 possible prisoners. ICRC was not allowed to visit these people.

21/8/95: The refugees suggested that UN should take control over the camp to provide safety. UNHCR is to establish a central warehouse for distributing the humanitarian aid. Most refugees don't want to go back to western Bosnia under control of the existing Government. JORBAT has established two medical centres in the refugee camp with two doctors and two nurses. They stay in the camp only during the day because overnight is dangerous. In one section of the camp called 'KVART 3' there are 4,383 people with 1,338 youngsters under the age of 18. [Of the total] 2,932 persons do not live in normal houses, there are some 80 heavily wounded people and about 20 diabetic patients without any insulin. There is a major lack of flour and the ration of bread is 125 grams per person per day. There is a need for canned food, milk and all kinds of baby food [and] although there is enough medical disinfectant material and soap, there is an urgent need for detergents and clothes.[27]

One more time the leadership qualities of Sead Kajtazovic were called into action as several international agencies rushed to the aid of a group of people who had now become known simply as the 'Abdic refugees'.[28] Needless to say, Fikret Abdic was not sharing their discomfort, preferring instead the luxury of his offices in Rijeka where almost immediately he began plotting his next political moves. For his misguided supporters and followers, however, the cyclical nature of Balkan life would continue unrelentingly but on this occasion there would not be another triumphant return to Velika Kladusa. After another period of self-inflicted exile the majority of them would eventually return to their broken bombed-out homes and attempt to re-build their lives, the alternative being to remain forever as refugees squatting in a state of permanent existential boredom. The political experiment that had come to be known as the Autonomous Province of Western Bosnia (APWB), or, more recently, the Independent Republic of Western Bosnia (IRWB), was now well and truly dead.

NOTES

1. UNHCR Report/Bihac: 3/5/95.
2. ECMM Team Bihac Daily Reports: 4/5/95 and 9/5/95.

3. ECMM CC Topusko Daily Report: 6/5/95.
4. ECMM Team Bihac Special Report: 6/5/95.
5. ECMM Team Bihac Daily Report: 8/5/95.
6. ECMM Team Bihac Daily Report: 9/5/95.
7. ECMM Team Bihac Daily Report: 10/5/95.
8. ECMM Team Bihac Daily Report: 14/5/95.
9. ECMM Team Bihac Daily Report: 17/5/95.
10. ECMM Team Bihac Daily Report: 19/5/95.
11. ECMM Team Bihac Daily Report: 22/5/95.
12. ECMM Team Bihac Daily Report: 23/5/95.
13. ECMM Team Bihac Daily Report: 25/5/95.
14. ECMM Team Bihac Daily Report: 22/5/95.
15. ECMM Team Bihac Daily Report: 30/5/95.
16. ECMM Team Bihac Daily Report: 1/6/95.
17. ECMM Team Bihac Daily Report: 2/6/95.
18. 'A Change in Attitude', ECMM Team Bihac Special Report: 15/7/95.
19. ECMM WIAS, 31 July/3 August 1995.
20. The last meeting of the parliament of the Republic of Srpska Krajina took place in Topusko on 28 July when, perhaps fittingly, Milan Babic became Prime Minister just in time to preside over the last days of a political entity which Milosevic and he had conspired to create in the heady days of 1990 and 1991.
21. The best Milosevic could offer was to address two letters to Izetbegovic and Mladic on 1 August, urging both of them to implement an immediate cease-fire.
22. In an interview with Tim Ripley, Zagreb, 21/12/97. See Ripley, Tim, *Operation Deliberate Force*, Centre for Defence and International Security Studies, Lancaster University (UK). Due for publication in autumn 1998.
23. ECMM WIAS, 4–10 August 1995.
24. Roderick de Normann, 'Operation Storm', *Jane's Intelligence Review*, November 1997.
25. In fact, by the afternoon of 8 August Izetebgovic, Rasim Delic and Mohammed Sacirbey were already walking the streets of Velika Kladusa, having arrived earlier by helicopter: ECMM Team Bihac Daily Report 8/8/95/
26. ECMM WIAS, 11–17 August 1995.
27. ECMM Humanitarian Activity Report, no. 33/95, 18–24 August 1995.
28. ECMM Team Karlovac Special Report: 13/9/95.

Epilogue

In the summer of 1998 rumours still abound that Milan Kucan and Slobodan Milosevic conspired together and made a deal which allowed Slovenia a relatively painless exodus from the Yugoslav Federation in 1991. In the interim the Slovenes have progressed to a point where democracy prevails, human rights are universally respected and the country is now probably on course for admission to NATO early in the new millenium – although EU membership may take a little longer. There will not be another conflict in Slovenia and it remains a moot point whether in fact there ever really was one there in the first place.

Croatia, on the other hand, no longer has a Krajina Serb problem. 300,000 people – men, women and children – were brutally evicted from their homes by the Croatian armed forces and the treatment dished out to those few elderly Serbs who remained in their homes was sufficiently reprehensible to delay Croatia's admission into the Council of Europe until November 1996. Today Croatia has become the most ethnically cleansed of all Balkan states. A problem remains in Eastern Slavonia where the Serb population continues to reside under OSCE supervision but as time goes by they too may well decide to quit their homes rather than take their chances under Croatian jurisdiction, where they would have to rely on the impartiality of a new police force specially trained at the Police Academy in Budapest under the watchful eyes of the FBI.

In Bosnia, where tanks, artillery pieces, missiles and thousands of small arms have been supplied to the Armija as part of the ongoing US-sponsored 'Train and Equip' programme, one can be forgiven for wondering whether this latest tactic is designed to reinforce a peace settlement or serve to ensure that if another round of fighting breaks out the Muslims will be better prepared than they were the last time. One can also be forgiven for thinking that no matter what initiatives are taken the International Community continues to sit uneasily on a time bomb which remains primed and ready to explode. While I-FOR and S-FOR have certainly imposed some order on the situation, and the initial presidential, parliamentary and municipal elections which were supervised by OSCE did for the most part turn out to be free and fair, notwithstanding a 107 per cent turnout in some areas, the stark reality remains that precious little else of substance has been achieved since the Dayton-Paris Peace Accords were signed.

Within the Muslim-Croat Federation divisions remain, with the inability to unify both armies the most spectacular failure.[1] Commentators consistently warn that when the Muslims are up to military specification they may well seek to redress all defeats they have suffered in the past. Tons of American hardware, an ethnically cleansed army, the perception of weakness in their enemies, a divided political spectrum and continuing paranoia in relation to the ultimate division of their country between Croatia and Serbia has facilitated the emergence of a strong Muslim military leadership. A question of consequence might now be how long the West can legitimately expect to retain control of them.

For their part the once-powerful Bosnian Serbs are still in total disarray. They have not been treated equally in the allocation of much needed international re-development aid, having initially received a mere 2 per cent of the total fund, although that situation may now improve following the election of a new RS Prime Minister, Milorad Dodik, in January 1998.[2] Nevertheless with obsolete equipment, few spare parts, chronic unemployment and absolutely no prospect of any support from either Serbia or Russia the Republic Srpska remains in a very precarious position and all the major players in the region are well aware of it.

In Belgrade Slobodan Milosevic still survives and presides now over what is left of Federal Yugoslavia, but the same man who in 1989 informed the Serbs in Kosovo that they would 'never be beaten again', and then be-friended Radovan Karadzic and Milan Babic, as he fanned the flames of pan-Serbian nationalism, now believes that 'the united forces of peace and development will celebrate an historical victory over hatred, violence, and conservatism'.[3] Karadzic, Martic and Babic were all sacrificed at the altar of political expediency as Milosevic grasped the lifeline thrown to him by Richard Holbrooke, but of late it would appear that he is having substantial difficulty maintaining that grip. Over 29 per cent of Serbia's population are living in poverty and even where salaries are paid to industrial workers the average wage comes to little more than the equivalent of £85 per month,[4] while in Montenegro the statistics are only marginally better. Today Serbia is also home to over 500,000 refugees from Bosnia and Croatia who are not in receipt of any state benefits and from whose existential boredom there appears to be no escape. The plight of these people and the social chaos their presence has caused was instrumental in Milosevic losing control of several major city councils at the 1996 local elections but rather than heed this warning he simply proceeded to annul the results, which in turn brought the 'Zajedno' protests on to the streets of Belgrade.

Milosevic must also grapple with the situation in Kosovo where recent attempts by the Kosovar Albanian majority to obtain some degree of autonomy have been greeted with savage police and military crackdowns. Violence has now resulted in hundreds of deaths, wholesale destruction of property and as of the first days of June an exodus of Kosovar Albanians across the border into Albania itself. This issue, which has been simmering for years, is currently boiling over, and Milosevic may well live to regret that no provision was made for this region when the Dayton deal was cobbled together. It would surely rank as the ultimate irony if the home of Serb nationalism since the Battle of Kosovo Field in 1389 was eventually sacrificed to ensure the final lifting of economic sanctions against Serbia and Montenegro.

Carl Bildt, the former European Union High Representative in Bosnia, was absolutely correct when he said that, 'We have no reason whatever to be complacent concerning the future peace and stability of this part of the continent. The price that Europe would have to pay if things went wrong [again], in terms of security, refugee flows and lost economic opportunities would be huge.'[5] In this context then we would do well to recognize that while much has been achieved since Dayton, something as basic as playing inter-ethnic football remains totally beyond the scope of most people's toleration. In Bosnia, for example, there are now three separate football leagues – one for Muslims, one for Croats and one for Serbs – and in many places former clubs can no longer use their old stadia because they are now located on the wrong side of an artificial monstrosity called the 'Inter-Entity Boundary Line' (IEBL). Two Serb football referees sitting at a bar outside Sarajevo summed up the whole situation rather well: 'When you spend four years seeing someone through gun sights you cannot [then] play sport with them. Maybe our grandchildren will, but not us.'[6]

In that context it is perhaps fitting to include the assessment of Lord David Owen, who probably had one of the best views of Yugoslavia's many battlefields as he interposed between all the parties at various times.

In the three and a half months from May to August 1995 the map of Croatia and Bosnia-Hercegovina was dramatically changed. The loss of life and casualties from the fighting were accompanied by appalling atrocities and ethnic cleansing by all parties on a scale that we had not seen before in such a concentrated period of time. The International Community looked on helpless and divided, its diplomacy in tatters, the UN forces irrelevant. A Balkan solution had been imposed on the battlefield, tearing up the Contact Group Map, destroying the Z-4 Plan and raising fundamental questions about the relevance of any of the various involvements from outside the region since 1991. The Security Council passed resolutions of condemnation but they were ignored by the Croatian government army in Western Slavonia, the Bosnian Serb army in Zepa and Srebrenica, and the Croatian and Bosnian government armies in the Krajina. The victors in the Yugoslav wars of 1991–5 have been the Croats and President Tudjman. The losers have been the Croatian [Krajina] Serbs.[7]

In Bihac Pocket Atif Dudakovic was also a victor and by the end of hostilities he had managed to significantly enlarge the area under his control following the 5th Corps' successful autumn 1995 campaign. As usual this was not achieved without a liberal sprinkling of controversy and it followed on directly from the events of 28 August in Sarajevo when yet another salvo of mortars were fired, with one of them again landing in the crowded market place. Although Dudakovic could not have known it at the time this latest atrocity would soon provide the 5th Corps with another opportunity to take the fight to the Bosnian Serbs entrenched around Bihac.

However, in the immediate aftermath of the shelling, UN officers in Sarajevo were again divided on whether the shell that killed thirty-seven and wounded nearly eighty others had actually been fired by the Bosnian Serbs. Colonel Andrei Demurenko, a very experienced Russian artillery officer, who was also General Rupert Smith's Chief of Staff, formally stated that in his opinion the shell could not have come from Serb positions, while a Canadian officer expressed doubts about whether the bomb had in fact been fired from a mortar tube at all and not dropped from the top floor of a building nearby. British and French officers were not initially able to find evidence that the Serbs were in fact responsible and not for the first time the finger of suspicion began once more to point at the Bosnian Muslims themselves, whose leaders coincidentally just happened to be attending an international peace conference, this time in Paris. Subsequent leaked reports from Russian military intelligence suggested that they had known of a plan to plant a bomb as early as 20 August and had already passed this information to the US, German and Croatian governments.[8] In any event US officers in Sarajevo, assisted it must be said by senior British officers close to General Smith, quickly overruled all of their international colleagues and claimed that they had found a 'fuze furrow' at the site of the impact as well as Cyrillic markings on what remained of the bomb casing. They were also satisfied that the bomb in question had bounced off the roof of a building nearby en route to the market below, and when adjustments were made to their calculations to allow for this, the point of origin could be placed on the Serb side of the demarcation line – just. There was also a palpable feeling in the city that this might well have been Serb revenge for a Muslim attack on a Serb funeral the previous day, and on 29 August NATO announced that it had established 'beyond reasonable doubt' that the Serbs were to blame.

The following morning NATO's air bombardment of the Bosnian Serbs began after Peter Galbraith had convinced Admiral Leighton-Smith in Naples that a new combined HV/HVO/Armija ground offensive could commence immediately as well.[9] The International Community had finally decided to go to war with the Bosnian Serbs and now effectively adopted co-belligerent status with the combined Muslim/Croat forces and their ever-increasing number of foreign advisors. NATO began a programme of strategic bombing which included everything up to and including the launching of Tomahawk cruise missiles. With several key BSA installations quickly demolished, and command, control and communications in tatters right across the country, the boot was now firmly on the other foot as Muslim and Croat commanders set about redressing Bosnia's military imbalance. The 'endgame strategy' had become the endgame.

It would take almost two weeks for Dudakovic to marshall his troops sufficiently to become involved in this latest offensive but on 13 September he again entered the fray by launching four brigades simultaneously against BSA positions to the east of the Pocket on a front which was over 20 km wide. Codenamed Operation Mistral 2, 511 Brigade re-took Bosanska Krupa just after midnight on 14 September, and 502 Brigade marched into Bosanska Novi at 0115 hrs on the 15th. Having achieved his primary objective, which was as always to push Serb artillery outside the range of the main towns in the Pocket, Dudakovic again conducted a 'relief in place' as the 501 Brigade and a reserve group consisting of very young teenagers were brought forward into positions on the new front line.[10] With the perimeter of the Pocket secure, and mistakenly thinking he had routed the Serbs when in fact most of them had simply conducted a controlled tactical withdrawal, it would appear that Dudakovic now decided to abandon his arrangements with the HV in order to make another drive for Kulen Vakuf. This was to make amends for his failed attempt to capture the town ten months previously and also just to get there before the Croats. Again the whole escapade went horribly wrong and culminated in what is commonly known as a 'Blue on Blue' near the village of Ostreli, just north of Drvar, at 0500 hrs on the morning of 15 September, when the HV and the 5th Corps ended up shooting at and killing one another.

There were other incidents too which forced commentators to conclude that either Dudakovic was operating exclusively to his own agenda or elements of the 5th Corps were now out of control – or that perhaps it had become policy in Sarajevo to begin frustrating the HV advance into Bosnia lest they become too comfortable in their new surroundings and might not want to go home. Whatever the truth, further independent actions by the 5th Corps continued and were typified by the bizarre attack undertaken by the 501 Brigade, which took them to within 6 km of Mrkonjic Grad only to be subsequently routed in total disarray, and an attempt by Dudakovic himself to capture Sanski Most, only to be systematically beaten back by a BSA counter-attack on the morning of 17 September.[11] By now relations had become very strained between the 5th Corps and the HV, who had both the 1st and

2nd Guards Brigades deployed close by, although obviously not now actually in support of Dudakovic. In fact cooperation became so bad that on 19 September Galbraith had to arrange a meeting in Zagreb between Tudjman and Izetbegovic in order to sort it all out and only managed to finally resolve the matter after a screaming fight with Defence Minister Susak, when 'extreme' US pressure was brought to bear on the Croats.

HV Commanders now gave Dudakovic a very wide berth as the 511 and 503 Brigades became overstretched in the north and the remainder of the Corps ended up making little progress in and around Sanski Most. Then, on 25 September, a BSA counter-attack seemed to catch Dudakovic completely by surprise and he ended up suffering several casualties as well as yielding large tracts of territory which had been hard won during the previous fortnight. Attacking south-west from Prijedor and due south from Sanski Most, General Momir Talic also threw the BSA's 43 Brigade from Possavina into the fight and this proved a decisive factor. Licking his wounds – and there were many – Dudakovic was now forced into yet another reorganization of his forces at a time when probably, but for his own eccentricity as a tactician, and the obscure instructions he was receiving from Sarajevo, he certainly need not have found himself in that position.

With the BSA now enjoying a limited respite, having finally recovered some composure and launching a series of minor counter-offensives, NATO's air campaign continued unrelentingly and by early October it was clear that the 'endgame strategy' now involved bombing the Bosnian Serbs all the way into the 51/49 division of their country which had been the cornerstone of the Contact Group Plan for so long. In the north-west, having apparently managed to patch up their relationship, another HV/HVO/Armija offensive began on 8 October. This time the operation was called *Juzni Potez* (Southern Move) and before the off a clear boundary line on the ground was identified between the Croats and the 5th Corps. On 9 October the HV rolled into Mrkonjic Grad without a shot being fired and three days later Dudakovic re-took Sanski Most as the Serb defence collapsed before him. By now the BSA were in dire trouble right across the country but particularly so in the north-west, where the biggest threat was no longer coming from the 5th Corps but from over 3,500 HV troops who were now advancing menacingly on Banja Luka. This was in a move clearly in line with President Tudjman's long-term plans for the ultimate division of Bosnia between Croatia and Serbia, a matter which he had already explained in detail to UK Liberal Democrat Leader, Paddy Ashdown, at London Guildhall on 6 May 1995.

An opportunity to commence this annexation was now at hand but for this to work a huge population transfer would have to take place. In the final analysis this was not something Holbrooke could sanction because it would certainly create far more long-term problems than it would solve.

Instead, limited offensives were permitted to continue in order to arrive at a territorial and ethnic balance which saw the eviction of over 100,000 Serbs from their homes across the country in areas which were now controlled by either the Muslims or the Croats. The Sarajevo government were openly none too pleased about exercising restraint when the Serbs were now clearly on their knees, but reluctantly they agreed to a cease-fire late on 10 October.

However this left unfinished business in several areas, where no clear physical delineation had been achieved on the ground. Not surprisingly several reasons were concocted to justify a postponement of the general cease-fire. While negotiations on these issues continued Muslim and Croat forces were afforded an extra few days to consolidate their positions, in addition to securing a number of key road junctions which would be vital in terms of re-supply once the confrontation line was finally frozen. There were of course other agendas still in operation too and, apparently oblivious to any overriding political considerations, Dudakovic announced that under his direction the 5th Corps were about to launch a new offensive against Banja Luka in which they would be supported by the 7th Corps, commanded by General Mohammed Alagic. In the midst of this confusion another general cease-fire was agreed at midnight on 12 October but Dudakovic immediately began qualifying his position by stating that as far as he was concerned if no overall peace settlement was in place then he did not feel himself bound by the terms of any cease-fire signed in Sarajevo. However, by 15 October, even Dudakovic was prepared to accept that a genuine cease-fire did appear to be holding across the country, and on that date the 5th Corps finally fell into line as well.

Thereafter all side dug themselves into deep defensive positions on either side of the confrontation line as a new division of Bosnia on strictly ethnic lines became a stark reality. The Dayton Agreement of 21 November, and formal signing in Paris on 14 December, effectively formalized these positions and with minor alterations prior to the arrival of I-FOR, the territory of Bosnia-Hercegovina had finally been battered into the 51/49 split that most mediators had deemed so appropriate. Having finally arrived at this position there were of course no guarantees that is was now going to work. Only time, the presence of NATO and a massive injection of Western finance would ultimately provide the answer to that.

Bihac Pocket remains today of critical importance to the Sarajevo government and it was no accident that Izetbegovic chose this location to make a major policy statement on 21 April 1996. In the presence of Ejup Ganic, Prime Minister Muratovic, Generals Delic and Dudakovic and a gathering of foreign diplomatic and military attaches, the President, having reviewed a huge military parade by the 5th Corps, announced to the world that the parade itself was 'a message to both friend and foe to make friends and rejoice, and to warn the enemy never again to raise its finger against our people.' He went on to say, 'I am here to tell you that the struggle for Bosnia-Hercegovina has not finished yet, that it goes on, and to wish you success on this long, difficult and honourable road towards a free and democratic Bosnia. The struggle will continue until Bosnia is unified and democratic.'[12] A few weeks later Dudakovic was even more specific. 'I am seriously preparing for the next war,' he declared. 'We see that all sides are trying to undermine the Dayton-Paris Accords.'[13]

For the moment Atif Dudakovic reigns supreme, having been promoted and decorated, while the 5th Corps, no longer encircled by Serbs of any kind, are now free to conduct patrols on their side of Bosnia's Inter Entity Boundary Line. In May and June of 1997 it was also possible to rotate the entire corps through four phases of training prior to them leaving for the Livno area in Western Hercegovina where, under the watchful eyes of American ex-service personnel currently employed by MPRI, they were put through their paces in greater detail, using newly Acquired T-55 tanks and M-63 APCs. Captain Fuad Sadikovic, a mechanized battalion commander in the 501 Brigade, was on hand to inform interested bystanders that the emphasis now was on training section, platoon and company commanders, and that he was particularly happy with the performance of his tank crews. Also on hand to oversee the exercises were Dudakovic and General Rasim Delic, with both expressing gratitude to their US tutors for the high standard which the Corps was now able to achieve.[14]

And finally, as always, there is Fikret Abdic, the perpetual thorn in the side of Alija Izetbegovic. On 8 April 1996 the Croatian Security forces arrested an armed group of six Bosnian Muslims (five male and one female) near the town of Senj, sixty miles south of Abdic's offices in the port of Rijeka, initially for a road traffic violation. Later, upon further investigation, it was discovered that the group belonged to the Bosnian government intelligence service, AID, and had planned to assassinate Abdic by firing a RPG 7 rocket at his car as he drove along the busy coastal road near the tourist resort of Opatija.[15] Two days later the intelligence operatives were indicted for attempted assassination and in the course of interrogation admitted to several other offences, not least among which was the concealment of a huge weapons cache in the Costabella forest near Preluka, as well as several previous unsuccessful attempts to rid the world of Mr Abdic.[16]

By the end of 1996 over 10,000 of Abdic's followers had decided to return to what was left of their homes in and around Velika Kladusa. Frightened and disillusioned, the reception they received was hostile. Harassment by the police proved to be a regular occurence and several families who returned from the Gasinci Refugee Camp near Djakovo in Croatia found themselves persistently discriminated against when it came to the distribution of humanitarian aid.[17] Equally many senior police officers in the area now operate to clear political agendas with several permitted to concurrently hold high level SDA appointments in several local assemblies. Rasim Sahinovic (Buzim), Casim Budimilic (Cazin) and Fikret Hadzic (Velika Kladusa) to name but three have all been candidates in Bosnia's recent OSCE supervised elections, with Sahinovic and Budimilic actually succeeding in winning seats at the Federation's Parliament.[18] Additionally those who remained loyal to Sarajevo throughout the war years have also been rewarded. Mirsad Veladzic, who was the wartime political coordinator in Bihac Pocket and permanent intermediary between Dudakovic and Izetbegovic, has now been made governor of the newly configured Una-Sana Canton. This has been without a doubt the most critical political appointment in the region and it literally guarantees a continuation of Sarajevo's hardline approach to both Abdic and those who still profess to follow him.

In November 1997 Bosnia's long-awaited municipal elections took place and through a 'voting in absentia' mechanism those Abdic refugees who had still not returned were allowed to vote in their camps in Croatia for candidates who might ultimately take their seats at assemblies in Bihac Pocket. This resulted in Husein Delic becoming Mayor of Velika Kladusa where Abdic's new political party, the DNZ,[19] succeeded in winning an absolute majority in the municipal assembly. However, despite his best efforts, Delic has thus far been unable to overcome the prejudices of the SDA who see him purely as a puppet of Abdic. Other DNZ members who won seats in the Cazin and Cantonal assemblies have not managed to take up their positions either because they fear they will be arrested if they attempt to do so. Their fears are well founded. When DNZ member Alija Besirevic returned to the area to pursue his political career he was arrested, charged with war crimes, and now languishes in a jail in Bihac town.[20] It is a fair comment that but for the presence of international observers in the region it is probable that Delic would not be tolerated either, and in moves now to frustrate him and further marginalize the DNZ, Governor Veladzic openly admits that he wants to transfer key municipal functions (police, finance, etc) to Cantonal jurisdiction where the ruling SDA would have complete control over them.

Nevertheless it is quite clear that in 1998 Fikret Abdic continues to exercise considerable influence in both Croatia and Bosnia, despite being branded a traitor by Sarajevo and tried in absentia in Bihac for war crimes in September 1996. He continues to reside in the Croatian port of Rijeka where his FINAB food company currently employs over 1,000 people. He also remains committed to returning to Bosnian politics via the DNZ and to one day reactivating the old Agrokomerc company in Bihac, in spite of the fact that Mirsad Veladzic believes he will probably be shot should he attempt to cross the international border. However the opportunity for a political comeback will present itself in the autumn of 1998 when the next round of Bosnia's parliamentary and presidential elections are scheduled to take place, although whether OSCE will be prepared to recognize his candidacy remains unclear.[21] But in Bosnia anything is always possible and with UNHCR expecting another 3,000 Abdic refugees to return to Bihac in the current year, and the remaining 2,000 some time during 1999, it would be unwise to write off their leader as a national political figure just yet. Currently in the process of stepping down as president of the DNZ to make way for the more moderate Izet Latic, Abdic's gesture should not be interpreted as abdication or capitulation in the face of continued SDA pressure. Rather it should be seen for what it really is – another tactical move from one of Bosnia's consummate political performers, the final chapters of whose chequered career have certainly not been written yet.

NOTES

1. ECMM Special Report on Croatian Republic of Herceg-Bosna: 15/3/98.
2. ECMM Special Report on the Formation of the RS Government: 19/1/98.
3. *Independent*, 2/11/96, p. 12.
4. Serbian Red Cross Survey, 1996/7.
5. Bildt, Carl, 'A Regional Plan for the Balkans', *The European*, 24/30 October 1996, p. 11.
6. O'Reilly, Dominic, 'Ethnic Leagues Divide Bosnia', *The European*, 21/27 November 1996.
7. David Owen, Lord, *Balkan Odyssey*, Indigo Press, p. 387.
8. Bodansky, Yossef, *Offensive in the Balkans* (ISSA), 1995, p. 15.
9. Ripley, Tim, *Operation Deliberate Force*, Centre for Defence and International Security Studies, Lancaster University. Due for publication, autumn 1998. Galbraith also admitted to Tim Ripley that both he and Holbrooke knew the bombing was going to happen. Was this just pure telepathy, inspired prediction or was he also aware of the Russian intelligence report which indicated that a bomb was about to explode?
10. Captain N.J. Fenton QDG, HQ 4 (UK) Armd Bde, *A Study of Federation Offensives against the BSA Nov. 1994–Oct. 1995*, IFOR, Sipovo, Bosnia, April 1996.
11. Major J.W. Ogden LD, *An Exercise in Force Protection*, 'C' Sqn, The Light Dragoons (UK), IFOR, Bosnia, February 1996.
12. Bodansky, Yossef, *Some Call It Peace* (ISSA), 1996, p. 130.
13. Op. cit., p. 132.

14. Dzanic, Enis, and Erik, Norman, 'Background Warriors', *Jane's Intelligence Review*, December 1997.
15. AID (The Agency for Investigation, Research, and Documentation) is Bosnia's Intelligence Service with responsibility for domestic and international security. The operatives arrested in Croatia in April 1996 were believed to have been part of the Bihac office of AID but operating with full approval from the higher echelons of the SDA and the Sarajevo government. The impetus for such an action may well have been Abdic's registration of his new political party in Mostar and Izetbegovic's continuing paranoia that Abdic would one day succeed him to the Presidency of Bosnia.
16. Op. cit., p. 54.
17. ECMM Special Report: 5/3/98.
18. OSCE Elections: September 1996.
19. DNZ: Demokratska Narodna Zajednica (Democratic National Coalition).
20. ECMM Daily Monitoring Activity Report, no. 10532: 5/11/97.
21. RC Sarajevo Daily Report: 4/5/98. Husein Delic stated that Abdic had officially announced his candidacy for the presidency of Bosnia-Hercegovina.

Select Bibliography

BOOKS

Almond, Mark. *Europe's Backyard War*, Mandarin Books, 1995
Baerlein, Henry. *The Birth of Yugoslavia*, Leonard Parsons, 1922
Bell, Martin. *In Harm's Way*, Hamish Hamilton, London, 1996
Bodansky, Yossef. *Offensive in the Balkans*, Int. Media Corp./ISSA, London, 1995
Bodansky, Yossef. *Some Call it Peace*, Int. Media Corp./ISSA, London, 1996
Caplan, Richard. *Post-Mortem on UNPROFOR*, Centre for Defence Studies/Brassey's, 1996
Civic, Christopher. *Remaking the Balkans*, Pinter Publishers, London, 1991
Djilas, Milovan. *Rise and Fall*, Macmillan, 1985
Eyal, Jonathan. *Europe and Yugoslavia: Lessons from a Failure*, Royal United Services Institute for Defence Studies, 1993
Honig, J.W. & Both, N. *Srebrenica – Record of a War Crime*, Penguin, London, 1996
Glenny, Misha. *The Fall of Yugoslavia*, Penguin Books, 3rd edn, London, 1996
Gow, James. *Legitimacy and the Military*, Pinter Publishers, London, 1992
——. *Triumph of the Lack of Will*, C. Hurst & Co., London, 1997
Gutman, Roy. *A Witness to Genocide*, Macmillan Publishing, London, 1993
Hukanovic, Rezak. *The Tenth Circle of Hell*, Little Brown and Co., London, 1996
Jasarevic, Senudin. *Aggression on the Bihac Region*, Una-Sana Canton, Bosnia, 1995
Judah, Tim. *The Serbs*, Yale University Press, London, 1997
Malcolm, Noel. *Bosnia – A Short History*, Macmillan Publishing, London, 1994
MacKenzie, Lewis. *Peacekeeper*, Douglas and McIntyre, Toronto, 1993
Owen, David. *Balkan Odyssey*, Indigo/Cassell Publishing, London, 1996
Pavlowitch, Stevan. *Tito: Yugoslavia's Great Dictator*, C. Hurst & Co., London, 1992
Reiff, David. *Slaughterhouse: Bosnia and the Failure of the West*, Random House, London, 1995
Rodhe, David. *A Safe Area*, Pocket Books, 1997
Ripley, Tim. *Operation Deliberate Force*, Centre for Defence and International Security Studies, 1998

Silber, L. & Little, A. *The Death of Yugoslavia*, BBC/Penguin, London, 1995

Singleton, Fred. *A Short History of the Yugoslav Peoples*, Cambridge University Press, 1985

Stewart, Bob. *Broken Lives*, HarperCollins, London, 1993

Tanner, Marcus. *Croatia – A Nation Forged in War*, Yale University Press, London, 1997

Thompson, Mark. *A Paper House*, Vintage Books, London, 1992

Vulliamy, Ed. *Seasons in Hell*, Simon & Schuster, London, 1994

Woodward, Bob. *The Choice*, Touchstone/Simon & Schuster, 1996

Woodward, Susan. *Balkan Tragedy*, Brookings Institute, 1995

ARTICLES

Ajami, Fauad. 'The Mark of Bosnia – Boutros-Ghali's Reign of Indifference', in *Foreign Affairs*, vol. 75, no. 3, 1996

Bodansky, Yossef. 'The Roots of the New Escalation of the Bosnian War, and Washington's Role', in *Defence and Foreign Affairs Strategic Policy*, 31/10/94

Bougarel, Xavier. 'Bosnia-Hercegovina: State and Communitarianism', in *Yugoslavia and After*, ed. by Dyker, D.A. & Vejvoda, Ivan, Longman Ltd, 1996

Boutros-Ghali, Boutros. 'Global Leadership after The Cold War', in *Foreign Affairs*, vol. 75, no. 2, 1996

Boyd, Charles, G. 'Making Peace with The Guilty', in *Foreign Affairs*, Sept./Oct. 1995

——. 'Making Bosnia Work', in *Foreign Affairs*, Jan./Feb. 1998

Civic, Christopher. 'Croatia', in *Yugoslavia and After*, ed. by Dyker & Vejvoda, Longman Ltd, 1996

De Normann, Roderick. 'Operation Storm – Attack on the Krajina', in *Jane's Intelligence Review*, 11/95

Djilias, Aleksa. 'Tito's Last Secret', in *Foreign Affairs*, vol. 74, no. 4, 1995

Doyle, Colm. 'An Investigation into the Bosnian Dilemma', MA thesis, University of Limerick, 1994

Dzanic and Erik, N. 'Background Warriors (MPRI)', in *Jane's Intelligence Review*, Dec. 1997

Glenny, Misha. 'Heading Off War in the Southern Balkans', in *Foreign Affairs*, May/June 1995

Gruden, Zivko. 'The Ustasha Revival', in *Feral Tribune* (Croatian weekly), 24/1/96

Hunter, Greg. 'Bosnian Serbs left isolated as Dayton continues to drift', in *Jane's Intelligence Review*, 9/97

Jagger, Bianca. 'The Betrayal of Srebrenica', in *The European*, 25/9/97

Kent, Sarah A. 'Writing the Yugoslav Wars: English-Language Books on

Bosnia, 1992–1996', in *American Historical Review*, vol. 102, no. 4, Oct. 1997

Kuljis, Denis. '20,000 Serb Soldiers from Croatia and Bosnia are entering Bihac', in *Globus* (Croatian daily), 25/11/94

Long, Angela. 'The Truth is limping on crutches in Bosnia', in *The Irish Times*, 12/18/95

Markovic, Mihailo. 'Dayton: The Inside Story', in *Newsweek*, 05/02/96

McManners, Hugh. 'Serbs "Not Guilty" of Massacre', in *The Sunday Times*, 01/10/95

Meron, Theodor. 'Answering for War Crimes', in *Foreign Affairs*, Jan./Feb. 1997

O'Shea, Brendan, 'Bosnia's Muslim/Croat Federation', in *Studies in Conflict and Terrorism*, vol. 19, no. 4, 1996

——. 'The First Battle of Bihac', in *The War Studies Journal* (King's College, London), vol. 2, no. 2, 1997

Reily, Jonathan. 'The Monitor Mission', in *ECMM Publication* (Zagreb), 1992

Ricker, Di Mari. 'Closing a War', in *The ABA Journal*, Jan. 1996

Rose, Michael. 'A Year in Bosnia: What Was Achieved', in *Studies in Conflict and Terrorism*, vol. 19, no. 3, 1996

Shehadi, Kamel S. 'Ethnic Self-determination', in *Adelphi Paper* no. 283 (International Institute for Strategic Studies, UK), 1993

Klemenic and Schofield. 'After The Storm', in *Jane's Intelligence Review*, 12/95

Stipetic, Petar. 'Storm', in *Oluja* (Croatian journal), Oct./Nov. 1995

Susak, Gojko. 'Interview: I am proud of the Croatian Army', in *Glas Slavonije*, 23/4/96

Svarm, Felip. 'Bosnian Rwanda', in *Vreme International*, 15/09/94

Tudjman, Franjo. 'No One Can Endanger Croatia Anymore', in *Glas Slavonije*, 23/4/96

Ustinov, Peter. 'Comment', in *The European*, 14/3/96

Vasic, Milos. 'The Yugoslav Army and The Post-Yugoslav Armies', in *Yugoslavia and After*, ed. by Dyker & Vejvoda, Longman Ltd, 1996

Vejvoda, Ivan. Yugoslavia 1945–91: Decentralization without Democracy to Dissolution', in *Yugoslavia and After*, ed. by Dyker & Vejvoda, Longman Ltd, 1996

——. 'To Avoid the Extremes of Suffering', in *Yugoslavia and After*, ed. by Dyker & Vejvoda, Longman Ltd, 1996

Woodward, Susan. 'The West and The International Organizations', in *Yugoslavia and After*, ed. by Dyker & Vejvoda, Longman Ltd, 1996

Zametica, Jovan. 'The Yugoslav Conflict', in *Adelphi Paper* no. 270 (International Institute for Strategic Studies, UK), 1992

Zimmerman, Warren. 'The Last Ambassador – A Memoir of the Collapse of Yugoslavia', in *Foreign Affairs*, vol. 74, no. 2, March/April 1995.

Index